The complete guide to

Selecting Music for Movies, TV, Games, & New Media

D0580308

Music Supervision

By Ramsay Adams, David Hnatiuk, and David Weiss

SCHIRMER
TRADE
BOOKS

A Part of **The Music Sales Group**
New York/London/Paris/Sydney/Copenhagen/Berlin/Tokyo/Madrid

Schirmer Trade Books
A Division of Music Sales Corporation, New York

Exclusive Distributors:
Music Sales Corporation
257 Park Avenue South, New York, NY 10010 USA
Music Sales Limited
8/9 Firth Street, London W1D 3JB England
Music Sales Pty. Limited
120 Rothschild Street, Rosebery, Sydney, NSW 2018, Australia

Order No. SCH 10138
International Standard Book Number: 0-8256-7298-8

Printed in the United States of America

Cover Design: Josh Labouve

This book and the sample agreement (s) contained within are designed
to provide general information in regard to the subject matter covered.
The information and sample agreement(s) are for informational purposes only
and are not dispositive of the many and complex issues that may arise
in this subject matter. This book is sold with the understanding that the publisher
and authors are not engaged in rendering legal, accounting, or other
professional services. If legal or other expert assistance is required,
the services of a competent professional should be sought. The publisher
and authors are not responsible for the readers use of any of the contents hereof.

Library of Congress Cataloging-in-Publication Data

Adams, Ramsay, 1969-

Music supervision : the complete guide to selecting music for movies, tv, games, & new media / Ramsay Adams,
David Hnatiuk, and David Weiss.

p. cm.

ISBN 0-8256-7298-8 (pbk. : alk. paper)

1. Music supervision. I. Hnatiuk, David, 1974- II. Weiss, David, 1972- III. Title.

ML68.A33 2005

781.5'4--dc22

2004030399

Table of Contents

Dedication

Ramsay Adams dedicates this book to his wife, partner,
and best friend, Ananda.

Dave Hnatiuk dedicates this book to his wife, Danielle;
Scotch Plains Music Center; and his entire family. Thanks.

David Weiss dedicates this book to his wife, Linda; son Broderick;
his parents Joseph and Louise and his brother Steven.

Acknowledgements

The authors of *Music Supervision* wish to acknowledge the many people who contributed both directly and indirectly to the making of this book. Thank you for understanding and supporting our vision!

Ramsay Adams would like to thank his two partners, Dave Hnatiuk and David Weiss, for their efforts in helping to bring this idea to fruition. Although it is our three names that appear on the front cover, so many people were critical in this book's development. My wife, Ananda Adams provided invaluable daily support and encouragement and I thank her deeply for that. Many thanks to our editor, Andrea Rotondo, for believing in this project and seeing it through, with valuable feedback along the way. Special recognition to my parents, John and Patricia Adams, whose own lifelong commitment to excellence has been a true inspiration.

Thank you Penny Jakubek for believing in me and supporting me and to Thorson for you gifts of wisdom.

My appreciation to a number of organizations including New York University and the Film Music Network.

There were many people who made significant contributions merely through simple referrals or advice. My thanks to Lance Adler, David Lasley, Abe Valez, Rob Reynolds, Mary Joe Mannella, Greg Curtis, Tom Swift, and Hooman Majd.

A final acknowledgement to those people in my professional life who served as role models for me in the field of music and music supervision. My sincere appreciation to David Krebs, David Fenton, Jeffrey Sachs, Ken Sunshine, and Richard O'Brian, Phil Garrod, and Reed Hays—all friends, mentors, and teachers.

Dave Hnatiuk would like to thank his wife Danielle for endless support, love, and motivation. Dave would also like to thank his parents Greg and Mary, as well as his brother Jeffrey for all their inspiration, encouragement, and advice. Mr. Hnatiuk would also like to thank Christian and Eleanor Rittman, as well as William and Valerie Hnatiuk for their strong backing and love of the arts, as well as their musical genes! Dave also thanks Scotch Plains Music Center, NJ for his life-long music education and St. Josephs's High School (Metuchen, NJ), as well as Monmouth University (W. Long Branch, NJ) for helping him discover his second love, his career. He would also like to thank David Sherman and Adelle Irving *ABC/Disney Music,* as well as Richard O'Brien *Fox News Channel,* Mary Jo Manella *Twentieth Century Fox,* Nocole Tecco *N.Y.U.,* Jamie Manalio *Rust Productions,* and Kevin MacKall MTV for allowing him the opportunity to define and refine his expertise in the art and business of music supervision. Mr. Hnatiuk thanks his corporation, Autonatic Entertainment, as well as The Film Music Network,Sprout Productions, Sonica Media Group, and The Music Supervisors. David also thanks The Kin, Lonnie Rutledge, The Strange, The Golden Dawn, Dana Fuchs, The Vanities, Sunshine Flipside, The Burn & Cry, Provolone Jones, and BLESTeNATION. Thanks to Tom Swift for his priceless legal guidance. Special thanks to Andrea Rotondo and Schirmer Trade Books/Music Sales Corp.

David Weiss would like to thank his family: His wife, Linda, who was behind him all the way, and son, Broderick, who showed up in the middle; his father, Joseph, who provided so much inspiration to write; his mother, R. Louise, for her artistic mind; and brother Steven for jamming in the basemen. Thanks to the Becks: Jim, Susan, Deborah, and Emily for all their help and support. Thanks also to the Russells, Curt, Jane, and Sharon. Musically, he is indebted to the many drummers who gave him the rhythm to play, read and type, especially master percussionist Larry McDonald. Many thanks also to Andrea Rotondo, our extremely talented managing editor and the dedicated team at Schirmer who helped make this book a reality. Thanks are also due to David Weiss' past and current magazine colleagues, who helped hone his journalistic skills, including Phil Hood and Andy Doerschuk of *Drum!* magazine, George Petersen, Tom Kenny, and Kevin Becka of *Mix* magazine, Kirsten Nelson of *Systems Contractor News,* and Frank Wells of *Pro Sound News.* Other people whose influence, advice, and efforts contributed strongly to this book include Audrey Berger, Budd Carr, the family of Irwin Coster, Evan Greenspan, Christina Kline, Mary Jo Mennella, Howard Sherman, Michael Simon, and Ria Spencer. Special thanks to Tom Swift for his valuable legal advice. Everyone who is profiled in these pages or on the book's Website was extremely generous with their time, and additional thanks is due to them.

Credits

Managing Editor: Andrea M. Rotondo
Copyeditor: Barbara Schultz
Cover Art: Josh Labouve
Production Director: Dan Earley
Interior Design: Len Vogler
Publicity Coordinator: Alison M. Wofford

About the Authors

Ramsay Adams has extensive experience in branding the look and sound of television, print and new media, from flash files to Web design and advertising. He was the music director for a major cable news channel (FOX) for more than three years. Prior to his television experience, he worked as a music manager, working with an A-list clientele that included Richie Sambora and The Trans-Siberian Orchestra. He has worked with James Taylor and Leonardo DiCaprio on environmental campaigns and helped DiCaprio on the Millennium Earth Day celebration.

Adams has also worked as the director for an urban parks advocacy group and as a columnist and editor for major print and online publications. He wrote an entertainment column for FoxNews.com and is an adjunct professor at New York University's Center for Advanced Digital Applications and has served as an editor for the advocacy publications Energy Futures, and Parks For Tomorrow as well as the news magazine The National Times. Ramsay also cofounded the band Bananafish Zero which and was signed to Edel Records.

The next piece of the puzzle is Dave Hnatiuk, an artist manager, published author, professor, show/film producer, and an expert on the field of music supervision for TV, Film, New Media, and Live Events.

Hnatiuk started his career at birth as the son of two successful professional musicians based out of Scotch Plains, N.J. In 1996, he landed a music-supervisor position with ABC/Disney, where he was awarded a Daytime Emmy for his contributions in Music Direction and Composition for a Drama Series, *All My Children*.

In 1998, Mr. Hnatiuk built the first music division of the Number One-rated Fox News Channel. It was there that he produced theme songs and sound design for shows including *The O'Reilly Factor, The Fox Report,* and all the rest…literally. With his move to MTV in 2002, he can now say that he's done music supervision at all the major networks (ABC, Fox, NBC, and Viacom).

On the film side, Hnatiuk served as the music supervisor for the 2005 Merchant Ivory/Sony Pictures Film and Soundtrack *Heights*, directed by Chris Terrio. Also, he music-supe'd Evan Oppenheimer's feature *Justice,* which competed in the 2003 Tribeca Film Festival and won at the 2003 Marco Island Film Festival. Hnatiuk also helped score his former rap group BLESTeNATION a hot spot in the Universal Film *Blue Crush,* as well as a spot on the film's Virgin Records soundtrack in 2002. Upcoming films include Christian Charles' *Nothing But the Truth* and Vinny Rubino's *Break-Up Artist,* which won awards at the Hampton's/IFC, Garden State, and Newport film festivals.

In early 2002, he developed and established the first ever curriculum for

Music Supervision at New York University. The Fall 2004 semester marked the tenth semester of the course's existence. Hnatiuk also delivers regular seminars on Music Supervision with the Film Music Network.

In 2005, he signed the New York City-based rock band The Kin *(www.thekin.com)* to his management and production company, Sprout *(www.sproutproductions.com)*. He manages several other bands and artists, as well as consulting for companies such as Breast Cancer Awareness, Harley Davidson, Bethel Center for the Arts, Radical Media, Artstart, Camp Interactive, Firebrand Productions, Hothead Studios, Temple of Soul, The NASA Space Program, The Ad Council, Tribeca Films, The Director's Guild, The International Academy of Television, Arts and Sciences, Nickelodeon, Employ.com, CHAMPCAR Racing, Who Did That Music?, 5 Alarm Music, ABC Sports, Newline Cinema, and more.

"Find what you love, and do it. Just don't hurt yourself trying." —David Hnatiuk

The third member of the *Music Supervision* team is David Weiss. Mr. Weiss is an internationally published freelance journalist. He is the New York editor of *Mix* magazine, the world's leading pro audio publication, and his work has appeared regularly in publications such as *Systems Contractor News, Archi-Tech, Digital Television, TV Technology, Time Out New York, Remix, Tape Op,* and *Drum!* magazine.

Weiss is the founder and music supervisor of the growing music-loop library, *www.meetyourbeat.com,* which features fresh content from some of the world's most talented musicians. He is also the founder of D Media, Inc. *(www.dwords.com),* a communications consultancy for the pro audio and broadcast technology industries.

Weiss is also a seasoned marketing/PR writer for the pro audio, broadcast, A/V, music, and fiber-optic industries. Clients have included the New York City video-editing facility Rhinoceros; communications firm Marcomm Group for clients including Canon, Ikegami, Chyron, Videotek, Vinten, and D Data; fiber-optic carrier Q Media; A/V specialists Essential Communications; and post house, Planet V.

Weiss graduated from the University of Michigan with a B.A. in Communications (1994). He lives in Manhattan with his wife, Linda, and son, Broderick.

L-R: Ramsay Adams, David Hnatiuk, and David Weiss.

CHAPTER one

The Evolution of Music Supervision

In **order to** look great, it has to sound great.

From ancient times to the Academy Awards, audiences have been moved by sound. It's true no matter what the performance: The chorus in a Greek tragedy, a tribal dance deep in Madagascar, a performance of Mozart's *Cosi Fan Tutte,* or the premiere of the latest Quentin Tarantino movie.

Today, more and more of the people who match sounds to visual media and events—film, TV shows, commercials, video games, Websites, Flash animations, DVD menus, cell phone ringtones, live happenings—have a title that clearly defines what they do: *Music supervisor.* A music supervisor is a person who selects and licenses music and sound effects for media, but you don't have to have that title to have those responsibilities. In fact, with the explosion of media experiences in every direction, music supervision is a job that producers, directors, editors, Web designers, programmers, animators, administrative staff, and many others are asked to handle on a daily basis.

Whether you're doing it by choice or by default, music supervision can be both incredibly rewarding and challenging. Besides the artistic appeal of perhaps taking one of your favorite pieces of music and sharing it with a wide audience via a movie soundtrack, there's so much more that goes into doing music supervision right. Great music supervisors have to juggle licensing know-how with budgetary skills, while tending to multiple relationships and staying on top of pop culture.

No matter what your job description, one thing is undeniable: The better the music supervision on your media project, the more effective, inspiring, and unforgettable it can be.

Music Supervision's Evolution: A Convergence Timeline

In the twenty-first century, the music supervisor's job is made even more important and exciting by the phenomenon of *convergence,* wherein diverse media eventually combine to create a new experience. DVDs are an extremely powerful example of convergence—not only do they offer high-resolution audio and video, but they can also be played on either a TV or a computer, and provide links to Websites and other interactive features.

Because audio is such an enriching part of the human experience, convergence leads again and again to the inclusion of music and sound effects within various media. In order to get the proper perspective on the complexities of music supervision today, it will be helpful to look at key developments and points of convergence in the audio/visual experience.

Pre-1800s

Starting with ancient civilizations, mankind accompanied its most sacred and important rituals with chanting and drumming. The Bible extensively documents music's presence in all facets of life, ranging from social to political. From Africa to Alaska to the Aztecs, official gatherings had an audio component, and someone whose job it was to make sure it came off right.

In culture after culture, live music—there was no other kind—and storytelling in the form of dramatic performance began melding to create new kinds of performances. In sixteenth-century China, *Kunqu* was a style of performance where soft singing was accompanied by drums and bamboo flute. In Europe, full orchestras were combined with powerful vocalists acting out a story to produce opera. By the 1700s, a system was even in place to keep track of royalties (for performances and the reproduction of sheet music). It was an important channel of income for popular composers like Mozart.

1890s to 1920s: The First Convergence

Big things were happening on the audio and visual front around this time. Thanks to the vision and expertise of inventor Thomas Alva Edison and his laboratory, still images came to life with his patented Kinetoscope, which could record and reproduce objects in motion. Meanwhile, phonographs—also brought into being by Edison—had been maturing since 1877. Early phonographs worked by wrapping strips of tin foil around a 4-inch-diameter drum that was hand-cranked at about sixty revolutions per minute (RPM). (To actually hear some of these amazing first recordings and get a deeper history of the origins of recorded sound, visit *www.tinfoil.com.*)

It was only natural that people would attempt to fuse the Kinetoscope with the phonograph. Throughout the next decades, multiple attempts to make the moving picture synchronous with phonograph technology were undertaken. Until this was perfected, it became clear that music was needed to accompany the otherwise silent movies that were proving enormously popular, and making mega-celebrities of performers like Charlie Chaplin.

The solution: An on-site organist, piano player, or a group of musicians who brought out the finer points of the story in the theater. At first, the musicians were allowed to improvise the music, but soon music publishers that specialized in making music for film sprang up. Likewise, filmmakers and movie studios started to dictate what music should be played at their screenings. Not surprisingly, performing-rights societies such as the American Society of Composers and Producers (ASCAP) were also founded to protect the increasingly complicated rights of composers. Music supervision for media was officially taking shape, and quickly.

1922 to 1941: Radio Takes Off, Movies Talk

Radio, which had been under serious development for decades—already used extensively by amateur operators and the military during World War I—finally entered primetime in the 1920s. Radio networks, including the National Broadcasting Corporation (NBC) and the Radio Corporation of America (RCA) came together, forming the basis for powerful media companies whose influence continues to this day. Most early stations were AM (amplitude modulation), and all broadcasts would be in mono—as opposed to stereo—for several more decades.

Entertainment turned an important corner in 1927, when the first "talkie" movie—boasting synchronized sound and picture—was released in the form of *The Jazz Singer* starring Al Jolson. Suddenly, there was a huge market for film composers who could create a signature song for the opening credits (or "titles"), closing credits, as well as musical embellishments throughout. The Academy of Motion Picture Arts & Sciences gave a nod to music in movies with a new category, "Best Score," at the Academy Awards.

Music supervision also took a big leap at this point. Working under the title of musical directors, skilled individuals oversaw what could be a large group of music editors, composers, and arrangers. Check the credits for a film like 1939's classic *Gone with the Wind*, and you'll see that stock music people were already in on the project (in addition to composer Max Steiner, who created its still-legendary theme).

1941 to 1950: Movietones and TV

As the United States got seriously involved in World War II, Movietones, or five-minute movie-house newsreels showcasing the exploits of the armed forces, became a cultural institution in and of themselves. The choice of the opening strains of Beethoven's Fifth Symphony for these pervasive newsreels would prove to be a high-profile piece of music supervision.

Meanwhile, television, which had actually been available to the public since 1935, was poised to make its move, beginning a pop culture dominance that continues to this day. After 1945, with the horrors and shortages of World War II finally over, many American families went on a spending binge and added a TV to their home, particularly in 1948 and 1949. With the arrival of this powerful mass medium, which funneled audio and video directly into people's houses and businesses, many more music directors would be needed.

Music supervision was about to get much more sophisticated—and interesting. In 1949, a convergence was happening in the form of radio series being adapted for TV. *The Lone Ranger* is one example. The issue of what music cues could carry over from the existing radio library, and how much they would cost TV producers and directors, reshaped music directors' and editors' practices for licensing, re-arranging, and re-rerecording.

1950 to 1970s: Multiple Convergences

A landslide of crucial developments in mass media, both audio and visual, occurred during this time period, so that the importance of music supervision was boosted in many ways.

TV and music became forever inseparable, with the success of a show called *American Bandstand,* which debuted in 1952. Hosted by Dick Clark from 1956 on, it showed a teenage studio audience dancing to mostly lip-synched performances by carefully selected, mainstream pop artists of the day, exposing national viewers to rock 'n' roll and breaking artists such as Jerry Lee Lewis in the process. One of the most important TV music events of all time would occur on February 9, 1964, when The Beatles appeared on CBS' *The Ed Sullivan Show.* It was a landmark performance that influenced an entire generation of music fans and musicians, changing music forever.

The TV medium itself also became a richer format, as RCA sold ninety thousand color TV sets in 1959 alone, and broke the one million mark in 1964. TV commercials, like radio before, would prove to be a rich source of income for composers and stock music houses.

While phonographs had been a staple of most modern homes for decades, music distribution took a step forward in the 1950s, as records changed from the brittle 78rpm format to 33⅓ and 45rpm vinyl records, which were much more durable.

At the same time, recording practices were becoming increasingly sophisticated, as studios developed multitrack techniques that gave artists, audio engineers, and producers heightened control over sound quality. Recordings also became multichannel, moving from one channel, or mono, to two-channel, or stereo, starting in 1957. In the mid-1960s, stereo became the industry standard for music recordings. An early form of surround sound, quadraphonic (four channels), would also appear in 1969.

Recording technology developments converged with radio in 1961, when the first FCC-authorized FM (frequency modulation) stereo broadcasts took place.

Meanwhile, movie scores and soundtracks would become even more diverse and influential than ever before. There was the startling sound of Wendy Carlos in *A Clockwork Orange,* Bob Dylan in *Don't Look Back,* The Beatles in *Help!* and *A Hard Day's Night,* and *Easy Rider* with its signature Steppenwolf song, "Born to be Wild." Music supervisors now played an increasingly important role in the sounds of cinematic pop culture.

1970s to 1984: VCRs, Computers, Video Games, and Cell Phones Arrive
As TV, radio, movies, and music were humming along, another key sector in communications technology—computers—started to develop. Xerox was a key contributor with its founding of PARC, the Palo Alto Research Center, a laboratory that helped speed along the maturation of microprocessors, Ethernet, modern GUI's (graphical user interfaces) and, eventually, Apple Computer. By the early Eighties, the computer was moving from a novelty to a necessary item for word processing and other tasks, both in the office and at home. Music supervisors were already using computers for spreadsheets and other organizational tasks, and before long they would become indispensable for auditioning, editing, and composing music.

Video cassette recorders (VCRs) hit the home market in 1972, adding a new dimension to home entertainment, and increasing the licensing complexities music supervisors would encounter as they negotiated royalties for cassettes, and domestic vs. international distribution.

The video game maker Atari was also established in 1972, making its debut with a single Pong machine in a California bar. The game was a huge hit, and Atari followed up with a home version in 1974 (Apple Computer founders Steve Jobs and Steve Wozniak were early employees.) There were other players in the home and arcade markets as well, including Bally and Magnavox, and Taito (Space Invaders), and by the end of the decade, video games, which already employed multiple sound effects and basic music, had become a multibillion industry.

In 1977, public testing of cell phones began. The first trials were by 2,000 customers in Chicago, followed by Washington D.C. and Japan. Early phones didn't have customizable ringtones, but eventually they would, introducing a new set of challenges for music supervisors.

Not long after, the development of the compact disc (CD) would come to fruition, bringing digital audio storage and playback to the mainstream. Developed in large part in a joint effort by Sony and Phillips, the standards for the CD that were set in 1979 remain to this day, including maximum program length (seventy-four minutes) and sample rate (44.1 kHz). Upon the introduction of the CD in 1983, thirty thousand CD players and eight hundred thousand CDs were sold. Computers and CDs hadn't come together just yet, but when they did, music and music supervision were fundamentally altered.

MTV debuted in 1981. The name itself, "Music Television," represented a convergence, and it would have a huge ripple effect on culture. The program directors who served as that channel's music supervisors wielded enormous power to make or break artists. The considerable influence of MTV and its subsequent spin-offs—VH1, MTV2, and more—-remains firmly in place today.

1985 to 1995: Commercials, Stereo Broadcasts, Movie Sountracks, and the Internet

Music supervision for TV commercials took an important turn in 1985 when rock legend Eric Clapton allowed his song "After Midnight" to be used in an ad for Michelob beer. Before this, rock artists had been almost unanimous in their refusal to license their songs for corporate use, and Clapton's decision caused a great deal of controversy at the time. However, it also helped open the door for other artists to do the same, and over the ensuing years, the licensing of hit rock tracks for commercial purposes would become a much more common—and artistically acceptable—practice.

Stereo TV broadcasts also began to be widely adopted by the networks in the mid-Eighties, after several years of development. As a result, a much larger emphasis was placed on the musical content of shows, giving music supervisors an increased role in the success or failure of a series. *Miami Vice* was one such series, a stylish show that became as well-known for its cutting-edge music as its on-screen action. Its theme song by Jan Hammer became a smash radio hit single.

Movie soundtracks continued to be big business, with the music supervisors in charge of them capable of launching big hits, boosting existing bands, and reviving older artists. Just two examples of massive hits from movies included Berlin's "Take My Breath Away" from the *Top Gun* soundtrack, and Ben E. King's classic "Stand by Me" from the movie of the same name.

While the concept of computers talking to each over a global network, or Internet, was not new, it wasn't until the early 1990s that it became easily accessible to everyday computer users. The name "World Wide Web" appeared in 1991, and the term "surfing the Internet" came up a year later. Due to bandwidth limitations, the ability to deliver music files digitally over the Internet was still out of reach to most. It wouldn't be long, however, before computers, music, and music supervision became completely intertwined.

1995 to Present: Convergence Mainstream

With computers firmly entrenched in home and business life, one of the most important factors in media growth became Internet connectivity. The number of people with access to e-mail and the Web grew very quickly. By 1998, there were already two million Web domains registered with Network Solutions. In a dangerous combination for the music industry, CD players/burners also become standard equipment on computers, completely eliminating all barriers to the worldwide sharing of digital music files, especially in the compressed MP3 format.

From this point on, Websites could act as Internet radio stations, playing music 24/7, or TV stations, with the ability to play video, animation, and other visuals with accompanying audio. All such digitized media could also be e-mailed person to person, or made available to groups of users in networks known as peer-to-peer (P2P).

At the same time, the ability to preview, send, and receive music over the Internet and Intranets radically re-shaped the workflow of the modern music supervisor. Online searches for licensing information, as well as the electronic ability to complete license requests and other licensing functions with performing-rights organizations and publishers gave music supervisors unprecedented efficiency and access to the world of music and sound effects at large. As bandwidth increased and music production software became more intuitive, music supervisors also had increased responsibilities towards the creation and production of TV, video games, and online entertainment. The advent of portable music players, such as Apple's iPod, meant that vast licensed playlists and numerous music supervisors were needed to create and update them.

In addition, another new form of digital media storage/playback became predominant, the Digital Versatile Disc (DVD). When it was launched in 1997, the advantages were clear: It can store a full-length movie, multiple bonus features, and surround-sound audio on a disc that's the same size as the CD. DVD-ROMs became integral to the huge increase in video game quality for consoles like Microsoft's X-Box. DVDs also meant that music supervisors were allotted a great deal more memory for high-impact music and sound effects. In another twist, video games could be played by multiple players interacting on line.

TV broadcasting made its own leap, as the industry gradually shifted from the long-standing Standard Definition (SDTV) to High Definition TV. HDTV offers not only increased image resolution but vastly superior surround-sound capabilities, meaning music supervisors will be organizing a great deal more surround content, as opposed to stereo, as the transition to HDTV continues. Video On Demand (VOD), also grew in popularity, giving television a much higher level of interactivity.

Throughout this decade, pop and electronic songs were heard in an increasing number of TV commercials. Permission to use songs both old and new, hits and obscure, became the rule, rather than the exception. Volkswagen tapped indie artists such as Velocity Girl and Nick Drake; Cadillac used Led Zeppelin music, and Moby's album *Play* was licensed by Ford and dozens of other corporations. Commercial music supervisors also showed the ability not only to pick hit acts but also to create them, fulfilling a role similar to record company A&R in the process. Mitsubishi's use of the song "Days Go By" by U.K. dance act Dirty Vegas propelled the act to new heights of popularity that it may not have achieved otherwise.

Because digital storage media takes up so little space, promotions involving music continued to grow in all directions. LidRock is just one example, as it struck up agreements with major record companies to have music by artists like Britney Spears and Avril Lavigne distributed in millions of soda lids on three- and five-inch CDs. The popularity of such promotions created an expanding field for music supervisors.

Cell phone adoption also became extremely widespread, growing to approximately sixty million users and a $30-billion a year industry in 2004, with those numbers being driven partially by the sale of custom ringtones. Ringtones themselves evolved from mediocre-sounding monophonic sounds to rich, highly expressive polyphonic tones, giving music supervisors vastly increased options and responsibilities for selection and licensing.

Next...

While this timeline shows some of the major events in media and the ensuing implications for the field of music supervision, it is only a partial list of significant developments. The state of media at any time is the result of the tireless efforts of thousands of people, making contributions large and small, famous and unheralded.

Predicting what will happen next isn't essential here, because people are finding new ways to use and combine media—especially digital media—on an almost-daily basis. What is important is that you keep your eyes and ears open for developments, or, better yet, keep ahead of the curve and create your own media experience. In the pages of this book, you'll meet people your own media experience. In the pages of this book, you'll meet people who have done just that. There will also be constant updates at this book's companion Website, *www.musicsupervisioncentral.com*.

Music and sound effects are crucial factors in the success of virtually every new medium or media service: People are more likely to share, purchase, and spend their time on media with audio that amazes, inspires, or just helps to tell the story. Music supervisors are leading the way in making that connection.

PROFILE
Budd Carr, Music Supervisor
Natural Born Killers and *Heat*

- A leader in film music supervision
- The evolution of the field
- Music supervising for Oliver Stone and Michael Mann

Meet one of the giants of film music supervision: Budd Carr. A trendsetter in the field, Carr's first-ever music-supervision gig was for the 1984 classic *Terminator,* starring Arnold Schwarzenegger—an experience so good, he never looked back.

Carr already had a great job, working as the manager for the seminal rock band Kansas, when he was recruited by the indie production company filming *Terminator* to assist director/writer James Cameron and producer Gale Anne Hurd in obtaining music for their relatively low-budget film. "The problem the producers were having was that they couldn't get anyone to return their calls, so they thought I could help them," Carr recalls. "I had lots of friends who were personal managers, and my job was to get on the phone with them and say, 'Jim Cameron wants a song from the Go-Go's; from the Police; from Prince.' After clearing the songs, I found out the movie didn't have enough money to license such popular tracks! From there, it was kind of a learn-by-doing process. I went home, opened my desk drawer, and pulled out cassettes from friends who were developing artists, played them for Jim, and he put them in the movie."

Terminator was a surprise hit, and with just one film under his belt, Carr had already made an impression on Hollywood. He was quickly recruited to music-supervise Oliver Stone's directorial debut, *Salvador,* and Carr suddenly had a whole new career. He's overseen more than fifty movies since, including the landmark soundtracks of films such as *Natural Born Killers* and *Heat,* as well as *Dirty Dancing: Havana Nights, Twister, Any Given*

According to Carr, his experience in managing bands was the perfect recipe for success as a music supervisor. "I found my knowledge of negotiating was an asset to a film director and producer," he says. "Therein lives the basis of music supervision. It's access and the ability to present ideas.

"For me, that skill springs from my background as an agent and a manager. What you do in those areas is negotiate for people who have ideas and creative desires. The challenge to actually accomplish that, and to be creative at the same time, is what attracted me to music supervision.

"I think the most important thing a music supervisor can do is enable the writer, producer, or director to fully realize their music desires within the framework of their budget. The important thing is to remember that, at the end of the day, it's not your picture, TV show, or video game. It's their project."

In his two decades as a music supervisor, Carr has seen a surprising number of changes in his field. "A film music supervisor grew out of the need of film producers and directors to get a more contemporary catalog of songs in their pictures," he points out. "At the same time, record labels and music-publishing companies did not have staff who marketed music to films, or even knew what they owned or how to license it. So in the early stages of modern music supervision in the late 1980s and early 1990s, it really became a bunch of renegade guys running around, trying to do stuff for indie film.

"In the Nineties, there was more attention placed on music for film, which provided more opportunities for music supervisors. Today you see more and more producers and directors hiring a person to liaise between themselves and the studios, whether on budgets or coordinating with the record labels. Music supervision is now a business—in the late Eighties there were maybe half-a-dozen to a dozen music supervisors, but I think the most current industry book has at least twenty or thirty pages of them."

Ask Carr what distinguishes a good soundtrack vs. a bad soundtrack, and he puts it this way. "You shouldn't really be distracted from the storytelling, and hopefully the music enhances the storytelling. I think that if you go to a movie and you love the music in the picture, it enhances the experience, and the same is true for TV or a video game.

"That doesn't mean I haven't approached it differently. I have deliberately put an irritating piece of music in a movie because I wanted people to feel uncomfortable—and they're not a hundred percent sure why they're uncomfortable—but it's because the music is not quite right. Film composers do the same thing: Instead of a typical action cue, they might spin reality by contrasting it with something beautiful, and it becomes scary. A classic example is Michael Mann's use of "In-A-Gadda-Da-Vida" in *Manhunter*. This was already a scary scene, but something about the music and the way it was shot scares the living daylights out of you."

One of Carr's signature films is the riveting 1994 serial murder saga *Natural Born Killers,* directed by Oliver Stone and featuring a wildly dark, diverse soundtrack that efficiently propels and underscores the disturbing action onscreen. "One of the benefits I've had working with Oliver is being brought in on the early stages of a movie. I read the script, and I'm there for the casting. Oliver is someone who will write music into his scripts, and in the early stages of *Natural Born Killers,* the script already had many music references. He also had producers around him who had concepts about particular types of music that either (lead characters) Mickey or Mallory would be into, or that the audience would appreciate."

To Carr, foresight and tight organization are the most essential qualities for success in music supervision. "If you're not prepared for the task, then it's going to be difficult," he states. "That means if you don't understand licensing, if you don't understand where to go to get material, and if you don't understand how to utilize resources, then the job's just going to be difficult. A good music supervisor is not just somebody who has a great CD collection.

"The other task is making sure that you understand what it is the director wants, so that you can provide solutions, while making sure that the director and the composer are actually speaking the same language. It's communication: If someone says they want a song with 'edge' in that scene, what does that mean? Do they want a punk song, a loud guitar song, an edgy lyric? Sometimes they don't know what they want, and all you can do is play them half-a-dozen choices. If somebody tells you, 'That's the worst idea you ever had,' then you go, 'Okay, at least I know what *not* to bring back.'"

For Budd Carr, the future of music supervision is wide open. "I look at every project as a brand-new challenge," he concludes. "I think as long as people continue to change the way they're producing media, then I think music supervisors will continue to be challenged in the way they search for music."

PROFILE
Joel Beckerman, President
Man Made Music

• The Discovery Channel, HBO, Jetix, ABC, and Showtime
• How to develop sonic branding
• Innovative business models in music supervision

What is sonic branding? The man to ask is Joel Beckerman, founder of Man Made Music (*www.manmademusic.com*). A talented composer and sound designer, Beckerman worked at several music houses in a number of capacities before he began his own, with the mission of combining music production, music supervision, and the science of sonic branding.

"The use of music in media is all about helping to tell stories. That's what it's all about. The more tools you can bring to bear to tell great stories in a great way, the more ways you can get music to contribute to that," says Beckerman, whose facility is complete with a full-fledged recording studio. "That's part of being exposed to new music and providing new resources that aren't traditionally thought of as music-supervision resources."

Beckerman's rapidly expanding firm, which he founded in 1997, has a fast-growing client base that includes HBO, Discovery Channel, and Disney's newest channel, Jetix. A key has been his sharp understanding and development of the field of sonic branding. "Sonic branding is the strategic use of sound and music to build brands," he explains. "What we did recently for Jetix is a good example. They said, 'This is what our brand is all about; this is the "emotional takeaway"; the touch points where people will see the brand—on line, on-air, products, theme-park rides, and a million other things.' So we were able to say, 'Now that we know all that, we'll tell you all the ways and places that music and sound design can make a difference.'"

One of Man Made's most visible roles in the Jetix campaign is a large "launch" package of promo IDs, lasting three, five, or ten seconds in length. "We worked with a design company called Spark Design out of California," Beckerman says. "We were both hired to create these IDs, and really develop what the brand was all about. The design company came up with the idea of this mascot named Jay, the client loved it, and the assignment essentially was for us to help create a real personality and language for him, as well as the sonic identity for the whole brand.

"Disney has a bunch of brands, including the Disney Channel which is a demographic. But for Jetix, the idea was to create an older boys' network, so we thought about the mascot—how he should appeal to people, the music that should be in there, how it should appeal to these kids. We realized the best way to reach kids in this age group was to actually target it to kids in the age thirteen to fifteen group. It's the 'older brother' thing. Jay the mascot became representative of the older brother you want to grow up to be like."

With the concept established, the next step was translating it into a unique sound. "What we determined is that Jay couldn't speak any known language—this is a multinational, multicultural, worldwide brand. So we actually took a human voice and processed it up in millions of different ways, and spent weeks and came up with a vocabulary of sounds.

"The sonic branding element of Jetix is an announcer saying, 'Jetix,' but it's also highly processed. The idea being that, at the end of each one of these international spots, the kids hear the sound of the character planting his feet [stomp, stomp], followed by 'Jetix.' Since the audience hears this in every break, in every association to the brand, it's become a mnemonic for the brand, or sound logo. These spots tell a whole story in ten seconds, because in TV, time is money."

The next step was to back it all up with the right music. "We began looking at and creating music that made sense for the Jetix audience," Beckerman continues. "The IDs featured stories that were quirky problem-solving situations, so music that was more celebratory made sense: Dance-hall music, things we did that were more for sports shows, and very frenetic, kids bouncing-off-walls stuff. In general, music for promotions of any kind has to have some energy to it. Very rarely is it slow or subtle; it's supposed to be a brand statement, which doesn't tend to be a mellow thing."

When Discovery Channel hired Man Made Music to supervise the overall sound for the entire cable network, Beckerman knew he had an equally interesting, long-term challenge to meet. "The trick for them sometimes is budget. If you're on a feature film, that's one budget. But for some of these programs that are not the top-tier series, they still need great music, because you can't have mediocre music on some shows and great music on others. We're all about budget. In those cases, we'd help them find additional music-library options, or help them find a great up-and-coming composer.

"It's not about trying to come up with a consistent sound across all of Discovery's shows. We describe it as passionate music that makes an

Discovery's shows. We describe it as passionate music that makes an emotional connection to the viewers. That opens up enormous possibilities."

No matter what the project, Joel Beckerman firmly believes it is most important to give the music supervisor a good head start. "We always say to people that the key is to bring us in early," he concludes. "The problem is when people come to us after the film has been shot and the story told. That's very limiting. The power of music supervision is letting us, as music supervisors, get into the mix early and really try to help influence the project. It's a combination of reflecting what the director's vision is, and then influencing their vision by exceeding expectations with what you bring to the table."

PROFILE
Joel Sill, President
Intermedia Music Group

- Pioneer in the field of film
- Music supervisor for classic films, including *Easy Rider, An Officer and a Gentleman, and Forrest Gump*

In the world of modern music supervision, there are few names that carry more weight than Joel Sill. His immersion in music started with his father, Lester Sill, the legendary music publisher and prolific record producer who influenced Joel to kick off a lifelong career in music that reshaped the scope and power of today's movie soundtracks. President of Intermedia Music Group (*www.intermediafilm.com*), Sill has an impressive list of film music-supervision credits, to say the least, starting with the groundbreaking *Easy Rider*. From there, he headed the music departments of Paramount Pictures and Warner Bros. films, overseeing music for motion pictures such as *Reds, An Officer and a Gentleman, 48 Hours, Flashdance, Purple Rain, Mad Max: Beyond Thunderdome,* and *The Killing Fields.* After Warner Bros., he independently supervised *La Bamba, The Fabulous Baker Boys, Forrest Gump, Cast Away,* and *Terminator 3: Rise of the Machines.*

How did you become a music supervisor?
It was by accident. I was working at Dunhill Records as a producer and music publisher. Steppenwolf was one of our recording groups. Burt

my father's and an acquaintance of mine. Burt wanted to use "Born to Be Wild" and "The Pusher." My father saw the film and loved it and suggested Burt call me for the Steppenwolf clearance. I wanted to see the film before approving the use. After seeing the movie, I knew it was going to have a great impact, so I went to work securing the rights for all the music. The costs of licenses then was minimal—maybe $750.00 for Hendrix or $250.00 for the Electric Prunes. We traded the vinyl pressing rights to Columbia Records for the Byrds and early Steppenwolf. We traded cassette rights to Warner for Hendrix and the Prunes. We could not get The Band from Capitol because of a non-coupling clause, so I re-recorded "The Weight" with our group, Smith, that was hot at the time. The film and soundtrack came out and were both enormous successes, and I became the flavor of the month as a music guy for film.

What can a good music supervisor add to a film, TV show, or video game?
I think one can help the filmmakers find a musical concept, help sell the film with good musical promotion, and save costs.

What makes a good soundtrack? What makes a bad soundtrack?
I think a good soundtrack supports the film emotionally and stylistically, and then steps up with performance numbers that leave the audience satisfied. Like *Risky Business, Flashdance, Pulp Fiction,* or *Oh Brother, Where Art Thou.* A bad soundtrack is made by bad ingredients, either the wrong mix of people making the project, the wrong mix of music, or both. Sometimes circumstances work against you with the rights of certain material or artists not being available.

Who are some directors you have worked with that help you to introduce great music into a soundtrack?
Taylor Hackford, Bob Zemeckis, Barry Levinson, Steve Kloves, Sydney Pollock, Dick Donner, Joel Schumacher, Warren Beatty. Certain producers are also great contributors such as Steve Starkey, Jane Rosenthal and Frank Marshall, Kathy Kennedy, and the late Mark Rosenburg.

What's your favorite soundtrack you've compiled, and why?
I have some favorites. *Easy Rider* (I was living the sentiment of the movie), *An Officer and a Gentleman* (the first of many projects with Taylor Hackford), *La Bamba* (I got to work with filmmakers who helped me reach the film's and my potential), *Tap* (It was a great experience with Greg Hines,

Sammy Davis Jr., and James Newton Howard, and I love the record), *The Fabulous Baker Boys* (musically off the beaten path and a challenge to cast the right musicians to display believability for Jeff and Beau Bridges, and providing Michelle Pfeiffer with Sally Stevens to help her refine her voice), and *Forrest Gump* (working with Bob Zemeckis is always a treat, but this was a feast), *K-19 The Widow Maker* (working with Harrison Ford and convincing the production to use The Kirov Orchestra and Choir with conductor Valery Gergiev and recording the soul of such great Russian musicians with a conductor who is revered as a force of nature). I think "The Why" is based on the overall experience of the project, not just the success.

What's most difficult about being a music supervisor?
Not getting the music to its potential, or having a studio executive tell you his son or daughter doesn't like the song.

What should today's up-and-coming music supervisors be aware of?
Paying attention to all their responsibilities, as well as the other elements that combine to make the film, not just the music.

What are your favorite aspects of music supervision?
My favorite is an emotionally satisfying outcome and seeing an audience respond to the material. I also love being in the editing room.

What is your proudest moment as a music supervisor?
When my father saw the scene where Forrest Gump was running from the truck with bullies and his braces came off. The source record was the Duane Eddy recording "Rebel Rouser," which my father produced. Also, when "Up Where We Belong" (from *An Officer and a Gentleman*) won the Academy Award for Best Original Song.

How do you expect music supervision to continue to change and evolve? What's next?
Because of the consolidation in the music business, competition will increase in the field and fees will be impacted. Reduced sales and more inter-label restrictions will make early preparations more critical to ensuring one gets the correct artists. I believe most productions realize that a music person is an essential component of the project, regardless of what the delivery system is.

CHAPTER two

Theory and Application

An overview of music-supervision theory and application in popular forms of media is in order. We'll break down important musical scenarios "cue to cue," from concept to completion. It's a detailed introduction to the standards and techniques used every day by working music supervisors.

Merging Sound With Vision

Media for the eyes and ears, ranging from television to movies and video games, rely on a seamless relationship between sights and sounds to communicate thoughts, feelings, and artistic vision. Whether a music supervisor is working in TV, where four hundred-plus productions may be in production domestically each week, or on one of the four hundred-fifty to five hundred feature films distributed in the United States annually, he or she is responsible for fostering that connection with an audience. It's no easy task, as music supervisors use an expert skill set while drawing from a vast body of knowledge covering music and visual theory and application.

Everything visual has a potential sound accompaniment. The key word here is *potential*, because there are events and situations that exist apart from sound. For example, if we were walking in space or floating on the Moon, the absence of air means there would be no sound—even though there would be mind-blowing visuals! Or, you could be sitting in a coffee shop looking out the window: You can see a couple outside and know that they're arguing because of their gestures and facial expressions, but you can't hear what they're saying.

Conversely, there are just as many scenarios that have a multitude of sonic elements, many of which stem from music. The music supervisor must be aware of all of these possibilities at all times.

Even in the absence of human speech, music and sound are everywhere around us. Wind makes sound when it passes through trees, and birds make sound when they communicate with one another. Man has long been influenced by these bird songs, wind textures, and all natural sonic elements, and they have often become part of the blueprint for musical works.

Imagine sitting in a city park like New York City's Central Park, with the ever-evolving natural orchestra engulfing your eardrums, senses, and psyche. What are you hearing, and how is your actual position—your location—affecting what you are hearing? If you're sitting in the middle of the park in the grassy field, would you hear a totally different mix of city sounds than if you were sitting on the northwest perimeter under a tree with some bushes at its base?

Location, Location, Location

Why is it important to consider all these factors in determining the location of the scene or cue, as in the park example above? Location is important because, as much as you may hear the same "set" of sounds in two different spots in the park, your *perspective* relative to these sounds is the more important element. Perspective is what the music supervisor of every TV show and film creates through the use of music and sound design.

Sound design is the art of creating and/or mixing sound effects for the purpose of complementing a particular visual scenario. Sound designers often mix common environmental sound effects, creating a completely original aural collage—much like the way a song is made. However, sound design does not have to be musical as much as it must marry itself to the visual in a way that communicates with the viewer.

Every commercial, show, and movie on TV takes place within its own location, or world. Some locations require music as their backdrops, and others need only natural sounds. Imagine yourself back in the city park: You hear birds, cars, trucks, horns, footsteps, a radio playing heavy metal, leaves rustling, people talking, a homeless man mumbling, and glasses clinking as a local restaurant sets up for the lunch rush. With all of this sound around you, it is your duty as a music supervisor and sound designer to remember what it is you're hearing and how you are hearing it, so that you can precisely re-create it in a post-production studio during the "sweetening" phase of your next project (probably using Digidesign Pro Tools, the digital audio workstation—DAW—that is the standard mixing platform for TV shows, commercials, and film).

Creating natural sound environments is most commonly the job of a designated sound designer, but a thorough understanding of sound design is an extremely important part of the body of knowledge music supervisors need to be successful. Typically, as you read in the first chapter, music supervisors choose and sometimes produce songs for productions. However, aspiring music supervisors today cannot rely on only those two skills to win them future projects. They must take their skill set to the next level: Combine an understanding of sound design with the practice of music supervision. (See an in-depth explanation of sound design and audio mixing in Chapter 4, Sound Design.)

Combinations of music and sound in visual media are infinite, but there are some basic building blocks that create the sound field and help to define the sense of location:

Score: Original music created by a composer written specifically for a TV show, commercial, movie, video game, or other media project.

Theme: The "signature" piece of music, usually score.

Background/Bed Music: Sets a tone and style for the work, and is often a variation on the theme. Good bed music is not necessarily even noticed by the viewer, but the viewer would notice its absence. For example, while watching the 1999 film *American Beauty*, take notice of the background music choices. Some are alternate arrangements of the film's main theme, and others are popular songs licensed for theatrical use. Again, this is usually score.

Source: Music with a visual connection to a source (radio, TV, headset) in the scene. Increasingly, "source" means any music in the project that isn't a part of the score.

Atmospheres: Drones or ambient music pieces that establish a mood or emotion and help set the scene.

Sound Effects: The whooshes, explosions, beeps, foghorns, and barking dogs that make for seamless transitions between scenes or give the viewer more clues to complete the picture that they're seeing. Managing sound effects can be a large part of the music supervisor's job. A good example is the 2002 film *Minority Report,* which relies heavily on original sound effects to bring to life ultra-modern technologies not commonly seen in real-life scenarios.

Natural Sound: Also known as "nat sound," this is the sound that was actually recorded at the same time as the video or film. Well-recorded dialog is nat sound that works for the picture, while constant traffic in the background is nat sound that may work against it.

Sound Delivers the Message

Think about any BMW or Chrysler commercial on TV today. With increasing frequency, spots from automobile manufacturers incorporate a recognizable song that was edited to the visual, with all the key actions highlighted, or it's a blend of sound design and music that communicates a specific message. Generally, the producer and the director of the production tell the music supervisor what slogan or message they want communicated. Once the supervisor understands that sonic goal, the planning phase of the job begins.

Clear Communication

Remember that the more you assume to be true at the project's inception, the greater risk you take. Music supervisors must make it their duty to get as much detailed information from their clients and production crews as possible. Simply put: Ask a *lot* of questions.

However, asking the right questions during the pre-production phase is only the beginning. The general rule of thumb is a variation on Murphy's Law: If something in the project can change, it probably will. However, if you can anticipate the change before it happens, you can potentially solve the problem in advance. Clear and constant communication with your crew and client will always help achieve your goal and meet your deadline.

There are a number of key questions to ask in the pre-production phase:

- Where does this production take place?
- Can I see an outline, shotlist, script and/or treatment?
- What is the music budget?
- From whose point of view will the message of this production be communicated and interpreted?
- Who is our audience?
- What time of day or night will this commercial air?
- What are my own technological capabilities?
- Are you (the client) using a temporary ("temp") reference track? If so, what is it?
- Have you (the client) given any thought to what kind of music you are looking for?

That last question is a particularly important one that often needs to be asked repeatedly throughout the production process. It's important to stay on the same page with your producer, writer, and director, so not to stray away from the common creative path of the team.

This can lead to another question:

- Are we composing an original song for this spot, or are we licensing a song?

The answer usually relates to your budget. In the TV commercial realm, currently, the average cost to commission an original song for one thirty-second track is $25,000 to $30,000. Once those fees have been paid, the client (in this case, the ad firm you're working for) owns the track and may run it forever. However, they must make the appropriate residual payments to musicians and singers (see Chapter 8, Licensing).

The costs to buy an existing pop or rock song, on the other hand, vary greatly. A song may be licensed for a few thousand dollars, or a million or more. Factors such as how long the commercial will run, for how long, and how many variations will be created are all factors that the publisher, record label, and artist will take into account in naming a price. (See Chapter 8, Licensing, for a thorough breakdown on how a song request is priced and negotiated.)

When the music supervisor has reached an understanding on the pre-production end, it's time to get to the drawing board. You'll hear thousands of different stories from music supervisors about how they decided on certain songs for their productions. Some refer to "the ping" as the most accurate method of narrowing down the correct song for any given scenario. "The ping" is a feeling of harmony that can be felt when visualizing a scene while auditioning music simultaneously. Most of us have experienced this in some form or another; it can be related to the emotion an actor feels when he or she comes as close as they possibly can to their character in a perfect performance.

Getting to "the ping" sounds almost meditative, but whatever you call it, it's really all about finding the right sonic fit. First, focus on the visual subject matter and all of the information that you have accrued throughout the pre-production process. When you are totally immersed in the scene, begin auditioning songs.

Auditioning the "Top 3"
Throughout this chapter you will notice the repeated use of the word *auditioning.* Here, auditioning means listening to music for the purpose of

choosing a "Top 3" list of songs for presentation. This Top 3 will be considered for the final production. Three is a good number, because it's not so many songs so as to confuse or overwhelm your peers. Rather, you will appear to have considered multiple options for the team to choose from, and given serious thought to communicating the advertisement or scene from more than one musical angle.

Often, music supervisors already sense which song is best for the job, even on first listen. Most times, your prediction for what is best will be consistent with the producer's or director's—after all, you did ask all of those detailed questions during the pre-production phase, so you know what they want.

The music supervisor must present choices that have arisen through careful research and auditioning, but it's also important to bring confidence to the cutting board and the entire production staff. If the staff doesn't agree with your choices and predictions, it is your responsibility to find out how you can redirect your search to better suit the production's needs.

Depending on your needs and budget, the perfect music for your project might already be recorded and ready to go, or it may be up to you to help bring it into existence. You'll have three main sources to sift through:

Library Music: Available on line or in CD collections ranging in size from miniscule to massive. These tracks are usually very well-recorded and are set up to be used fast and licensed with extreme ease. They can also be generic, boring, and/or the exact same sounds that all your peers are using. Nonetheless, in a time crunch, library music be your best friend.

Popular Music/Commercial Hits: Turn on your radio, or try and remember what you heard on the radio a decade ago. By far the most expensive option, well-known music can also be the most effective. Currently, the price to license a non-hit song typically ranges from about $15,000 to $40,000, while hits or semi-hits from more established artists can command $500,000 to $1,000,000.

Custom Music: Songs, score, themes, beds, or atmospheres composed specifically for the project. Here, the music supervisor plays the crucial role of middleman between the composer and producer. Your job is to pick the right composer the first time, and give that person accurate direction.

Getting back to those three ever-important song choices: How did you come to them? Did they make you feel like you were there in the project's visual scenario? It is important to be sure that the feelings you are identifying with the music you're auditioning are consistent and accurate.

This goes back to your experiences in a place like Central Park, as discussed earlier. Once you've been there, you can confidently say that what you heard there is one hundred percent real and true. Can you say the same about some random high-speed street scene that takes place in Abruzzi, Italy, with two BMW sports cars? Maybe not, unless you've been there, or to a place with similar acoustics, such as the Greenwich Village neighborhood of New York City, with its many narrow, cobblestone streets and nineteenth-century buildings.

The point here is that, when you make judgments on the sound or musical backdrop of any given scene, you'd better be confident in the accuracy of your judgment, and you should have prepared a very thorough explanation of the artistic parallel you are attempting to make. Every song has a meaning, and in every meaning there is a message. Music supervisors are masters of interpreting these sonic messages, whether they are expressed through lyrics, chord progressions, tempos, or sound effects. And, quite often, it is the music supervisor's responsibility to sync up the audio with visuals.

DAWs Make the Difference

Often a song will convey a message that is consistent with a visual, but the timing of the song is wrong for the timing of the visual. Let's say you're working on the :30 BMW commercial and you've got just enough money in your budget—$50,000 or so—to license the song you want.

You choose "A Little Bit More" by Lava Records recording artist Tony C and the Truth. There's only one problem: Your choice song has a :60 section that communicates the exact emotion and message you are looking for. Now you're trying to get :30 out of :60. Manual tape-to-tape, razor-cut splicing used to be the only way to solve this common problem, but today, we can achieve the same goals at much higher levels of efficiency through the use of Digital Audio Workstations (DAWs), such as Pro Tools (the current industry standard), Nuendo, or Digital Performer, to name a few.

DAWs have revolutionized what music supervisors and all audio engineers do with music editing, sound design, recording, and mixing. What used to amount to a full day of studio work can now be accomplished in a matter of minutes (much to the dismay of studio owners who charge by the hour). DAWs allow sound engineers and music supervisors to cut, manipulate, mix, and master any piece of music that exists on any format. DAWs can do this extremely quickly if the user is proficient in the program. All you need is the appropriate source equipment, monitors (speakers), and the multiple inputs of a standard mixing board.

Why do music supervisors need multiple inputs? Without multiple inputs, they would not be able to bring in sounds and music from multiple formats, such as vinyl, CDs, cassettes, VHS tapes, betas, and more. All of these formats have respective playback devices (i.e., sources) that every well-resourced studio engineer has or can easily access or rent. Remember, be prepared for the most difficult situations. You never know what format of media a client will bring you.

As the BMW commercial deadline approaches, the music supervisor now has the song and the money to get the job done. The final challenge is to make it fit. With a DAW, the supervisor can quickly and easily import a song into a session and edit it using cuts and time compression so that it works as originally planned (generally a standard :30 or :60). Once you have received the approval of your producer and/or director on the creative end, the only thing left to do is to be sure the proper licensing and clearances have been completed.

Licensing

You got the song you wanted at the price you wanted, and you edited the song significantly to get it to make sense with the advertisement. Therefore, you are required to get two different licenses in order to finally secure the use of "A Little Bit More" by Tony C and the Truth. You'll need a master use license and a synchronization, or "sync," license. It is among your foremost responsibilities to thoroughly understand what different kinds of music licenses exist in the world of television, film, and live events. (We'll explore this in depth in Chapter 8, Licensing.)

Exploring a Music Supervision Scenario, Cue to Cue

Music supervision is multifaceted. Just as there is no one way to draw a picture or take a photograph, there really is no one right way to supervise music for a project. When you put music to a moving image, you're trying to give as many viewers as possible the impression that it's a natural part of the film, video game, TV show, or commercial.

Inevitably, somebody will think the music is bad or could be better, which is perfectly acceptable. The goal of a music supervisor is to make the media sound the best that you can within the constraints given to you.

Key factors for picking the right music include:

- Budget
- Time-frame
- Genre

• The personalities of others involved in the project

Wouldn't it be great if the project you're working on had a music budget of $500,000, you had a year to get it together, the musical genre was completely up to you, and you were the sole decision-maker on the sound? Unfortunately, the more likely scenario is that you have little or no money to start, the music must be selected and licensed immediately, and the director has final say on what the music will be. It is your task to facilitate and navigate through these constraints.

Indie Film Scenario

Let's take a look at a hypothetical music-supervision job: You are hired to supervise the music for an independent feature film—a two-hour romantic comedy with a total budget of $75,000. Most of the money has already been spent on actors, filming, editing etc., but the director has agreed to give you $8,000 for the music, plus $2,000 for your time, and three points (percentage of ownership that act like shares) on the movie. The movie has already been shot, the director has dropped popular music that he likes into the scenes, and the movie has been roughly edited. The director's goal is to get the movie finished in three months in order to show it at the independent film festivals.

So your job is to take $8,000 and find music for two hours worth of film in less than three months. This is not a big budget for film music by any measure, but that is your limit, so you have to do your best. Further, all of the music that the director has put in already seems financially way out of your league: The Rolling Stones' "Sympathy for the Devil," Red Hot Chili Peppers' "Californication," John Mayer's "Something's Missing," Dido's "White Flag," The Mamas and the Papas' "California Dreamin'," and "The Hotel Ambush" from the score of *The Matrix* (1999) by Don Davis as the main theme.

Clearly, you cannot license all of these tracks with a budget of $8,000. In fact, you probably can't license even one of them for that much. In addition, the track from *The Matrix* won't work because it is so well known. So what are you going to do?

First, you want to make it clear to the director that the budget is a limiting factor and that popular music will be difficult (or impossible) to license within the financial limitations that he has given you. Make sure he understands that you will be replacing all of the music with tracks that you can license for the budget, and most likely it won't be music he has heard of.

This is a critical juncture, because often the director, producer, or music editor who has selected the "temp" tracks has become attached to them. Often, nothing you give them will be "as good" as the temp tracks they selected. Unfortunately, given the budget, they must be replaced. This is a circumstance when clear communication and diplomacy must be used. You must firmly but politely inform the production team that second-best is what you are looking for, and that is the way it has to be.

Getting music for an independent film with a limited budget is difficult but by no means impossible. There are thousands and thousands of licensable tracks that fall well within your budget from music libraries such as Killer Tracks *(www.killertracks.com),* Video Helper *(www.videohelper.com),* and Mega Trax *(www.megatrax.com).* There are also thousands and thousands of independent bands, who don't have publishing or management deals but are making great music and would love to have their recordings used in an independent film.

Most of the music libraries have free online previews and the ability to download CD-quality full versions of the songs when you're ready to buy them. Sites such as *www.audiogalaxy.com, www.sonicbids.com,* or *www.broadjam.com,* and others, which host independent bands and other music, allow you to listen and download music for free. So, with a computer and a high-speed Internet connection, you can preview thousands and thousands of tracks without having to spend a penny.

Once you find the music that you want, negotiate with the music libraries and the artists directly. The music libraries do this all the time: You tell them the scope of the project and the terms, and they give you a rate. If you only want to license the music for the festivals, as opposed to forever, you can get the music even cheaper. The same goes for bands: If you tell them you want to use the songs for festivals only and will then renegotiate when the movie is picked up for distribution (a "back-end" deal), you may get the right to use the song for a very small fee or for free.

This raises another important point: You may be able to use some of that popular music that the director liked after all. When an independent movie shows at a festival like Tribeca, Sundance, and even Cannes, the movie isn't making any money. It's being shown in the hope that it will be bought by a distributor. In that case, you could contact the artist's management and find out if you can use their song for "Festival Use Only." There are no guarantees that you will be granted permission for free, but on the other hand they might say, "Go for it. Contact us when the movie gets sold. We will negotiate with you at that point."

So in review, your limitations are:

1. You only have $8,000.

2. You need approximately eight songs.
3. You have less than three months.

Your possible solutions are:

1. Call the management companies for the songs the director picked and find out if they will grant you a "For Festival Use Only" license.
2. Take advantage of the vast world of music libraries.
3. Find songs by bands that haven't been signed and offer them a nominal fee and some excellent exposure.

Now, of course, this hypothetical scenario is just one random combination of possible constraints. The budget could be smaller or much larger, or the kind of music needed may not be easily found from unsigned artists. However, the point is that no matter what the limitations, you can find music that will make your project sound brilliant. It just takes time and creative thinking.

The Different Roles of a Music Supervisor

Music supervisors play diverse roles in the creative process of films, television shows, commercials, and other media. Let's take a look at the different hats you can expect to wear—often simultaneously—during a project.

Liaison Between Production Staff and Composer

Sometimes the music supervisor is brought in at the beginning of a project and has the opportunity to work with the director as the film or show is being shot, providing input at every step of the way. The music supervisor can also be the connection between the production staff of the project and the composer of the score, given that producers and directors often know what kind of music they want but may not have the musical knowledge to articulate their ideas to the composer. Meanwhile, composers aren't always the best at understanding what production people want when they speak in layman terms.

So, one of the music supervisors important roles is as the liaison. For example, a director might say, "I want a piece of music that sounds edgy and hip. You know, something that creates some tension because in this scene Bill is going to fight with Ted."

What does that actually mean? After all, "hip" is a relative term. What was hip three years ago is probably severely outdated today. "Edgy" is also a relative term. Many people would think *The Matrix* was edgy, while some others would think it was not particularly worthy of note. But your job is not to judge, it's to get to the bottom of the request. To do this, re-engage the production staff and ask questions: "Hip like hip-hop, or hip like Moby? Do you want elemental music or melodic music? (Melodic music has a melody and a beat, and often it is easily hummable. Elemental music is raw and unstructured, containing drones and noises and very little or no melody.) Do you want electronic sounds or orchestral? Do you want the music to sound 'minor' and foreboding or just a little bit tense and anticipatory?" This way, the producers are forced to articulate in layman's terms more specifically what they are looking for, and you discover that they want driving electronic music—not hip hop—that is tense and minor.

Now that description can be articulated to your composer. You can also peruse the music libraries for tracks that seem to fit that description, and then play them for the production staff to see if they're similar to what they had in mind. If they are similar, than you are right where you want to be. The next step is to give the composer a reference track and say, "It should have a similar kind of feel to this."

Diplomat

When selecting the music, it is always important to remember that the music is not the star. The lead actors are the stars, and the film itself is the star—the music simply plays a supporting role, and its purpose is to make the movie much better. Don't try telling that to a composer, however! For many composers, music is the star and the movie is but a platform for their own art, which makes diplomacy a necessity here, as it is in so many other aspects of the music supervisor's work. Your job is to continue letting the composer think that the music is the star, while assuring the director that the music is playing second fiddle to the movie.

In fact, a great deal of what the music supervisor does is practice the fine art of diplomacy. Very often on creative teams there are conflicting egos, and the music supervisor must continuously be the mediator. Every project also has a different pecking order. For example the executive producer may be actively involved in the project (they raise the money), or the senior producer, or the director, assistant director, the composer, the sound editor, the actors, etc. The hierarchy changes on each project, and it is critical for you, as a music supervisor, to determine what the real hierarchy is. The hierarchy is often different on paper than in reality. For example, the director may be in charge, but it is the assistant director who is actually picking the music cues. You must feel out each working scenario to determine who actually answers to whom.

Sometimes the message you get is, "Hey music supervisor, this is *your* gig. We do movies not music. Make it sound great." On the other hand, sometimes your client or colleagues say, "This is the music I want. Now go and get it for me." Often, what you get is something in between, and they say, "This is what I think. What do you think? Can we try this? Could we license this? How do you think this sounds?"

There is no one way this job unfolds. The best music supervisors understand this, and they can walk into any situation and turn it to their advantage. They understand the dynamics and what role they can play to make the most of the situation, and they understand that their job is to accept the constraints of the situation and make the best of them.

PROFILE
Peter Greco
Executive Music Producer/Senior Partner
Young & Rubicam, New York City

• Selecting music for advertising
• Musical diversity and expertise

Rapid changes are taking place in music supervision for advertising. Beyond just picking the best sounds to promote a product, advertising music supervisors are now demonstrating the ability to set and sustain musical trends, and even to break new artists faster than the best A&R person.

The advertising agency of Young & Rubicam in New York obviously takes its music seriously. For Peter Greco, executive music producer/senior partner, his job is a fast-moving sequence of musical, diplomatic, and logistical decisions.

"This job is fun because it's new and different every day," he confirms. "It forces me to keep current across all musical styles, and I like crisis management. Since our time frames are probably the tightest of all music supervision possibilities, it forces you to rely on your gut. You have to think on your feet—I really love that about it."

Before Greco started his decade-plus stay at Y&R, he was a trained guitarist who moved from video production to various positions at music composition companies (music houses) and ad agencies. "It's been a great home," he says of Y&R. "I'm basically the senior-most of three producers in our department. The three of us have tremendous independence with our own accounts, but if there are issues to be dealt with, the others will run it through me."

Their responsibilities at Y&R are diverse. "A producer's job is twofold," says Greco. "There's tremendous creative responsibility, but also a responsibility to both formulate a budget and adhere to it.

"From a creative standpoint we are called upon for our musical expertise. Our colleagues will consult us while they are forming their idea for a commercial, and they can be coming from one of several perspectives. One is, 'We have this idea; what do you think we should do musically?' It's not always about music either, it can also be about sound effects and design, as well as dialog. Other times people will come to us—especially in the current realm of what we see in commercials—and say, 'We think we'd like to surround this message with a piece of equity music [a recognizable hit song]. What song do you think would have the best application for this idea?'"

At that point, the commercial may very well already be shooting, so the race is on for Greco to try and license the equity music, as well as pick a composer to handle original music that could go into another spot in the campaign. "There are no two jobs that are exactly the same," he says. "No two song negotiations are exactly the same."

When music-supervising for a multi-spot campaign with different music requirements, Greco reminds people to stay focused. "The key word is *campaign*," he notes. "The campaign is your umbrella. That is your central driving force, and you want things that are related—sometimes obviously, sometimes not. You could have three diverse musical ideas and still have them relate from a conceptual point of view, but it's all in service to the campaign, as opposed to a commercial that's a one-off and its own entity."

Music supervision in advertising sounds stimulating and exciting, but keep in mind expectations from your peers run high. "Our pressures come from a number of different areas, and they're unique to our situation," Greco says. "We work with much tighter time constraints than a TV sitcom or drama. We're usually at the end of the production food chain. We do a lot of pre-production work and work-shopping to help us be prepared for final production, but at the end of the process, we might only have two or three days to fully produce the music.

"We must sometimes overcome the pressure from clients who feel uncomfortable with a more adventurous musical direction than they have used in the past. Since it is critical to be able to speak in both musical and corporate terminology, you must use that ability to explain clearly and convincingly why the direction you have chosen is the correct one. It's important to remain flexible and be prepared to find a middle ground that will satisfy the clients concerns and still be a great creative product."

The way to navigate those waters is to constantly listen to as much music as possible. "I think because advertising music supervisors run into so many different situations, we have to be tremendously well-versed in all styles, from trip hop to classical," says Greco. "We're involved in so many diverse projects, and each idea requires its own unique piece of music."

To Greco, the rapidly changing nature of his job is a direct reflection of the fast-transforming music business. "You've got this huge shift in the landscape," he points out. "The record industry is going through amazing changes right now; many of them are negative, and they're now looking at advertising as being much more of a partner than in the past—we are a really strong revenue possibility for them.

"I think record companies have really shifted their approach to us, in terms of not only their vast song catalogs, but their talent pool. We have access to people who previously were unapproachable. Artists who were not interested are now very much taken with the idea of working on a commercial. Commercials are now better than they were twenty years ago, and we're not talking about dinky little jingles: We're talking about cool, cutting-edge tracks."

PROFILE
Paul Glass
Supervising Music Director
ABC's *One Life to Live*

• Music supervision for daytime drama
• Building a library
• Pro Tools expertise

"Daytime drama" is a good description of the reality of music supervisors working on the soaps. This genre has progressed far beyond the radio days of organ music; it's a hectic environment that calls for sharp ears, Pro Tools chops, and the ability to stay on track with the fast-moving production schedule.

"It's relentless," confirms Paul S. Glass, Supervising Music Director for ABC's *One Life to Live*. "We do five shows a week, for a show that's been on for thirty-five years. Every day, you're trying to find a way to make each show as good as it can be. You come in each morning looking at a blank screen, and you have an average of ten hours to score a one-hour show. You're trying to use the music to set the pace, intensify, an emotion, establish tension, and much more. That's why all the preparation in advance is so important, because there is no time to let up."

Before Glass was at *One Life,* where he has won three Emmy Awards, a BMI, and a DGA award for his work, he had gone to Berklee College of Music to study composition, and then set his sights on a network music job. Eventually, in 1992, he got his foot in the door at the now-defunct ABC daytime drama *Loving.* "The music director said I could fill in for him when he was on vacation. I would go in there every day and observe him, following the story, scoring it on my own and seeing what his decisions were, preparing for when I would be given the chance."

Glass' gumption paid off, and finally, in 1996, he got his current post at *One Life* and established a groove to stay on schedule. "I read the long story months in advance, then I start planning the library," he says. "I have a group of composers that I work with, including Dominic Messinger in L.A. and David Nichtern here in New York. The composers record the music, then send me the cues with percussion, piano, strings etc. split off, so I can build the music as if I'm scoring to picture."

With more than two thousand custom-made cues already in his library, you'd think Glass wouldn't need any more, but he actually needs new music made constantly. "We're doing over two hundred-fifty shows a year—I have to keep the sounds changing," he points out. "For instance, if there's an extreme dramatic situation, something filled with so much emotion—confusion, sadness, tension, passion—a new cue needs to be written for this moment. At times, I can't imagine something in this library that would be that specific."

In such a case, Glass might compose a general idea at his home studio, then e-mail the files to Nichtern's studio to flesh it out fully. "When commissioning a cue series, I'll relate it to cues we already have so it's not just hypothetical. I'll say, 'It's like the oboe in this cue, and the ostinato in this one,' or a specific set of sound design [elements] I'm looking for. I know the different composers pretty well, so if I call them, they know when I'm looking for a specific thing."

Glass takes pride in the fact that ABC adheres strictly to American Federation of Musicians (AFM) practices when it comes to recording and renewing the cues. "In a union session, the musicians get paid and that's good for a year," says Glass. "After that, we have to renew or retire the sound cue, and if we decide to renew, then there's a residual payment that goes to the musician or musicians."

In addition to his library of musical cues, Glass also needs to keep developing his arsenal of songs that serve as source music and other uses. "From a music-supervision standpoint, the other aspect is to find songs, which sometimes requires planning months in advance, because we have to do all the necessary licensing, and the directors may even decide to plan their shots around the song. Usually the choice involves exploring many styles since we broadcast to a wide demographic. Since we have such a diverse audience, I try to satisfy a wide range of musical tastes."

In addition to coordinating everything far in advance, Glass still has to assemble it all, every day, to form the soundtrack for the show. That means synching the video to his Pro Tools system early in the day, choosing the spots where cues and source music actually go, editing them, and then overseeing the mix that ties it all to the dialog. The producers then watch the mixed show and alert Glass to anything they want changed. Once approved, the actual master media of the show is what airs—no time to dupe a copy! "I'm trying to satisfy the executive producer all the time," he says. "You have to read their minds, make them happy, and at the same time be creative enough to have a scoring sense that captures the moment, and then onto the editing and technical end of it. This has become a pretty specialized job, even more so with the addition of post-production to the process."

Paul Glass loves his job for a ton of reasons, but the biggest reward is rediscovering the impact that the right sounds can make on the moving image. "Every time I put music to video, it makes me feel something different," he says. "Ten different music choices can make you feel ten different ways about what you're seeing: It can make you feel sorry for one person over another, or root for one person over another. I constantly find the music's impact amazing."

PROFILE
Jason Bentley
Music Supervisor
Machine Head

• DJ-turned-music supervisor
• The music of *The Matrix*

If you want to know how Jason Bentley, music supervisor for the stunning *Matrix* trilogy of movies, became a trendsetter in the field, do a résumé check. Before he began assembling scores and soundtracks that would rewrite the relationship between electronic music, classical sounds, and audiences, Bentley was a club DJ, music journalist, A&R executive, radio show spinner—and always a rabid music fan with one foot on the dance floor.

"Music supervision became a way I could continue to exercise my excitement for underground music in a way that took it to another level," Bentley says. "I found there were a lot of similarities between music supervision and DJ'ing. As a DJ, you come into a place, assess the environment, and decide which way to go and what direction to take people. Whether it's a cocktail party, dance floor, underground rave, being with people live, or over the radio, it's about sets that draw people and take them somewhere.

"All of those skills helped me hone my abilities as a music supervisor. Once I was sitting with music editors and directors, I could flex the same sets of muscles, and bring the same boxes of records I took to DJ gigs. It was a more intimate conversation than in clubs, but it was about the same thing, which is trying to find the right songs for the moment."

Sounds fun, right? But Bentley is quick to point out that his DJ experience and sharp ears were only the beginning of his successful journey into music supervision. "That's just the creative side. As a music supervisor, you're at the intersection of a lot of different people, needs, and interests. You're the liaison to the soundtrack's record label—they have an agenda—you're in contact with the composer, you're trying to serve the director and the picture."

Bentley first made his mark when he was working as an A&R executive for Madonna's Maverick Records label. He had just one major-studio music-supervision gig under his belt (1997's *City of Industry*) when producer Joel Silver called him to check out an upcoming film that would need a good deal of licensed music. "It was called *The Matrix,* and I was very impressed," Bentley recalls. "I said, 'We've got to do this.' So I was thrust into this situation with the Wachowski brothers (directors Andy and Larry), forging a friendship with them and understanding what they and Maverick wanted to do. That turned into a three year-plus project.

"Moving through to the third installment, *Matrix Revolutions,* I got to be closer with the composer Don Davis, and got to develop more of a continuity between the composer's world and my role as a music supervisor, introducing him to people he could collaborate with for a hybrid between underground electronic music and traditional Hollywood score."

Bentley shaped the movies' distinctive musical direction only after developing a clear idea of the Wachowski brothers' concept. "It was very much a part of the directors' vision of a futuristic world," he explains. "They felt like *The Matrix* was a world where all cultures had intimately collided and become interwoven. On 2003's *Reloaded,* they demanded that there be a natural-feeling integration of the two worlds, not cut-and-paste classical score ends and electronic beginnings. Through the conversations and a lot of deep philosophical discussions with the directors, I'd play them ideas, and we'd discuss potential candidates to work with Don and meld their sounds.

"For the 'A list,' we tried really high-profile people like The Prodigy, Billy Corgan, Nine Inch Nails, but there's so many issues you have to manage. That's the biggest thing about music supervision is managing rock-star egos. It's one thing to conceptualize something and come up with it in conversation, but to make it happen…that's the tough part."

Bentley called on his other life as a DJ to reach out to a list of top electronic producers, such as Paul Oakenfold, Fluke, Juno Reactor, and more to get their interpretations, and then make the best artist matches possible. "In some of the sequences, like the highway chase, what we tried for was a really organic integration of fresh electronic music score. We just did our best, and there are some moments which I feel are signature to me, such as the sexuality of the Zion dance, which is a dance record from Fluke—that's a little piece of me there."

Bentley has his own theories as to why the musical character of the *Matrix* trilogy stood out in a sea of soundtracks. "I think there was enough there to be appealing to a mainstream audience, enough that it was a discovery to that audience. A middle-of-the-road music fan could appreciate that, and the first film had five Platinum-level artists, like Rage

Against the Machine, Deftones, and Marilyn Manson, and balanced well with six or seven tracks that were entirely new to people."

For Jason Bentley, the *Matrix* movies represented a complete journey through every aspect of music supervision. "The first *Matrix* was all licensed music—I didn't have time to have things written for the film," he says. "So it was the label side, lining up a compelling soundtrack and filling up open cues, but with very little connection to the composer or history of the project. Then I was trying to introduce Don Davis to new musicians from the U.K. to create a musical hybrid that the directors insisted on, with electronic music and dramatic score. At that point, it was not simply about filling available cues; it was about originating an innovative and hybrid score, almost the other end of the spectrum in terms of range of responsibilities for music supervision. The *Matrix* movies taught me the full range of what a music supervisor should be prepared to do."

PROFILE
Ray Castoldi
Music Director
Madison Square Garden, New York City

• Music supervision for live events
• The setup at Madison Square Garden

Although music supervision is usually associated with TV, film, video games, and other media that require post-production, that's not all there is. New arenas and stadiums that host live sporting events—from major-league baseball to college basketball and beyond—are being built every year, and a well-coordinated audio experience is an increasingly important part of the arena experience.

As Music Director for the fabled Madison Square Garden, Ray Castoldi may have a complicated job, but he has a simple reason for loving it. "They pay me to come to the games!" he laughs. "I've always been a sports fan, and I remember when I was a kid going to Fenway Park or Yankee Stadium and thinking, 'Wow—there's somebody up there playing the organ!"

Before Castoldi started drawing a paycheck for being the loudest fan at the Garden, he was a classically trained pianist who was also producing dance music and DJ'ing at night clubs. Just when his turntable skills had really ramped up, he heard that auditions were taking place at MSG to fill the organist spot. Now, instead of inspiring kids to get up and dance, he's enhancing the experience of tens of thousands of other fans of the Knicks, Rangers, WNBA Liberty, plus numerous boxing, track and field, and other events

Castoldi was uniquely qualified to get the gig in 1990, and his late-night sensibilities have been paying off ever since. "I could immediately sense that there were a lot of similarities to playing in a large nightclub," he says. "When you're talking about what songs drive people, definitely something with a strong beat. A lot of times, it's really simple songs with a big beat, simple hook, and something to chant along to. The other thing is finding the right moment to launch it."

Besides having a good ear, Castoldi must have a great sense of timing and the ability to read and reflect the crowd's mood. "Someone had once described this type of profession as live film scoring, and I like that. You're responding to the drama on the ice or the court, and there's this ebb and flow of emotion. You have to ride the emotional tide with the audience, and try to give them musical gestures that reflect and amplify on that. And if I'm playing, 'Let's go Knicks!' on the keyboard, I'm really saying what the audience is saying. You also don't know how any given night will go; it's not like scoring the same movie every night, and you can't build a set the same way you would in a nightclub."

To work the games, Castoldi enjoys the view from a well-equipped booth on the arena's upper level. At his disposal (and often an assistant's as well) are electronic keyboards, an Instant Replay playback unit with hot keys for instant sample triggering, a pair of CD turntables that allow live scratching, and a collection of two thousand CDs, about three hundred of which might get used on any given night. As the contest unfolds, Castoldi manages the often furious action with the help of a game script that keeps him coordinated with music cues for the Knicks City Dancers during TV time outs, or tells him to stay quiet as marketing promotions unfold on the giant video screens. Headset communication with the game director on the floor keeps him on top of late-breaking developments.

A common misapprehension is that Castoldi can actually affect the outcome by making the team play better. "That's really stretching it," he says. "I can amplify what the fans feel, and I think that the fans can give energy to the players. If I play a record that gets the fans up and cheering, that gets communicated to the players, and that can help. Some classic examples are Garry Glitter's "Rock & Roll Part II," 2 Unlimited's "Twilight Zone," while newer stuff includes a remix of Ozzy Osbourne's "Crazy Train," and "Song 2" by Blur with the "Woo-Hoo!" chorus."

While he is upholding tradition with his organ sounds, Castoldi is equally committed to introducing new sounds and music into the MSG arena experience whenever possible. Besides getting new music from the "Promo Only" subscription service *(www.promoonly.com)*, Castoldi constantly monitors the radio, record stores, front office marketing needs, player preferences, and tips from friends. Acting in a quasi-A&R capacity, to be the first to discover an arena hit is also a major incentive for him to keep his ears and mind open at all times. Once he makes a pick, it gets cleared by the team officials for family-acceptable content, and the song gets added to the playlist. Because MSG pays a blanket performance license to ASCAP, BMI, and SESAC, he has the luxury of leaving reporting and cue sheets off his desk.

"Then it's the moment of truth: Try it in an arena," he says. "Usually, I'll try out a song in a more neutral situation in a game, like an early time out. Some things don't lift people the way you think they will, but it can still be useful."

While his workplace may be highly unusual, ultimately Ray Castoldi is every inch a music supervisor. "Absolutely, I'm a music supervisor," he confirms. "I'm responsible for maintaining the CD library and knowing where the music is. If someone needs a Rod Stewart album because he's playing the Garden in a couple of weeks, and we have to program that in at the ticket lobby, I take care of that. I'm also working on databases so that people know what we're playing, because we have accountability and certain standards.

"We're also a big part of branding. It goes back to the idea of setting up the musical database, and asking, 'What types of songs do we use to communicate?' It's all about branding the sound, and branding the experience."

PROFILE
Rupert Wainwright
Director

• Director/music supervisor interaction
• Choosing a music supervisor
• The music of *Stigmata*

An actor turned Fulbright scholar turned director, Rupert Wainwright (*www.rupertwainwright.com*) is a moviemaker who understands the intense connection between music and film. He made the leap from directing landmark music videos, such as MC Hammer's "U Can't Touch This" and NWA's "Straight Outta Compton," to the big screen with *Stigmata*, an updated take on the classical horror film. A feast for the eyes and ears, *Stigmata* shows one Hollywood director's perspective on the importance of a great music supervisor (Budd Carr, in this case).

What does a music supervisor bring to a film?
A good music supervisor expands the movie. They make little moments really fly as opposed to just sort of sit there, and they help mold the tone of the movie by identifying the songs that would fit in. Also, a good music supervisor is instrumental in helping you to choose the right composer, and in helping choose the temp music, which can be quite instructive as the movie's tone is coming together. Then they'll help you through the final mix, helping you fine-tune the overall feel of the film.

What was your goal for Stigmata, *musically?*
We wanted to get a bunch of music that was contemporary and edgy to bring the story to life. We wanted to tell two different stories: Gabriel Byrne's part, which would be more scored. The other was Patricia Arquette's—being more of a night owl and a party girl, she was going to have a wide range of cool music that would get through to the audience.

How do the director and music supervisor work together?
You sit down, watch the movie together, and start identifying where you want source music, which is music that's already been written that you want playing in the background, or in a source-type way—not music that the composer will be writing. That's called spotting: You choose spots where their choices of music will come in, and the editor is typically there

as well. So usually the music supervisor will start to bring choices of music to the editing room, and you'll be playing them as you watch the scene. Some choices you think will work great, and you put them up against picture, and they're just horrible; and others you don't think will work and you say, 'Why aren't we trying this?' You place them and, bang, it's perfect. The third part is cutting them up, rearranging the verse and chorus, rearranging the music to fit the picture and help tell the story better.

What songs really worked in Stigmata?
"Angel" by Massive Attack was a great piece. In that scene, Gabriel had gone away, and when he came back, Patricia had changed but he didn't really realize it. This music was playing under the dialogue, as if it were playing in the background, but gradually we brought it up more and more so it was score, not just source—it's a really moody piece that helped. Though the name of the song is "Angel," it's scary and works very well.

The first third of the movie seems to be very rich from an audio perspective, and then the amount of music and sound effects decreases for a while. Was this an intentional part of the way you paced the movie?
Once Gabriel and Patricia start getting together, the whole movie starts to work in a different way. It's less about sensation and shock, and their relationship opens up. Hopefully, you've got the audience hooked at the front, and then once those two characters are together, you want to just settle down and be a third person in the room.

How does the music supervisor help with the pacing you want to achieve as the director?
A music supervisor will never say, 'Here's the song. Put it in.' and that's it. A music supervisor hopefully knows a hell of a lot more about music than you do. Hopefully, they're giving you five or six choices, three of which you would never have thought of and get you thinking, 'I've never heard that music at all. That's great!' and it helps the film in a way that you wouldn't expect. So hopefully they have an encyclopedic knowledge of music, especially contemporary music, which really helps you. The music supervisor is kind of like the second composer. They're not writing the music, but choosing it to make a musical statement, as if it were specifically written for the project.

Overall, what would you say is the sonic feel of Stigmata?
Hopefully very varied—sometimes very soothing, sometimes very shocking, sometimes very spiritual, very demonic. One has to balance all of those.

How does the music supervisor's work with the music budget and licensing affect the picture?
That's constant battle. You don't really get that involved in the budget as a director until they say you can't afford something! There is a big element of budgets and licensing going on that they have to deal with. That's probably the mark of a good music supervisor, is to keep you out of it.

What's your advice to up-and-coming music supervisors?
Know a lot about music, to start off with! I know that sounds like an obvious thing, but there's enough people knocking around the movie business who know about film. Knowing about film is important, but knowing about music is what sets you apart on the set.

Where is music in film headed?
I think it's just getting more and more important, because most movies mainly have to appeal to a younger audience, and the younger audience is more interested in music than the older audience. So by and large, the music as a part of a movie is more and more important as a selling point, which means music supervisors will have to be more critical—and they'll have to work harder!

CHAPTER three

Tools of the Trade

The software, hardware, and audio gear that music supervisors use can range from stripped-down to complex. While one music supervisor's workspace might have a computer, a pair of speakers, and not much else, another's might be a full-blown recording studio. Like a great deal of other occupations, the field of music supervision has been drastically altered by digital technology. Knowing what types of systems you'll be interacting with in the digital world—and keeping track of technological changes—is crucial for excelling as a music supervisor.

Analog and Digital Worlds

Whether you're employed at a major TV network where the infrastructure is in place for you, or you're setting out on your own as a freelance music supervisor for indie films or other media, the challenge is the same: How do you get the video or animations into your computer, make them compatible with your audio software, and then export them so the next person in the chain can use everything easily?

Although there's little question that, at some point, virtually all media will be produced and delivered digitally, a great deal of videotape is still used to move footage for TV shows, commercials, and movies along the production chain. Video that has been shot to VHS tapes, and the multiple copies that are made of these tapes, are known as *analog* format. Likewise, audio that has been recorded to tape is called analog audio. Meanwhile, media that is recorded straight to digital formats, like video on Digital Betacam (Digibeta) or audio recording directly to a computer's hard drive, is digital.

On the most basic level, the difference between analog and digital is this: Older recording and sound transmission systems used analog technology, which involves changes in electrical voltage that mirrors (or is analogous to, hence analog) a continuous wave. Digital recording, on the other hand, takes thousands of samples per second of the information along the wave, and then translates them into a string of 1's and 0's. As a result, digital sound and video are much easier to process, compress, copy, and edit. Whether digital is more or less aesthetically pleasing is another question altogether.

Understanding all of the scientific differences between analog and digital media is extremely important for producers and engineers, but probably not as important for music supervisors. The key for music supervisors is simply to be able to recognize when their media is being delivered in analog format and when it's digital, and then process it accordingly. No matter what form the audio or video takes when it begins its life, when it comes time for the music supervisor to work on everything and move it efficiently, the project will almost certainly have to be digitized.

Some examples of analog-format media that you may encounter include:

Video: Film, VHS tapes, Beta SP
Audio: Vinyl records, tape cassettes, 8-track (very rarely)

Some examples of digital-format media that you may encounter include:

Video: HD, Digibeta, FLINT, FROST, .avi, .RM (compressed file for Real Player), .wma (compressed file for Windows Media Player), Apple's QuickTime multimedia player
Audio: CD, .wav files (PC format), .aiff (Mac), MP3 (compressed audio)

For our purposes, the most important difference between analog and digital formats is that digital information can be copied again and again with no loss in resolution, providing all systems are working properly. Just as importantly, working with digital media allows for nonlinear editing, meaning that any point on the timeline is instantly accessible. Using analog tape, however, necessitates linear editing (locating edit points by rewinding and fast-forwarding), and subjects the audio and/or video information to degradation each time it goes through another processor, or gets re-copied. Due to a variety of issues including convenience, field-worthiness, budget, legacy systems, personal taste, and plain old stubbornness, analog recording systems still see quite a bit of use. However, the days of analog are numbered.

The delivery method for the digital media you receive can vary greatly. Physically, files can arrive on CDs, DVDs, Zip discs, iPod, DAT, USB portable media, FireWire drives, and floppies, to name a few. It can also be sent quickly over a high-speed network in uncompressed format, or downloaded more slowly over the Internet, either uncompressed or compressed.

Computer Specifications

Before going into any detail about internal and peripheral devices to add to your computer, it's worth noting that the best way to work is with the most powerful computer that your budget will allow. Working with video, music, and multimedia in general causes a great deal of drain on system resources, and the more operations you ask your machine to do within this environment, the more it can slow it down. To work at maximum speed with minimum crashing, invest in (or demand from your employer) a computer with the fastest chip you can get, as much RAM as possible, and physical room for adding high-capacity internal hard drives for extra storage, as well as slots for professional-grade sound cards and video cards.

Your video monitor also makes a difference—the larger the better, with the recommended minimum being 17 inches. Increasing the amount of real estate on your monitor will make it much easier for you to deal with multiple audio tracks, as well as see your video better.

The question of whether the PC or Mac platform is preferable for music supervision-related tasks really boils down to personal preference, and what software you already own. The best thing to do if you can choose your own system is to find out what your colleagues are using: If you're in a post-production environment where everyone else is on a Mac, then easy compatibility with your peers is a top priority. If you're working out of your own home office, then make a list of the software you know you'll need (in addition to what you're already using), and then make sure it's all compatible with the platform of your choice. Then find the best deal on your hardware specs and go from there.

Getting It Digitized

For a lot of would-be music supervisors, one of the biggest technological challenges can be how to take a video tape with a movie or TV show's rough cut and digitize it. Having to take responsibility for this step can be time-consuming, but it's important to be prepared when it comes up. After all, if you won't take the time to digitize a VHS tape, that indie film music-supervision gig could easily go to someone else who will. No matter who gets the job, the guerrilla method of playing the footage on a VCR while you play music tracks on a CD player is good only for the most elementary spotting stages. If you want to get any further with your services, you'll need to be able to play that video back inside your computer.

A video-capture card is the device needed for directly hooking up a VCR (or other analog video source) to a computer. Even the cheapest cards will allow you to get video into your machine decently through a VGA connection on the card. Plug the VCR into the card (once you've installed it on your computer), and it will record the video into your machine in real time. Just be sure to have plenty of disk space. Every four-and-a-half minutes of uncompressed video takes about a Gig of storage. Fortunately, the video can be compressed easily once it's inside your system. Available products run from prosumer solutions to high-powered systems from Avid, Adobe, Pinnacle, and others. Remember that some cards are more expensive purely because of the quality of the editing software they come bundled with, so be aware of the features that you need and don't need.

Selecting the right sound card is an even more important process for the music supervisor. The sound card is a specialized interface for your computer dedicated to managing audio performance. While your computer probably comes with a basic one for playing back CDs and streaming audio from Websites, the recording and higher-resolution audio demands of music supervision—especially any kind of music editing or recording—call for something better. If you want to work with the industry-standard DAW, Pro Tools, then the decision is made for you; Digidesign Pro Tools comprises both software and hardware, including a sound card. Other sound cards are available from a wide range of manufacturers, and their cost depends on their capabilities. The better ones include such things as a headphone amp, higher-quality analog-to-digital (A/D) and digital to analog (D/A) converters, increased input/output (I/O) options, and support for a higher bit depth and sampling rate.

Bit depth and sampling rate are terms that you can expect to come across frequently, usually in the form of numbers that look like "16-bit/44.1kHz," which is the current specification for CD audio, for example. The higher the bit depth, the more accuracy and volume (or dynamic) range can be achieved. Sixteen-bit is better than the noisier 12-bit recording of many DV cameras, but not as good as the 24-bit spec toward which digital recording is moving.

Sampling rate also contributes to how accurately a sound is reproduced. For example, 44.1kHz, or 44,100 samples per second, is very good—it can carry a 20kHz audio signal, which is pretty much the standard for high-fidelity sound. The broadcast and pro video standard is 48kHz, but, due to other technical factors involved in playback, 48kHz sounds identical to 44.1kHz. Nonetheless, if you're delivering audio for use with broadcast video, you'll need to convert it to 48kHz at some point as you work with it. Fortunately, making that conversion can easily be done inside your audio editor or DAW— it can usually be done in one or two mouse clicks.

The sounds you work with can be delivered in different channel configurations: Stereo, mono, or surround. The differences are as follows:

Stereo: Two channels of sound, consisting of a left and right side. Anything with two speakers or a pair of headphones and a stereo receiver, including a decent-size TV, boombox, Walkman, iPod, and many more are stereo devices. Currently, this is by far the most prevalent delivery format. Most of the music that a music supervisor works with will be delivered in stereo. Music that has been recorded and mixed for stereo often has elements that have been panned, or moved, left and right, for a more aurally interesting or lifelike sound.

Mono: One channel of sound, with no left side/right side separation. Anything with one speaker, like a small TV or a cell phone, is a mono system. On the other side of the spectrum, extremely large venues such as arenas or stadiums may have multiple speaker clusters, but still operate in mono to avoid the complications of left/right or surround separation that could take place in such a sizable space. (New York's Madison Square Garden, for example, employs a gigantic mono system for sporting events.) Audio that's usually delivered to a music supervisor in mono includes VO (voice-over) and some sound effects. It's often necessary or convenient to convert mono sound files to stereo in your audio editor, but they will not be "true stereo" when this is done. The mono signal is now simply being carried identically on the left and right channels of the track. Likewise, stereo or surround files can easily be converted to mono if your final delivery system demands this; however, the left/right or surround panning effects will no longer be apparent.

Surround: Also referred to as "multichannel surround." Just like the name implies, surround refers to sound that is mixed to be not only left and right, but behind the viewer/listener as well. The most common format of surround is 5.1, but other formats such as 7.1 and 9.1 do exist, and theoretically, the sky's the limit. In the 5.1 configuration, the "5" refers to the speaker configuration L (left), C (center), R (right), LS (left surround, or rear), and RS (right surround, or rear). The ".1" refers to an additional subwoofer. Audio that's mixed for cinematic release, DVD, and many video games comes in surround format, as does an increasing amount of content for HDTV. Mixing for surround is an art and science all to itself that demands a pristine listening environment, and in most cases the music supervisor will not be asked to take on this task. However, a good surround speaker setup is necessary for a music supervisor to audition and monitor playback of multichannel material. If you're going to work with surround media, be prepared to accommodate your expanded listening needs with the appropriate monitoring.

Music supervising for ringtones also has its own set of standards. At some point, cell-phone manufacturers will doubtless advance to the point where uncompressed, CD-quality audio can be downloaded into the phone. Currently, however, the big leap has been to move away from monophonic ringtones and toward more complex and pleasing polyphonic, MIDI-based ringtones. New formats are constantly being developed and licensed to phone manufacturers.

The limited resources and narrow bandwidth (as opposed to a full-on Internet connection) available on a cell phone put some challenging restrictions on what a music supervisor and/or composers can create and transmit. Expect standards to change constantly, but in general the specs to keep track of include download bit rate, the network limit on ringtone file size, sampling rate output, and phone-speaker frequency range (a subwoofer and deep bass are probably still some time away). A good resource for keeping track of developments in this area is the site *www.sonify.org,* which focuses on news regarding Web and wireless audio.

Ultimately, whatever the medium, it's the music supervisor's responsibility to keep track of changing transmission and delivery formats. DVD-Audio, DVD-Video, HDTV, 5.1 Surround, and cell phones are just a few examples of the ultimate destination for your music and sound effects. If you're involved in the production or post-production chain, it could very well be up to you to know what bit-depth and sample rate are expected, and how to get there. If you're not sure, ask! Clearing up confusion between formats can save you, your co-workers, and your clients a lot of time on the front end of a project.

The Software and Hardware Music Supervisors Encounter

Music supervisors can find themselves working in so many different scenarios—on their own, in a mobile production facility, in a networked post-production environment—that it would take an entire book to cover the technology requirements for all of them. Nonetheless, let's take a look at several categories of software and hardware that you can expect to encounter.

Audio Editors: These are the most basic programs for copying, editing, applying effects, and recording audio files, as well as displaying video. They can be extremely powerful and should be regarded as an essential part of the music supervisor's software suite. Popular examples include Sony's Soundforge for PC *(mediasoftware.sonypictures.com),* Steinberg's WaveLab *(www.steinberg.net),* and BIAS Peak for Mac *(www.bias-inc.com).* What differentiates audio editors from DAWs like Pro Tools is that they are not multitrack systems. In other words, you can only work with one mono or stereo track at a time. Although this may sound limiting, in fact it is often a better way to focus on, micro-edit, and fine-tune individual tracks than if you were trying to do the same operations in a DAW. In fact, many DAWs (like Steinberg's Cubase) allow you to select a track, work on it in your audio editor, and then bring the changes directly back into the DAW.

It's important to note that audio editors (like DAWs), are not just playing back the sound over the speakers, but are also displaying the waveform—a graphic representation of a signal's sound pressure level or voltage level over time. Having this "picture" of the sound is extremely helpful in carrying out a variety of operations, and an experienced music supervisor or audio editor can discern a great deal of information about the sound they're working with simply by looking at it.

Audio editors are also excellent for mastering, or finishing your audio. Whether you have assembled multiple tracks in a DAW, or never left your audio editor, you will ultimately boil it down to a single rough stereo or mono "program" mix that will be married to your media. (You could also have a 5.1 surround mix, but that would have be mastered in a DAW.) Applying EQ, volume level, and dynamic range changes across the entire program mix is an essential step in readying it for delivery to the next stage. It's also a convenient way to assure consistency from mix to mix as you work with different program materials that are intended for the same medium or client.

DAWs: The letters here stand for "Digital Audio Workstation." DAW used to refer to a stand-alone system with its own dedicated controllers, but today the term mostly refers to software solutions that will work on your everyday Mac and/or PC. Designed expressly to record and mix audio, as well as sync it to video, DAWs tend to be very deep, powerful programs, and they can basically allow your computer to do what it used to take a fully equipped recording studio to accomplish. (Again, much to the dismay of studio owners.) Working with a DAW, you can arrange countless mono and stereo tracks of VO, music, and sound effects, and then export it as pristine audio for use with your media. As in other areas of music supervision, the more you understand and study the principles of audio engineering, the better you can make use of these software suites. That said, these are also extremely intuitive programs whose basic operation can be learned relatively quickly, and a degree in audio engineering is not required to get started with them.

The industry-standard DAW is Digidesign's Pro Tools, which has become so widespread that many people simply refer to *any* DAW as "Pro Tools," much like the way "Kleenex" has become a pseudonym for "tissue." Pro Tools became such a strong leader in the space because it got there early, developed a relatively easy-to-use interface, and comes bundled with dedicated computer hardware that handles the heavy number crunching.

Naturally, there are a great many more choices than Pro Tools, and all of them can work with or export to the ".aiff" file extension of Pro Tools, meaning that they're ultimately compatible. Leading programs, especially for those who also sync to video, include Digital Performer for Mac from Mark of the Unicorn (a.k.a. MOTU, *www.motu.com)*, Logic Pro for Mac *(www.apple.com)*, and Steinberg's Cubase or Nuendo suites for Mac or PC *(www.steinberg.net)*. If you're building your own system, be sure to take the time to determine which package is best for you. After all, once you start working with your DAW, you want to get into a rhythm with it—hopefully, you'll be using your system for a long time.

Looping Programs: Not audio editors or DAWs, these are audio programs with video support that fall into their own category. Using applications like Apple's Soundtrack or Sony's! Acid allows you to create a soundtrack out of music loops and one-shots. If you purchase loops from the manufacturers of the many music libraries that design for these programs, you have fully licensed music that's ready to go and relatively easy to sync. Although they won't be used much by top-tier music supervisors, they can be an excellent solution for short indie films or animations, especially since they require very little musical expertise or know-how to get up and running.

NLEs: This stands for Non Linear Editor. NLEs are video-centric, and their name refers specifically video editing. However, there are some NLE's that also happen to be very good for music supervisors who want to multitrack audio but don't need the heavier-hitting capabilities of a DAW. Sony's Vegas family, as well as Apple's Final Cut Pro software, will often provide all the multitrack audio capabilities that a music supervisor needs, as long as you also have a strong audio editor on your machine. Using a quality NLE as your DAW also ensures more flexible video capabilities, and having some rudimentary video-editing skills can be a great asset to a music supervisor.

Media Management: These systems come in the form of software, and can have hardware as well, depending on how powerful and compre-hensive they are. Products like mSoft's ServerSound and MusicCue *(www.msoftinc.com)*, or Sonomic's Total Library Server *(www.sonomic.com)* incorporate servers custom-tailored to the needs of music supervisors and other media professionals, making it extremely easy to store and locate sound effects and music without putting a strain on your desktop system. They incorporate easily searchable databases, huge amounts of audio and video data, and they work easily across networks.

In addition to software, there are some key hardware components that a music supervisor will benefit from having. These include:

Monitors: In this case, we are referring to audio monitors, not a video screen. Whether you're listening for mono, stereo, or surround, the objective is not to have the most high quality, audiophile-grade listening environment possible, but an accurate one. You need to be confident that the way the audio sounds coming from your speakers is very close to how it will sound in your end audience's typical listening environment. Start with a decent pair (or set if you're in surround), and be sure to compare what you hear with the finished product that eventually goes over the air, onto the Web, etc. Through trial and error, you will gradually learn which bass and treble frequencies your monitors are either lacking or overemphasizing in your own environment, and you can EQ accordingly, or add acoustical treatments to your room.

Mixers: These handy analog or digital devices allow you a great deal of flexibility in auditioning, mixing, and balancing various sounds together. Whether you're working with audio tracks within your DAW, controlling levels of multiple playback devices, or recording your own original sounds or VOs, mixers have multiple tracks with faders and other controls that make for a fast, hands-on way to work with audio.

Patchbays: Depending on how complicated your audio routing becomes, a patchbay may come in handy. A patchbay is a panel with connectors that make it extremely easy to move signals from one device to another. Without a patchbay, connecting a mess of devices like CD players, computer, mixer, microphone, etc., can become time-consuming and confusing. With a patchbay and a supply of short cables, however, life can get a lot simpler. If you find yourself spending a lot of time behind your gear unplugging and plugging cables, it may be time to consider a patchbay.

DigiCarts: Music supervisors working in broadcast may very well have one of these in their setup. A box for playing and storage, the Digicart can deliver audio on Zip disks or over a network in a form that allows music cues to be triggered instantly. These come in handy for audio mixers working in live-sound environments, like news.

Systems For Visual Designers and Editors

Depending on where you're working and what type of medium you're working on, you may be dealing with a complex production or post-production environment. Besides the tools that music supervisors use directly, it's also handy to understand the various video/imaging sources that your media could come from, or go to after you're finished with it.

NLEs: While there's a chance you may use nonlinear editors to carry out your own music supervision duties, if you're working in TV or film, it's almost certain that one or more of your video-editing colleagues will be working with them. One of the industry standards is Avid *(www.avid.com)*, whose Media Composer system has proven tremendously popular with video editors everywhere. As with Apple's Final Cut Pro, Adobe's Premiere *(www.adobe.com)*, Discreet's fire and smoke *(www.discreet.com)*, Media100 *(www.media100.com)*, and other solutions, video editors can work on projects in their proprietary file formats, and then save them to compressed video formats such as AVI (video for Windows), MPEG, WMV (Windows Media Video), or others. The important thing is to let your colleagues know what works best for you, so that they may deliver it in that format on CD or Zip drive, or FTP it up to a network for you to download and insert into your video editor or DAW with a minimum of labor.

Graphics/Compositing: There are a wide variety of systems and software packages used to create high-quality 2D/3D graphics and visual effects. Many of these systems are also capable of compositing, or combining multiple layers of graphics and video into one image. Their visuals fill everything from Discovery Channel documentaries, to lead-ins for CNN, to video games, Websites, and more. Heavily used systems come from companies like Quantel *(www.quantel.com)*, which made a huge impact on the industry with products like Hal and Paintbox. Chyron *(www.chyron.com)* makes a variety of products that have become ubiquitous in visual media, especially with its character generators (CG), which specialize in creating onscreen text graphics. Solutions abound, but the most common and popular ones currently include Adobe After Effects *(www.adobe.com)*; Softimage *(www.softimage.com)*; Media100; Discreet's inferno, flame, flint, combustion, and 3ds max; and Alias Wavefront's Maya *(www.aliaswavefront.com)*.

All of these systems have been designed with the networked production and post-production environment in mind, and should be capable of outputting images in a compressed format that the music supervisor can easily play back and sync to his or her own system. Likewise, most, if not all, feature audio playback capabilities and will be able to add your finished soundtrack to their project.

Just as your visual effects and editing colleagues know how you want your video compressed, you'll need to communicate with them to find out what form of audio they need. In addition to agreeing on file formats, you might need to know, for example, if they want the audio track you've built to come back tied to compressed video so they can preview the integrated project, or if they want audio only, allowing them to drop it directly in with their high-resolution visual file. There may also be timecode for everyone to keep track of, or it may be up to you to align the beginning of your audio track with the video, and subsequently deliver it so the audio lines up with that video back in your colleague's system.

Getting it right all depends on personal preference, the workflow, and how fast everyone has to move at a given time. The key is two-way-street thinking, which opens the door to the multiple versions, tweaks, and constant improvements that are essential for creating a standout product.

Emerging Technologies

Like virtually any other occupation you can name, the field of music supervision will continue to evolve along with digital technology. Some changes will result from improvements that affect everyone in media, such as faster PCs and widespread adoption of DVDs. Other innovations are created expressly for music supervisors and their colleagues.

Perhaps the single most powerful factor guiding these developments will be that of convergence (as explored in depth in Chapter 1, The Evolution of Music Supervision). Convergence is a word with multiple meanings, but again, for our purposes it refers to the continuous recombining of media to form new kinds of content and outlets.

Newspapers like the *New York Times* used to only be available printed on actual paper—today it is also a high-traffic Website *www.nytimes.com* with audio and video content. Likewise, televisions with digital set-top (cable) boxes are increasingly providing much more than just TV channels to view, but also high levels of interactivity, including supplemental information to shows; the ability to order products, services, or video-on-demand (VOD) via the remote; and more. A DVD can be inserted into a computer and launch a Website. Cell phones can shoot video and e-mail it. These are just four examples of convergence.

If a new way to combine and/or deliver audio, video, animation, text, and graphics can be thought of and exploited, it will be. Today's media-savvy populations are ready, willing, and able to learn and spend money on all types of convergent media.

As new combinations of media are created, all the stages involved will be affected, including content creation, distribution, and consumption. While all these scenarios will doubtless cause some upheaval and confusion as they're rolled out, one ultimate result is going to be an ever-increasing demand for music-supervision services. The delivery of music and sound is almost always a desirable component of media, and the ability to manage that need efficiently is going to become increasingly valuable over time.

Online Music Supervision

Among the greatest assets for music supervisors are the continuing development of Web resources and the increased availability of high-bandwidth connections that make it possible to move audio files fast. Besides making it easier for music supervisors to obtain high-quality sounds instantly, the increasing bandwidth is making the companies that target this business more innovative and willing to come up with online products and services.

New Websites and business models are developed all the time, so don't take the following as a comprehensive list. Let these sites point you in the right direction for your own Web searches. If you can't find the type of service you want or need, consider developing it yourself.

Music/Band Searches

The performance-rights societies are an outstanding point of departure to track down a great deal of music. If you're looking for a band or song that you've heard of, be sure to start with *www.ascap.com, www.bmi.com, or www.sesac.com* Also, check with this site maintained by the Harry Fox Agency: *www.songfile.com.*

The demise of *MP3.com* took away a tremendous resource for finding unsigned/underground talent. Other umbrella sites for scouting are growing as a result. Some examples include: *www.broadjam.com, www.raw42.com, www.sibeliusmusic.com,* and *www.hitquarters.com.*

Make use of sites that allow musicians and composers to audition for jobs by sending you an electronic press kit over the Web, rather than mailing you a physical package. (All those CDs and bios pile up quickly!) One such site is *www.sonicbids.com.*

There are many music and sound-effects libraries out there, but some are expressly set up for completing the entire process on line, with a graphic user interface (GUI) that supports complex, highly tailored searches. Two top examples include *www.primesounds.com* and *www.sonomic.com.*

Music Supervision Applications/Services

Innovations that can be found on line for music supervisors range from desktop applications to conceptual.

A good example of a computer applications for music supervisors is the program Producer from TransMediaExchange, which serves as an online media production and third-party content resource. See details at *www.transmediaexchange.com/Products/producer.htm.*

An example of a company with an innovative concept directed at our industry is MovieMakerMusic, which is developing a catalog of hit songs re-recorded by artists like Cheap Trick, Irene Cara, and more, allowing the company to license these songs much more affordably. It's a good example of creative thinking with music supervision in mind: *www.moviemakermusic.net.*

Music publishers are also making better use of the Internet to expedite the music supervisor's search process. The Royalty Network is just such a publisher, with an online "Music Supervisors Request Form" *(www.roynet.com/music_supervisors.cfm)* that allows you to submit a request, with criteria including:

- genre sought
- type of use
- timing
- territory
- term
- budget
- scheduled release date
- media requested
- brief description of scene

Upon receipt of the form, publishers will search for applicable material in their catalog and quickly get the selections to the music supervisor for their review.

Watermarking

One of the most closely watched technological innovations in music supervision over the next few years will be the progress of digital watermarking. Companies like Verance *(www.verance.com)* have developed systems to monitor TV broadcasts and verify music used in commercials and programming.

Many aspects of their services are extremely useful for media management and tracking, and may be a great relief from the drudgery of cue sheets. In theory, a composer who has an account with Verance, for example, would be able to have their music encoded with a digital watermark that Verance's data center would detect as it monitors airplay for encoded content in major United States media markets. The composer would then get an airplay report, which they could then submit to their performance-rights society. This would free the music supervisor from worrying about submitting cue sheets for them, and it would ensure a completely accurate tally of the composer's performances.

In practice, however, ASCAP, BMI, and SESAC are still in the process of developing standards to accept such reports as a basis for performance-fee pay-outs. One possible reason for their cautious approach to digitally watermarked information is that the organizations are wary of accepting such reports from composers, believing that such data could be manipulated to inflate the amount of money composers are owed.

With luck, the questions on digital watermarking will be resolved soon and this type of media verification can move forward. It stands to save music supervisors a great deal of time, as well as assure that composers get all of the performance royalties to which they are entitled. Also, the performance-rights societies understand the value of perfecting such a system, since, once in place, it will ensure much higher levels of accuracy and service in their accounting.

As digital technology progresses, the bottom line is clear: There's never been a better time to be involved with music, and there's never been a better time to be a music supervisor. With media being one of the largest and most high-profile beneficiaries of improved computing power and entertainment options, music supervisors can do more—for more outlets—than ever before.

PROFILE
Michael Lau, Manager, Strategic Marketing and Catalog Development
Warner Chappell Music

• Music supervision for online entertainment
• Adapting to new technology
• Pro attitudes

How many different ways are there to be a music supervisor? As Michael Lau knows, the possibilities are limited only by how fast mankind can invent new forms of media. Armed with his degree from Berklee College of Music, Lau put himself on the music supervision fasttrack by working first with a music library company. That connected him to CBS, which made him the music supervisor for both the 1994 and 1998 Winter Olympics.

Lots of composing and music supervision gigs followed, ranging from Miramax movie trailers to the storied images of Warner Bros.' Looney Tunes mega-franchise. Working for Warner Bros. got him involved with Warner Bros. Online (WBOL), where he became an expert in getting great-sounding music and sound effects to fit within the limits of Flash animation. (Check out some of his work at *www.looneytunes.com* or *www.cartoonmonsoon.com.*) After learning how to program in Flash, and getting a solid working knowledge of how to make his audio files integrate smoothly with voice-overs without overtaxing the file-size requirements for smooth streaming, Lau serves as a living example of how staying on top of technology can pave the way for success in music supervision.

"I do what I do because I like stress!" Lau admits. "I like to multitask, and being a music supervisor, you wear a lot of different hats. One moment you're dealing with negotiations and contracts, then you're being creative, a music librarian, and a coordinator. If there are sessions with the composer, you're involved with that, too. Music supervision today is all-encompassing."

As music supervisors branch out from TV and film to the realms of DVD authoring, streaming content, and ring tones, Lau points out that they have responsibilities that extend beyond merely picking music and executing the licenses. "It's about understanding the technology—what's possible and what's not," he says. "If the producer says, 'We'd like to do this,' and you're the music supervisor who's the go-between to the composer, you have to be able to decode and say, 'The composer has to do this, the composer won't be able to do that,' or that it will be too difficult. It's too overwhelming for [the composer] to figure it out. They want to *create*. You need to be able to say, 'We have to make this music modular' and be able to build things. That's really the importance of understanding, so you can interpret and be the magic decoder ring."

Lau points to the use of Flash *(www.macromedia.com)* as a good example of what a plugged-in music supervisor can do for the project. "As far as Flash, it really comes down to understanding how the program works, especially if you're the go-between and you'll assemble it once it's composed," he explains. "And if there are separate things they want to do with the audio in Flash, who's going to do that? Will the composer or the developer program that? You need to know how to give it back to them to make their life easier, or you need to know the process, so you can start it for them.

"It's really about staying abreast. When a new version comes out, did they change anything? Did they make it better? You have to be your own advocate to make your life easier, and you need to know other programs—DAWs, Flash, etc.—where you can pull from experience and say, 'Why don't we do it this way?' The moral of the story is that the sky's the limit for how much you want to get involved, and the more you can do—especially on the interactive medium—the more they'll love you."

Lau points out that music supervisors who maintain a cutting-edge level of knowledge, besides helping their projects, are also helping their level of knowledge, besides helping their projects, are also helping their own careers. "It's the schmooze thing. They'll say, 'Wow, you can make my life easier? I want to work with you.' As opposed to handing your client a CD of music and saying, 'Go for it.' Plus, in terms of contact with the client, it keeps you in their face if you can do more for them. For WBOL, we had five or six conversations a day over IM, and since we were really entrenched with what they were doing, we became part of the team."

As both a composer and a music supervisor, Lau looks forward to the time when technology can truly streamline the cue sheet process for improved performance reporting. "As a composer," he says, "you hope and pray that cue sheets are done. Fifty percent of the time, that doesn't happen unless you have a really good relationship [with the music supervisor]. Or it's not processed correctly by BMI or ASCAP. However, there are emerging technologies with digital watermarking. Verance, for example, has ears and sensors in all the markets for verification of broadcast airplay. The problem is it's prohibitively expensive for the small guy, and, at this point, BMI and ASCAP do not accept this information. The societies really need to accept digital watermarking."

Lau notes that technical skills are useless without interpersonal skills. "First and foremost, music supervisors have to be able to deal with people," he concludes. "Producers and directors are hot-tempered. Early in my career, I'd get calls from a producer saying, 'What did you do? I didn't ask you for this music!' Even though two days before, that's exactly what she asked me for. Two days later, she called and said, 'Great job!' But that's the way it is: You have to get rid of the chip on your shoulder, and say, 'It's not about me. It's about the project.'"

PROFILE
David Schwartz, President
Essential Communications

• Emerging technologies
• Music supervision for retail environments

If you are looking for an indication of the real potential for music supervision, advanced software, and hardware to interact, check out the retail environment. The stakes are high when it comes to keeping customers comfortable and happy in the store, restaurant, or hotel lobby

Essential Communications *(www.makeasoundinvestment.com)* knows that correctly selecting and managing music for retail environments is critical.

"The business has developed into a multimillion dollar industry," Schwartz reports. "The current statistics state that only fifteen percent of all business in the United States is touched by business music, so it seems like there's still a big market to go and get. I've always had an interest in programming music for business; what they try to do is create a positive experience for people with music. It's a distraction, and it's a science. A lot of companies use music to move people in and out, like traffic: Do you want people to sit and linger or move on? Shop down the aisles or get out?"

Besides installing great-sounding audio systems in his clients' environments, Schwartz is also responsible for attaching the system to an effective music and sound source. He may opt for a hardware/software/online service like the one offered by Trusonic *(www.trusonic.com)*, or he may go for an entirely software-based solution like MuMa *(www.ycd.net)*. Whatever he selects, he faces the same challenges.

"The biggest aspect has always been, 'How do you consistently and continually play the appropriate music for that environment without intervention?'" he says. "If you have architects, designers, and owners with all sorts of ideas on how the place should look and sound, and the minute the manager turns his back the bartender pops in a heavy metal CD, that might blow the vision of what it's supposed to be, so everyone's looking for the music technology that can take that out of the hands of the end-user.

"The other problem has been getting the right music to play at the right time of day. If it requires a human to slip it in the CD player, it could still get forgotten: Customers are rushing in, the restaurant gets busy, and they're playing dreary music at 5:00 P.M. when it should be happy and bouncy. But with the advent of the Internet and computers, and prices of those service and devices coming down, people have developed the technology that will deliver targeted content at the appropriate time of day without human intervention."

While there are plenty of solutions to deliver music to the workplace that employees can't alter, such as the proprietary CD systems offered by companies like Muzak and DMX, Schwartz maintains the main advantage offered by emerging technology is automation. "Computers can do what human's can't: Run on a clock," he points out. "If I build a schedule into a computer, I can tell it to wake up every day and play breakfast music from 7:00 A.M. until noon. Then I want lunch music playing, and at 7:00 P.M., I want dinner music. Those are events you can program. While they have come up with CDs that, through compression, can hold twenty hours in length, that's twenty hours of bulk music. It's not really music supervision, is it? That's music by the pound."

Using Trusonic is one way Schwartz solves his clients' music-supervision problems. The system consists of a hardware box installed in their environment, which connects both to their sound system and to the company's central server in California via high-speed Internet. Store/restaurant/hotel owners using the system can easily interact with it via the intuitive online interface called Music Manager, which allows for convenient programmed play and song-selection features, daily modifications to schedules, and more. "It solves the physical transfer problem," Schwartz says. "We don't have to touch it. I can put it in a closet and know that at 7:00 every morning it's going to come on, and it will play exactly what we want it to play at that time. Trusonic is a music-delivery service. The delivery is where it shines and, in my eyes, sometimes the delivery outweighs the content itself." Music supervisors at Trusonic, in turn, select and license the music for the playlists, which run the gamut from classical to techno.

With MuMa, users can turn their computer into a musical jukebox, storing thousands of music pieces, and organize them into easily manageable libraries. While it gives users a great deal more control over the music, since they put it into the system themselves, it also has drawbacks. "MuMa's not cheap," says Schwartz. "You've got to pay for the software, buy the music, and pay the license."

These systems, and others like them, are a huge improvement over the bare-bones alternative, which has employees using consumer devices like CD players or iPods in tough commercial conditions. "CD players get changed in restaurants all the time—grease is the number one killer for a CD player," Schwartz says. "They're just not designed to be used sixteen hours a day, seven days a week."

Keeping track of places that need music, and new ways to deliver it, is one more way to keep moving in music supervision. In the case of music for business, these kinds of technologies allow music supervisors to handle the sounds, while employees in retail environments can focus on what they were hired to do. "We want to create positive associations with the products that we're selling, and music is one of the ways that we do it," Schwartz adds. "The most appropriate way is having the right style of music playing at the right time of day, and nothing beats having an appliance to do that."

CHAPTER four

Sound Design

Just like music, sound effects change the way we experience media, and sound designers are the ones to thank for that. From Foley recording to forty-track sessions, sounds and sights come together to communicate a wide range of emotions and thoughts for video games, films, TV, online media, and more. A great many music supervisors find that their job description not only includes selecting music, but tracking down the right sound effects and editing them all together. It's a lot of work, and it goes far beyond what you might expect. It also happens to be one of the most potentially fun and creative aspects of being a music supervisor.

The Effect of Sound Effects

Similar to light, sound waves reflect and change form as they pass through or bounce off objects such as brick walls, people, trees, water, tunnels, musical instruments, wood floors, etc. By nature, the human ear is designed to pick up sound waves, just as the human eye is designed to pick up light. The eyes and ears also act in unison, with the help of the brain, to interpret sound and light accurately.

This audio/visual/cerebral relationship allows people to perform any number of tasks, such as answering questions during class, or simply interpreting what's happening while watching a movie, commercial, or TV show. Sights and sounds live in seamless harmony in this world, and the human body is designed not only to interpret them but also to create them.

The job of the sound designer—and the music supervisor, who is often asked to serve in that capacity—is to be an expert on the nature of sound in countless real-life scenarios. It's also the sound designer's job to create sound environments for situations that do not necessarily exist in natural life as we know it. Sound designers rely on a variety of tools to get their job done on a daily basis, so it is important for music supervisors to be aware of what those tools are and how they're used.

Sound-design jobs can be found in a wide variety of entertainment-related fields, and as you will learn in Chapter 10, Getting the Job, anything can be achieved with hard work, focus, and a constantly expanding network of contacts. Music supervisors who skillfully double as sound designers will have a lot more to offer their potential employers, and should be able to explore more options in developing their own careers.

The Phases of Production

Pure sound designers are usually hired in the post-production phase of all major films, TV shows, radio and TV ads, Webpages, live events, DVDs, CD-ROMs, children's toy development, and more. Post-production is, for all intents and purposes, the third key phase of the production process, in that it occurs after the pre-production and production phases. The pre-production (also known as "prepro") phase is for creative and technical planning, as well as preparation. This is when the writers write scripts (and sometimes sketch out musical concepts), producers scout shooting locations, technical directors prepare necessary equipment and personnel, directors plan shots, and costume designers create the wardrobe.

The production phase is when the production team executes what they planned and prepared for in the pre-production phase. Once this phase is complete, the location has been chosen, the cameras have rolled, and the actors have played their parts. It is in the post-production phase that much is done with the footage and sound-on-tape (SOT) before a finished product can be distributed to the general public. This is when sound design is required.

Video is usually edited and approved by the producer or director before it enters the sound designer's hands. The video will come to the sound designer with a story and/or a message that must be expressed clearly. The sound designer makes it his or her explicit duty to understand the individual message and storyline of any project or scene before starting to work. This message is delivered to the sound designer by the project producer, director, and/or creative director. We'll get back to this specific communication in further detail later in this chapter.

Music Supervisors and Sound Design in Action

Once the message is understood, it is time for the sound designer to get to work. Let's say that the project at hand is a :30 "open" for an NBC show on "Extreme Snowboarding," and it includes real video, custom graphics, and animation. The function of a show open is to prepare the audience for the contents of the entire program, every week. It's also a branding tool, usually incorporating an original or licensed piece of music that music supervisors will most often get the chance to choose or produce from scratch. If the project includes a dedicated sound designer who is not also the music supervisor and/or composer, the sound designer will team up with the music supervisor and composer in the post-production phase. This is when the music supervisor's mentality enters the sound designer's world.

Remember, the sound designer is working around music that they either know will be selected, or music that's already been picked. Music supervisors usually pick the music, and a sound designer uses sound effects to enhance video. These are two different tasks, but when they come together, it's a beautiful thing.

If the sound designer is not the one composing or producing the music, often the video editor or graphic animator on the project will provide the sound designer with an Open Media Framework (OMF) file to begin the mixing session.

OMF: A file that can be read as an audio session by Pro Tools through a one-step conversion process facilitated by the program DigiTranslator. (See details at *www.digidesign.com.*)

Once the file has been created by DigiTranslator, the sound designer can open it as a Pro Tools session and use it as a scratch audio session that maintains standard broadcast timecode, within which the editor/animator is working as well. As the sound designer and/or music supervisor, what you will see on your interface is a Pro Tools session with pre-edited clips of audio, edited pieces of sound with definite beginning and end points, arranged in time sequence as per the video to be married to it.

The video editor or animator who gave you the OMF has an option to make the file with or without "handles" before giving it to the sound designer. If you're given an OMF with handles, that means you'll have extra audio before and after the clip that can be utilized to mix the session precisely. For example, mixing a Pro Tools session with handles allows you to create smooth crossfades and/or fade-ups or fade-downs.

Crossfade: When two pieces of audio are literally blended together seamlessly, as if they were originally composed and recorded that way.

Crossfades can be done with sound effects, dialogue, and music. Fades have to do with volume level per clip. A fade-down will be a gradual lowering of volume, and a fade-up will be a gradual rise in volume. A crossfade will encompass the lowering and raising of volumes together, which can be very useful for video transitions from scene to scene.

Introducing Timecode

If you're a sound designer or music supervisor, you're going to be getting pieces of video—perhaps a movie scene or maybe an animation—to cut your audio to, and you need to understand what the timecodes are and what their relationship is to the video. Films and other fairly involved video projects use SMPTE timecode, which was developed by the Society of Motion Picture and Television Engineers as a method for putting a unique number on every frame in a videotape.

The numbers from internal timecode generators are shot on film and read visually during post-production, encoded digitally on the film's edge, or recorded on a high-definition (HD) timecode track. SMPTE timecode is accepted as the standard for keeping everything in sync as videotapes move through post-production, as well as for the purposes of music supervisors, composers, and sound designers.

Timecode tags each frame with numbers for hour, minute, second, and frame. Keeping track is easy for film, which is 24 frames per second (fps), so every frame would count 00:00 through 00:24, then add a second and resent the frame counter to 1:00. PAL video, the European standard, counts at 25 fps, and many audio applications go at an equally easily divisible 30 fps.

The American/Pacific Rim standard NTSC video, however, makes things more confusing by running at 29.97 fps. Due to the complicated math that this disparity creates, frame numbers need to be constantly added and subtracted to keep everything even (just like leap year). This creates two more subsets of timecode that music supervisors also need to be aware of, as explained by Jay Rose in *Audio Postproduction for Digital Video (CMP Books):*

"*Drop frame* (also *drop* or *df*) timecode [is] used by broadcasters for program production. *Non-drop frame (ndf)* code is easier to deal with in commercial production. Standard practice is to begin each :30 spot at the start of a minute, so the editor can see that when seconds and frames read 29:29, the commercial is over. But in drop frame, most minutes begin two frames in; a :30 spot starting there would end at an unintuitive 30:01. So post-production facilities—particularly those dealing with advertising—usually prefer non-drop frame." (Used by Permission.)

Working in the world of Pro Tools, sound designers must be aware of whether or not the project they're being handed on tape or by OMF is drop or non-drop. How can you tell?

Usually if timecode is burned to tape properly, or the OMF is exported properly, Pro Tools will communicate to you whether or not the original video session was drop or non-drop through the actual timecode display window on your computer screen. If a clip is drop, you will see a semi-colon in the timecode display. If the video clip is non-drop, a colon will be displayed. The latter is probably what you'll encounter most often.

It's not necessary to go into the advantages and disadvantages of working in drop and non-drop frame worlds. What's important is to recognize that both worlds exist and that you are able to determine what you're working with at all times. If you are working in a drop session and the tape clip you were given is non-drop, it is probable that your session will lose synchronization in the final layback process (if you are laying back audio directly to tape).

Layback: The process of marrying final audio to final video.

Layback can be done either by a video editor/animator on a variety of platforms, from Avid to Final Cut Pro, directly to a standard Digital Beta video deck. It can also be done by a Pro Tools sound engineer/designer to the same types of decks as the video editor. It's preferable as an industry standard that the sound designer/audio engineer layback audio straight to the final video on tape as he/she is the "sound expert" and should be in control of the final process.

Remember, whatever digital platform is outputting the audio to the tape where the visuals live is also communicating a pre-established timecode message. This maintains perfect synchronization throughout, from frame 0 to the final frame of the project. Although the current standard is 29.97 frames per second, as we move forward technologically, higher-resolution visuals will continue to develop. Be aware of these standards as they change.

It would be really nice if the above timecode-related scenarios were the only ones you had to be concerned with encountering, but unfortunately this is not the case. There are music supervisors and sound designers that have to work in a world guided by timecode on the visual end, but also without it in their final layback process.

In these situations, it comes down to editing your audio directly to picture without the additional reference of timecode. In such cases, it is important that the video editor supply you with a clip that is cut to what is known as absolute zero.

Absolute Zero: Video that starts from absolute zero displays the first frame of visuals for air with no front-end pad attached.

Front-end Pad: Any video that exists before the first frame of "air video" which is the video that viewers see when they watch it.

When you talk about timecode for a movie, sound designers and music supervisors are usually more interested in the timecode of a particular scene, as opposed to the extended timecode of the entire production.

Communicating the Vision With Sound Design

Let's get back to the "Extreme Snowboarding" scenario where the producer now provides the sound designer with the edited final video and a hard copy of the script to use as a guide. It is important to note that some show opens will have a voice-over and others will not. If there is a voice-over, nine times out of ten the sound designer will record and coproduce the voice-over in the presence of the producer. After all, a voice-over can be an integral element in storytelling.

Sometimes, voice-overs end up becoming part of the sound design and will guide the flow of how the spot goes. It could even guide the music edit if it were personalized enough. In this case, the sound designer has to be proficient in using certain types of gear, such as microphones, preamps, mixing boards, patch bays, DAWs such as Pro Tools and Logic, and audio editors like SoundForge.

Each step of the sound-design process must reflect the message of the script/final video in order for the final product to be effective. The top priority is that the central message is communicated without question, and actually further enhanced by sound design.

Assuming the message of our "Extreme Snowboarding" open has been made clear, the sound designer chooses his or her method of attacking the project. What elements need to be added to the picture? It's apparent that extreme snowboarding should feel fast and dangerous, yet soulful and beautiful at the same time. What about the human element? Who's riding the snowboard in our open?

Let's say the open has been shot from both the boarder's point of view and from a helicopter-camera point of view. This means that video footage of both perspectives will be incorporated in the final video.

Final Video: The term used to describe any video that has been been fully approved by a producer or director for a designer or editor to work on.

At this point, a decision will be made as to whether it's best to communicate elements of both positions or just one. The answer can be found by asking the director or producer: From whose vantage point is this story being told? Is it being told by the camera operator in the helicopter, or from the snowboarder on the mountain? Or neither? Let's say the snowboarder is telling the story. Of course, you will draw your own conclusions about these questions based on your interpretation of the final video, but as we said earlier, it's critical that you understand exactly what the director or producer wants to express before starting sound design.

When the sound designer has a good idea of the message being communicated and the story being told, new questions arrive. What sounds are needed? What sounds are necessary for a high-speed race down a huge mountain with rough, dangerous terrain?

Here are some examples to get started with: Wind blowing swiftly behind the boarder's ears, the friction sound of a snowboard on the snowy slope, and the sound of a human reacting to and performing the action. It's up to the sound designer to know where to find these sounds quickly and accurately. There are a number places where they can be found, as well as a number of ways they can be created if not found.

Dependable sound-effects catalogs are constantly being produced and made available on CD, as well as on line. Many come from the same companies that create production music libraries. Well-known resources include Killer Tracks *(www.killertracks.com),* Sound Ideas *(www.sound-ideas.com),* Sonomic *(www.sonomic.com),* Megatrax *(www.megatrax.com),* and others. If you're lucky, you're at a facility with its own dedicated sound-effects server. (See Chapter 3, Tools of the Trade.)

If you have the technical resources to record your own sound effects, this can sometimes be an easier and faster way to get the sound you need, rather than spending hours tediously sifting through sound files. Imitating sounds (like the classic case of moving a pair of shoes across a board to simulate footsteps) is known as Foley, and is named after Jack Foley, who made significant advances to the art form in the 1940s. The crazy sounds you can make with your own mouth are also a perfectly acceptable source of sound effects, provided they're recorded well. Once you have your sound effects in digital format, they can be placed into your DAW or audio editor and tracked and processed just like music.

Sound Design Sorcery

One of the great tricks of sound design is using a sound to fool the eye. Hard cuts in video will look like a hard bad cut, unless your ears and eyes trick your brain first. The real art and challenge of sound design is that, by using whooshes, bangs, and any other transitional elements that move from place to place, you can take choppy video and give it a seamless flow.

Reverbs, delays, and EQs are probably the most common plug-in effects used by sound designers in digital mixing platforms from Pro Tools to Logic. These effects alter sounds to further enhance the video sonically and aid in performing crossfades or tough edits.

Reverb and delay are often confused, because they are both time-related, but they are actually quite different effects.

Reverb: Short for reverberation, is the ambience that surrounds a sound source and represents thousands of random reflections that a space— either real or virtual—and its dimensions, walls, ceilings, seats, and other physical properties contribute to the sound. Reverb can happen in the real world in a cave, club, or banquet hall, or it can be simulated with software.

Delay: A single repeat of a sound.

EQ: Short for equalization, or the tool that allows you to work with it, the equalizer. Very simply, EQ is a precise tone control that allows you to change the timbre of a sound by making one part of the spectrum louder, or another part softer.

People spend their entire lives studying the best way to use these three tools. (Trained experts who can record without using EQ, relying only on their selection and placement of microphones to get the sound they want, can earn the special designation of tonemeister.) A music supervisor who takes the time to study audio engineering and truly understand the nature of how these and other audio tools work will definitely benefit.

Applications of Effects

A common reverb found in many Pro Tools studios worldwide is the Renaissance Compact Stereo Reverb from Waves (*www.waves.com),* and it can be used if your goal is to make your audio sound as if it were being produced in a long hall, church, bedroom, bathroom, basement, metal tank, or even within PVC pipe. These are all examples of places where you'll hear room or hall reverberations for an extended amount of time.

Adding reverb to a sound effect makes you remember that a sound happens, especially if it's only for a few seconds. If you take that reverb off, the sound is dry and abrupt, or staccato. With reverb, you give the ear time to register what can be a lot of information in a short period of time.

So how do you sound-design so the eye and ear of the average listener can catch up with the message? Utilizing effects like reverb can help. All of the locations listed above have distinctive types of reverberations that happen as a result of their size, shape, and construction materials. Sound designers can take advantage of digital plug-ins in Pro Tools to mimic those real-life scenarios.

Delays are similar but not the same as reverbs. Delays can actually loop a sound repeatedly in time for as long as you want it to, depending on how you set it up. A delay is going to repeat the effected sound region, but it will gradually dissipate as if you were fading down on it over a period of time. Used properly, a delay can turn a sound effect into a powerful, highly emotional transition.

EQs are used to manipulate the high, mid, and low frequencies of a sound. For example, if you have a Jay Z song that has been approved as the theme for our "Extreme Snowboarding" open, chances are it could be bass-heavy, since one distinguishing feature of hip-hop is generous amounts of low-frequency drums, percussion, and bass guitar. An EQ can be used to remove or accentuate any frequencies within a sound clip. In the Jay Z piece, maybe it's the low end that needs to be relieved, or maybe it's the mid- to high-frequency guitars or cymbals that need to be pushed a little more. EQs can do all of this.

Mixing

It's a rule of thumb that mixes for broadcast television, for example, shouldn't be too bass-heavy. Why would someone be concerned about a bass-heavy mix going to air for broadcast television? Whether you're mixing for TV, film, video games, cell phone ringtones, or live events, your ultimate goal should be to create sonic balance throughout your project. Highs, mids, and lows must all have their place, but at the same time, they should never overpower one another.

As much as it is possible that some home and commercial theater systems can support bass-heavy mixes, sound designers must always remember that they're mixing for the masses. The most basic common-denominator viewing demographic has a TV set in their living room, kitchen, or bedroom, with one or two 1-inch stock speakers in it. One-inch stock TV speakers traditionally don't push bass or low end like 12-inch speakers with a floor subwoofer.

In the same way that mixes can't be too bass-heavy, they also can't exceed specific decibel levels (dB) when transmitted to the viewing public. However, there are varying points of view and standards as to what dB level is optimal to transmit. Generally, if the mixing board transmitting the final air signal is calibrated to zero, the standard decibel level at which audio is delivered is -10dB. This means once master control has determined that -10dB is the standard, every audio mix they receive will be boosted to -10dB no matter what dB level it is when they receive it.

Master Control: The entity/department/location where all final mixed audio/video is broadcast for TV, cable, and satellite.

For example, if the people at master control receive an audio mix for a Coke commercial that is -20dB, they will boost that mix up to -10dB so it meets their standards. Conversely, if they receive the same mix at -5dB, master control will compress it down to -10dB. The problem with compressing a mix down after it's already been mixed and mastered is that the mix usually ends up sounding "blown out." This means that the mix will end up sounding "blurry," or so loud that it begins to break up.

The sound designer has a responsibility to be aware of the standard broadcast level at which their respective master control is working. If the sound designer is aware of the master control-standard broadcast level, he or she should output mixes at the exact same level in order to complement master control.

One of the most effective ways to ensure your mix is set to the correct output level is by using a limiter.

Limiter: A device that limits the level at which the entire mix or master mix is broadcast and heard.

In ProTools, one of the more popular limiter plug-ins is the L1 or L2 limiter. If you put a -10dB limiter on a mix that averages at -30dB, the whole mix will boost up while maintaining the mix automation that you've already set. In other words, a limiter is not remixing your session. It's a direct sonic projection of the mix you've created, but it makes it all sound louder—in this case from -30dB to -10dB, a difference of 20 decibels.

What you never want to do is put a -10dB limiter on a mix that is louder on average than -10dB. As stated above, whether it's you or master control who's doing it, limiting a mix to -10dB that's louder than -10dB already will always sound "hot," "blown out," or simply so loud that it cannot be heard properly. What you are actually trying to achieve when using a limiter is the loudest possible signal you can get without blowing it out. To do this effectively, you must try to achieve optimum headroom.

Headroom: An averaged amount of breathing space that a mix is provided with to fluctuate within a limiter.

If the mix cannot breathe and bounce a little within the confines of a limiter, it will blow out or sound overly compressed. Note that that there is no standard here. Proper headroom is different for every sound designer, audio engineer, music producer, and music supervisor. Just be aware of it and study as many mixes with and without limiters that you can. Be aware of what master-control standards there are and how they relate directly to what you are doing. It is the sound designer's goal to output proper mixes so that they sound exactly as they did in their studio when they hit the ears and eyes of millions of viewers across the world.

With the music supervisor also often acting as the sound designer and the audio mixer, it is a big part of that individual's job to keep the capabilities of the lowest common denominator's sound system firmly in mind. Whether it's for a film, TV show, or video game, running the final mix through an inexpensive TV—instead of a high-end pair of studio monitors—is frequently considered to be the final test of quality in many top postproduction houses. If the sound that comes through is well balanced, clear, and intelligible, that's when it's ready to reach the public.

You can view and hear examples of the application of sound effects and mixing at this book's companion Website, *www.musicsupervisioncentral.com.*

Contrary to popular myth, technical ability and creative thinking are not mutually exclusive! Knowing how to use the vast array of musical technology available can only increase your value to a project.

IN-DEPTH
Mixing for TV

• Top techniques
• Fox NFL Sunday
• Mastering? Sure!

The quality of television viewing has been open to debate ever since RCA's first experimental transmissions in 1929, when W2XBS in New York began airing still pictures of a paper maché Felix the Cat. No matter how good or bad the storylines are, however, the TV sets themselves are the best they've ever been, with sharper screens, HDTV penetration, digital broadcasting outlets, and home theater-quality sound systems all on the rise.

Along with the vastly improved audio delivery capabilities that even mid-priced TVs can now provide come increased expectations for the mixers, composers, and sound designers who deliver the sound. Although relatively few of the pros who perfect the music and sound effects for broadcast set out to work in TV, even fewer of them would go back and trade their careers for anything else.

"The challenge that I feel is re-creating an environment that is not there," notes Patrick Giraudi, owner of the Las Vegas-based VirtualMix whose TV credits include *Xena, Warrior Princess* and *Tales from the Crypt*, as well as numerous films. "Like any movie, you need to re-create and emphasize all that you see onscreen and what you don't see on screen. Like George Lucas said, fifty percent of film is sound, and you can create suspense just with music and sound design. You don't need dialogue."

Still, the presence of dialogue is one of the key differences between making music for a TV show or commercial and making a music-only CD, and composers who forget that probably won't stay in the business for long. "You have to know the limitations of the medium," says Peter Fish, an Emmy-winning composer and partner in the New York City music house Tonic. "The limitation really is time, but another limitation is the usage of the sound spectrum sense of the music. In other words, if it's background, you have to treat dialogue as your lead instrument. There's no sense in having your guitar wailing with Claptonesque grace and beauty if it's going to conflict with two people having a conversation."

The wide range of TV audio systems out there—from tinny mono speakers to subwoofer-packing surround systems—and the multiple stages of transmission can also make TV mixing and composing a tricky science to master. "By the time something hits TV, there's usually so much frequency loss from transfers, dubs, and broadcast compressors that you have to compensate for that while you're mixing," says Phil Garrod, a partner in OSI Music, which creates themes for FOX News, ABC, CBS, and ESPN, among others. "You have to make it punchier than you would have for a record."

"Since you're dealing with people with surround systems in their home, as well as mono speakers, you have to make sure the bass and top end translate and are articulated—what's going on in the low mids is a very important thing," adds Reed Hays, another partner in OSI Music. "We try to deliver the equivalent of a mastered record to our people, so you could play it directly from your CD player. That process includes using fancy EQs like the GML programming equalizer, limiting it with an SSL compressor, and running it through a ½-inch analog two-track to try and get it as close to mastered as we can."

At OSI Music, virtually the only part of the process that's digital is recording to a Tascam MX-2424 hard disk. The heart of this analog-based studio is a 48-input SSL console. "The longer we do this, the less we rely on the computer for helping us out," confirms Hays, who, along with Garrod, has composed such well-known broadcast themes as *Fox NFL Sunday*. "For anything you want to sound good, it's very hard to beat an analog console. Even with all the new technology in a digital mixing board, it all falls way, way short.

"When we recorded the *Fox NFL Sunday* theme, for instance, we used a whole bunch of live players, which is the way to make it sound good. The instruments included trumpets, French horns, trombones, strings, guitar, and in some cases it was augmented with samples."

Once the sounds have been laid down, experienced composers know what to boost and what to cut before handing their work off to the mixer. "I don't track differently for TV, but I mix differently," says Fish. "On a record, if I have the hi-hat or shaker just where I want it to be, on TV all I'll hear is hi-hat. It's almost the same thing with kick drum—if it's right for a record, on TV I won't hear it. There are no rules, but in general a good starting point is that 200Hz is more audible than 100Hz, and sounds in the 5kHz range can be overpowering. It's knowledge born with time."

Still, TV is a volume business, and while doing amazing work is a nice objective, just getting it right should be considered an admirable feat in itself. "You have twenty-four hours of TV a day with a thousand channels—

not everything can be perfect," Peter Fish points out. "We have to set a level of expectation for our work and make it realistic to the marketplace. This is a tough industry to be an artist in. If you're going to be in TV, you should really have the goal of being a good craftsman."

By David Weiss. Reprinted with permission from Audio Media, *published by MAS Publishing, Inc.*

IN-DEPTH
Sound Design and Sound Effects Creation

• Tips from the pros
• Reality TV
• Hollywood
• Audio Post

For those seeking the path to professional audio nirvana, a career in sound effects is worth some serious meditation. The tools available to the fortunate group of men and women who help make the soundtracks to movies, TV shows and commercials, and radio programs have undergone vast improvement over the last decade, making their crucial niche more satisfying than ever.

"The bar keeps rising," confirms Scott Gershin, a Sound Designer Supervisor and Creative Director for Soundelux DMG. "Whether it's something that makes people think, cry, or a real wow factor, sound effects means trying to utilize techniques, technology, and the artistry of audio to come up with something that is both realistic and believable. At the same time, it has to have some psychological impact to further enhance the story that we're telling."

While FX specialists all seem to have heated opinions about the current definition of the term "sound design," their work enjoys the same range of expressiveness a sound designer or music composer has from project to project: From psychoacoustic subtlety to over-the-top wallop. "Some jobs need what I call 'invisible sound design,'" says Frank Verderosa, a mixer at Nutmeg *(www.nutmegrecording.com)* in New York. "I love taking a piece of video MOS [meaning "without sound"] and making you feel like you're there. You're looking at an open field and you feel the wind blowing, hear the grass moving, a bird goes by, and if you didn't know someone did the sound design, you'd think it was ambient sound. The other mission is to make hyper reality where everything is really whirling by, with the idea being not to take away from what you're seeing."

Composer Russ Landau, who has scored top reality shows including *Survivor, Fear Factor,* and *Dog Eat Dog,* to name a few, allows that his work often blurs some lines. "I'm sometimes asked to create music as sound effects," he states. "Scoring is a collaborative job. Along with the producer, director, and editor, we strive to tell the story to the viewer in the best possible way.

"For example, as an act-in from the commercial, you have to wake up the audience to tell them we're back. The scene may open with Wescam helicopter shots of rolling hills breaking out through the trees to a huge expanse of ocean. If that was in a long-form picture, I would score it pastorally, but in this scene we're slamming you over the head with a huge drum and a swell with a backwards vocal that leaves you in the air with a high female voice, backed by percussion with an orchestral cadence. That is an effect! But it's music."

Before FX designers even walk into the studio, they better come equipped with their imaginations and a lot of patience. "A lot of our work is trial and error as we work with different sounds, speeding them up and slowing them down," says Gary Gerlich, a veteran supervising sound editor whose credits include the movies *American Pie, Speed, Predator 2,* and *Alien 3.* "You can come up with some interesting tonal qualities that way: If you slow crickets down, it almost sounds like a subway screeching. In sound design, you try to keep an open mind and not be afraid to try things. A sound doesn't have to be literal. You don't have to use the scream of a human for a scream; you might use an animalistic scream and add to it for the spookiness."

Gershin's most powerful FX engine isn't a piece of hardware or software, however—it's his vocal cords. "I do a lot of vocal effects," says Gershin, who has been the voice of Flubber, Godzilla, and the dragon in *Shrek,* among others. "The reason I use my voice is I can do a lot with it. It gives me an organicness that a synth can't give me, and I can create it, sculpt it, do things. Whether it's creating an avalanche or a creature, I can sit there and actually contour it to picture."

While every sound FX pro has a personal style, one thing they have in common is the use of sound libraries. Whether these massive collections of doors slamming and birds chirping come from well-known companies like ILIO or Sound Ideas, secret sources, or their own meticulously produced field recordings, a comprehensive and flexible sound library is one of the

FX department's best friends.

"Sound libraries are very important," Landau notes. "They're part of almost every cue. I own almost everything from Spectrasonic and ILIO, and certainly everything that Eric Persing does. He designs great sample libraries like *Distorted Reality 1, 2p,* and *Metamorphosis.*"

Equally important to having a phat bank of sounds is a system for storage, retrieval, and backup. With a large number of people, including sound editors, sound designers, composers, producers, and directors at various locations needing access to the sounds at any time, easy mobility for all that lovely data is key, especially in Hollywood. Gerlich keeps his sounds in motion with a mini server for his studio/office at home, bolstered by a 600GB FireWire drive. Slide-out hard drives from Kingston Technology, which Gerlich reports are pretty much ubiquitous around Hollywood, can interface at any dubbing stage in town.

The way Scott Gershin sees it, the technical evolution of sound FX is moving so fast now that things are almost as scary as one of those monsters he helps make. "We're getting to a newer age where it's much more computer-oriented, and it's a little nerve-wracking to see how it's all playing out," he observes. "With the computers now fast enough to handle certain DSP functions and do a certain amount of mixing within systems, I think the relationships between mixers, designers, and editors are becoming much tighter."

By David Weiss. *Reprinted with permission from* Audio Media, *published by* MAS Publishing, Inc.

PROFILE
Walter Werzowa
Composer/Sound Designer
Musikvergnuegen

• Sound design as music supervision
• Designing "Intel Inside"

Musikvergnuegen—actually, it's kind of fun to say once you get the hang of it. That's German for "enjoyment of music," according to composer Walter Werzowa, who, along with his company of that name *(www.musikvergnuegen.com),* has become a leading expert in communication through music. Werzowa, a star in the field of mnemonics ("mnemonic," according to Webster's New Collegiate Dictionary: "intended to assist memory"), shot to the top of the game in 1994 when he created the five-note, three-second theme for "Intel Inside." You know, the one you hear in every commercial for Intel and the other computers that use its chips?

Since then, Werzowa's gone on to compose and sound design for a bunch of other things you've also heard: From film trailers for *The Last Samurai, A.I., Spiderman, Enchanted April,* and *Troy;* to memorable commercials for Nike, Budweiser, Microsoft, Mastercard, and Expedia; audio "logos" for IBM, Sony, Lifetime, and Comedy Central; and more, including feature film scores and/or partial scores for *Taking Lives, Minority Report, and Stillwater.*

The way Werzowa tells it, you might think his Intel success was of the overnight variety. In reality, the skills that produced what UCLA marketing professor Margaret C. Campbell calls "one of the best audio signatures that exists today" were hard earned. And although Musikvergnuegen's spacious, loft-like Hollywood headquarters are prosperously furnished with a combination of expensive European antiques and trendy modern icons, Werzowa's beginnings were humble enough that he had to take out a loan to purchase his first Roland Jupiter 8 Synthesizer.

"Everything is ten times more expensive in Austria anyway," comments the soft-spoken Werzowa, who was born in Vienna. "That keyboard was a huge expense for me."

Originally trained in classical guitar, he left-turned into techno pop, garnering a Number One Euro-hit with a band called Edelweiss and their novelty song, "Bring Me Edelweiss." After that, there were film music and commercials, but, as he says, "Austria is very small." The U.S and studies in film scoring at USC beckoned, then a big break: Scoring film trailers for Disney, which, Werzowa admits, "I didn't take seriously at first. To apply for the job, I sent a tape where I talked about Austria, with some sound effects and cowbells and yodeling. But they called me up, and I got the job."

Making movie trailers, of course, is prime education in the craft of communicating lots of information in very little time. Werzowa took to the task like a natural, noting, "It was the best school ever. I loved it. There was a time when I'd go to a movie theater and see four trailers I'd done!"

Werzowa claims he didn't take the Intel assignment seriously at first. "I'd become friends with Kyle Cooper and Garson Yu, who are amazing visual designers," he relates. "One Friday Kyle called and said, 'We've got this little project, three seconds long. It's the Pentium thing.' Back then I only used Apple/Mac, so I had no clue what Pentium was, or what a mnemonic was. He showed me the storyboards. Three seconds of music? That felt like a joke: 'Who wants to have something like this?'"

At first everything Werzowa tried sounded, he recalls, "a little stupid, or, at least, inappropriate and cut off." But he dug in for the weekend. "Friday," he says, "nothing. Saturday, nothing. Sunday, I started to freak out. No melody felt right. I had to find a different angle. It had to be accessible, and—in a good way—generic. 'Intel Inside' is four syllables, so: Four notes. And it's the fourth and the fifth, which are the most common intervals in every culture. I put them together with a little divider note—a 'clink' at the beginning, and played it for Kyle. We presented it to Intel, and they loved the idea. It was done, basically. I just changed colors and made it more interesting." (Actually there are more than twenty sounds in the first tone alone, including a tambourine, an anvil, and an electric spark.)

Werzowa reflects that the Intel project not only changed his life by vaulting him into commercial prominence, it also changed his thinking about music and its purposes. "It started to be very conceptual for me," he explains. "It's not about a melody, really, or about a sound. It's about, why do you need that melody or sound?"

The bustling Musikvergnuegen now boasts a staff of nine, including two additional full-time composers, John Luker and Justin Burnett. Each composer's studio is tied to a central, studio bau:ton-designed recording space, lined with both antique and modern instruments, used for recording music and sound effects.

Besides creating original music and sound design for commercial film and television clients, Werzowa keeps his hand in the classical world, teaching music to design students at the Pasadena Arts Center, and composing for ballet and opera. To him, it's all one. "A lot of people, especially where I come from, are afraid of being commercial," he reflects. "Not being taken seriously because you're on the charts doesn't make any sense to me. After all, Mozart or The Beatles were commercial! I think it's great."

By Maureen Droney, July, 2004, reprinted by permission of Mix *magazine.*

CHAPTER five

Production Relationships

As with almost any other profession, the personal connections that music supervisors cultivate, maintain, and build on are among the biggest keys to success. Whether it's with the project's producer that hired you, the composer you hire, the artists you license, or the legal advisor you communicate with, knowing how to manage relationships can make all the difference between an award-winning production and a forgettable soundtrack.

Communication Basics

The relationship of the music supervisor to the other personnel in a production setting differs a great deal from facility to facility, as well as from project to project. In addition to everything that is expected from music supervisors on the creative end, a music supervisor must ensure that whatever music is used in a production is "cleared"—or fully licensed—legally. Furthermore, it is the music supervisor's responsibility to coordinate contact information with job details (i.e. licenses, contracts, cue sheets etc.), as well as keep a complete correspondence record of communication with those who own the rights to the music being used.

The methods outlined here will help you develop productive working relationships as you build a project. It all hinges on maintaining critical, ongoing communication with key peers in the production environment.

First, you'll need to create templates for your methods of operation. These templates can be used and reused to save valuable time during the production process, as well as keep what can be an overwhelming amount of information in order and ready for quick access. Simply put, the more organized you are, the more efficient you will become—and time is a very precious commodity in this field.

Get Organized

Start by developing a contact list of people that you become acquainted with throughout your work day, and incorporate the maintenance of that list into your weekly music-supervision regimen. When dealing with contact information, license requests, cue sheets, budgets, official letters, faxes, and e-mail correspondence, common Mac- and PC-compatible programs like Outlook and Microsoft Office provide all the tools you will need to start. A comprehensive database program, such as FileMaker Pro *(www.filemaker.com)* is customizable to your particular needs, and is a must-have as your list of industry contacts grows.

In your Word program, have a separate folder for each project, and always keep track of conversations, phone numbers, and basic daily information-related updates. Make sure all folders and subfolders have names that will quickly tell you what they contain, and keep the document for an active project open on your desktop at all times, to encourage yourself to add to it.

Most importantly, maintain a personal log of conversations regarding music usage so you can refer to it later. You should always document more than you think you're going to need. You never know when a well-organized information flow—contact or otherwise—is going to come in handy. Also, keep a separate backup folder in your database for e-mail and faxes that have been sent and received for easy access to past correspondence.

It's a Small World

Developing productive relationships is key in music supervision, especially since publishing and master rights for many popular music tracks are held by a handful of major music companies, and you'll find that there are relatively few people who handle requests for music used in film and television. Generally, they include:

- Performing-rights organizations/societies whom you'll most often use as a "rights holder contact information resource"
- Movie-production companies, which often hold master rights to film scores
- Publishing companies who hold the rights to publishing
- Artist managers
- Music attorneys

- Production music and sound-effects libraries
- Record companies that also hold the rights to master recordings of albums by artists or bands

These entities are in the business of licensing their products to people like you. Remember, the professionals who represent music rights have their own tried-and-true mechanisms for negotiating with music supervisors. They follow a basic method of communication and correspondence, but each of them will have specific preferences that music supervisors must be willing to adapt to and remember for the next negotiation.

Stay on top of the different needs from company to company and person to person, while continuing to streamline your approach to the world of music supervision with every new conversation, letter, license request, or e-mail. After all, if you demonstrate that you know how a particular person likes to communicate, you're also making his or her job easier, and it just may make the person feel inclined to tip a negotiation your way.

Artist managers, in particular, are working to further the careers of the artists and bands they represent. They will most often find licensing opportunities as favorable business moves and may end up acting as players in your corner when trying to secure the master and publishing rights to a song.

Time constraints and basic geography make cell phones, the Internet, and faxes your closest friends. You may also want to consider using a pager as a backup contact method for last-minute dealings.

Communicating With Rights Holders

Once the music supervisor has determined who the rights holder is for a particular piece of music, a request for permission to use the cue must be issued. Use *www.ascap.com* and *www.bmi.com* (the music performing-rights societies) to research and find the contact information for publishing rights holders and master rights holders.

Once an agreement has been struck between the rights holders and the production company, a process for tracking airings and usage must be established in order to determine proper compensation for the rights holders.

You may also, depending on your specific project responsibilities, have to maintain ongoing communication with the performing-rights organizations ASCAP and BMI for the logging and tracking of music performances on TV and radio. For example, if you're the music director of a cable news channel like CNN, it's your responsibility to log and submit all the music that airs on the network twenty-four hours a day, seven days a week. These usages must be submitted in official cue sheet format (see Chapter 7, Cue Sheets) to

ASCAP and BMI on a regular basis, so that the proper master, writing, and publishing rights holders get paid their due performance royalties as close to on-time as possible.

Keep in mind that it's common that ASCAP and BMI run three or more months behind the actual air date on performance-royalty payments to writers and publishers for performances on TV or radio. This delay is understandable when you consider the amount of paperwork the performing-rights societies require to manage usages and performances worldwide on TV, radio, live venues, and new media. If a rights holder you have dealt with is impatient to receive royalties, you may want to politely remind them of this fact, so they understand that you are not the source of the hold-up in their payments.

Stay on Top of Reporting

Due to time constraints, procedural failures, and just plain laziness, it's an unfortunate fact that music supervisors and others often don't try very hard to ensure accurate usage reporting. Once they've secured the rights, they often report the initial, most obvious uses and then speed on to the next project. As technology improves over the next few years, reporting performances is going to become much easier—and hopefully automatic—but until that time, keeping on top of music performances you commission is important to maintaining your good reputation.

Composers are becoming increasingly litigious to recover under-reported rights, and it's obvious that these talented music-makers are not going to want to work again with the music supervisors whose production companies they're suing. Ultimately, by taking the time to do the rights-reporting paperwork, you stand to make yourself very popular among rights holders, which just may speed your next negotiation with them.

Handling Music License Request Rejections

When a music license request gets rejected, a music supervisor can and should question the reasons behind the rejection, but should always understand that it is not a personal matter. Don't take rejections to heart. Your license request is not being turned down because the representative doesn't like you, so maintain a level head as best you can at all times.

The most important thing when being rejected is to make sure that you fully understand why it's happening, and continue to keep records of your correspondence. This is because, when fielding the rejections of music license requests, the producer, director, or other executive you are reporting to will expect a fairly thorough explanation, as it will most definitely affect the project in some way.

Keep everyone informed, and if you ever have a legal question, contact a lawyer or your legal department for consultation. Logging this information will also save you a fruitless negotiation if the same song is requested later down the road for another project. If you already know that it can't be licensed for a similar scenario or budget, you can strongly advise your colleagues to pursue another song.

As you would likely predict, license rejections are most commonly associated with weak music budgets. However, behind every artist is a group of companies acting on their behalf, and another common reason includes their perceived over-exposure of the artist, or inappropriate branding/imaging in connection with your piece of media.

Whatever the reason, always remember that you will perhaps be requesting a future music license from the person who just turned you down. Therefore, it is crucial to maintain positive and open working relationships with each of your business contacts, and keep your emotions out of the picture if things don't go the way you want.

Again, this is all a part of developing working relationships with other media professionals. The best way to have productive relationships with other people in this business is to understand that they have obligations and loyalties that must be respected, even if they conflict with your own needs. An easy method for keeping calm and collected before you enter a situation or conversation that you think may be challenging is to clear your mind for thirty seconds or so, while taking slow-paced deep breaths and thinking positive thoughts. Try it—it works!

The Amorphous Role of the Music Supervisor

The music supervisor needs to maintain a complete database of information on music usages for every project. This database must always be complete with the following entries:

- song title
- composer
- publisher
- record label
- phone
- e-mail
- mailing address
- record of all correspondence

This list is necessary because the role of a music supervisor, and therefore his or her relationship to others, is constantly changing. Music supervisors must be chameleon-like in their business dealings, with the ability to adapt their methods and behavior to the needs of every new production environment or executive office. If you have all of the necessary information at your fingertips, you can expect to be successful in providing quick answers to anyone who needs them, at any stage in the production.

Corporate music supervisors have a much different role from independent film music supervisors. Likewise, video-game music supervisors and live-event music supervisors also deal with different specialists and play different roles. As stated before, whom you deal with and how you deal them will be drastically different from job to job. For example, in a corporate setting the music supervisor is very likely to answer to a creative director; while a music supervisor for an independent film may answer to the executive producer, producer, or director; and a videogame music supervisor could answer to the game's original designer or creator.

You can find downloadable examples of timesaving organizational charts at this book's companion Website, *www.musicsupervisioncentral.com*.

Basic Rules of Relationships

The above scenarios may seem confusing, sporadic, and inconsistent, yet there are some basic principles that will help to guide you in your projects.

First, you must know who your boss is. While this seems obvious, it's a theme that will come up frequently here, because the hectic nature of production environments and varying levels of bureaucracy can make this difficult to determine at a glance. Make it your first priority to answer this question upon being hired for a project: Who's ultimately in charge of approving your work and deciding what music will end up in the production? Figure it out, and don't forget it. This is the person who needs your expertise. You should tailor your work for this person's needs.

It is your responsibility to understand the creative perspective or direction of your direct report—your immediate supervisor. This person may or may not be the highest person in the executive ladder, but he or she will be the one to observe and approve your work on a regularly scheduled basis. Also remember that your direct report is always, in turn, fulfilling the needs of his or her own boss—unless your direct report is already the highest on the food chain, like executive producers, presidents, and/or CEOs.

Navigating Conflicts

With all of these different roles being played in the general production environment, there are often competing interests throughout the chains of command. One place this can happen is at the *temporarily placed for approval* stage, which means you have tried the piece of music yourself to the scene but have not yet gotten executive approval on the placement.

As an example, imagine a scenario where you're working with a director and a producer who both appear to be equally empowered, versed, and qualified to make music-related decisions on your project. What if you've listened to/auditioned, and "temporarily placed for approval" to picture more than one song for the scene at hand, and the producer and director end up differing on their song choices?

Under conflicting circumstances such as these, when the producer wants one type of music and the director wants another, it is best to try to mediate and seek out common ground. Again, you should determine—before you start the creative process on your project—who officially has the final word? That will help you determine whose opinion to weigh more heavily.

If it comes down to it, you may be challenged with trying to find an entirely new musical solution that bridges the gap between the differing creative interests and goals of both parties. Don't rule out that this commercial or video game could end up having a completely different musical direction or concept than you originally envisioned. When you experience this type of "executive approval conflict," you might choose to start over completely and pitch a whole new musical idea for a scene, rather than go to battle for—and against—one side.

In this stage, you might even go so far as to pitch songs that you know in your heart are *wrong* for a scene, which will underscore all the positive aspects of the original choices. This method can be helpful, because it could influence the director and/or the producer to come to the realization that one or the other of the originally pitched songs/ideas was actually correct. This happens frequently. Pitching songs that are wrong for a scene, in addition to songs that are right, will make your peers realize clearly when you choose a song that is perfect.

Equally important, the starting over process may spawn yet another new musical idea that no one ever considered in the first place. This musical brainstorming process can be interesting, engaging, and fun when done in the right company.

Again, the music supervisor wears many hats and must balance the needs and desires of many different players. As described in the above scenario, we find that often principals such as the director and producer have different ideas of what the music should be like. For example, a film's director might want music that is artistically creative, unique, and offbeat to give the film a creative edge. The producer, on the other hand, might want radio-friendly, marketable music to drive a soundtrack.

As a result, the producer wants pop music from star artists while the director balks, insisting that they don't want anything to do with radio pop material because it will diminish the creative credibility of the film. This puts the music supervisor in an interesting situation, where two competing interests with power over the film have two totally different ideas of what the music in the film should sound like.

The music supervisor must walk the fine line by supplying quirky but commercially successful music that will help drive a soundtrack's sales, while enhancing the artistic credibility of the film. It's a lot of responsibility, but this is where your extensive knowledge of the current musical landscape will aid your diplomatic efforts.

Timing is Everything

One important thing to realize is that often someone doesn't like a song or sound effect the first time they hear it, but it eventually becomes their favorite after additional listening sessions. It is equally important to get a feeling for *when* it is the right time to play music for people. Getting a sense of a decision-maker's mood is a good start. Experienced music supervisors often wait for the right time when planning a musical attack (read Sun Tzu's *Art of War* when you're done with this book, if you haven't already).

When someone seems happy and alert, it's a good time to play them music. If that same person seems tired and frustrated, try your best to come back another time. It's not a good time to play them a song, and all your hard work may get shot down for reasons totally unrelated to the quality of your effort. Human nature is such that when a person is tired, that person is less likely to find music exciting and inspiring.

Often, experienced music supervisors wait for a moment when producers, talent, directors, writers, etc. are on top of their game and feeling positive. Even if you get them on a good day, they still might not like the piece you picked. But at least you're getting an honest opinion, instead of one colored by frustration and exhaustion.

Constant Communication Makes the Difference

In a successful production relationship between the music supervisor and the rest of the team, clear verbal and written communication is the key. Feel free to talk to the creative director about what kind of music he or she envisions in the video game. E-mail the producer and work to determine what genre and style he/she thinks will drive a TV show, and then do your research to see what fits.

There is often mediation in this process, with the need to find common ground among the various interests. In television production, the on-air talent will often have an idea of what they want their show to sound like, while the producers and directors have different feelings. As the music supervisor in this situation, your job is to get the right music in the show without alienating or offending the talent and the production staff.

One important step towards doing this is taking at least a few minutes to get the opinion of everybody involved, even if they don't really have any authority in the matter. If they feel their voice has been heard, they may be satisfied that the subsequent music choices were influenced by them in some way, and that's one less battle you'll have to fight.

Throughout the process you will have formulated your own concept of what the media needs, who you think the characters are musically, and what you think the show's direction is. It's important for you to feel confident in saying, "While I understand why you want to do this, I see it this way…" As a result of these open lines of communication you've worked to establish, you can come to a unified conclusion that will, hopefully, please everyone.

Technical Relationships

Music supervisors constantly find themselves wearing multiple hats—having to juggle the relationships within the production team while facilitating licensing negotiations in the outside world.

In addition to the administrative relationships that allow music supervisors to acquire and license music and sound effects, there are also the relationships within the production team that must be dealt with on your own end to ensure that your work is properly integrated into the media at hand—the technical side. These include relationships with directors, producers, editors, and other technical support staff you need to work well with in order to make the music in your project the best that it can possibly be.

Music supervisors must be prepared to work with the entire creative team on a project. Dealing with designer/animators, video editors, sound designers, sound editors, producers, directors, talent, and all of the other production staff requires a breadth of knowledge about your profession and a set of effective people skills. If you don't like people, this might not be the job for you.

Animators and video editors expect music supervisors to be able to deliver audio tracks in the proper format with accurate timecode and production notes, so it's your responsibility, from shop to shop, to know what computer platforms, software, and cooperative formats different people are using. This information is attainable simply by speaking with each and every one of them as often as your and their schedules allow. Respect your colleagues' time and space, and you will increase the likelihood of your time and space being respected.

Before you can fully understand what you are required to do for any specific person in the production environment, you must first understand what it is *they* do. As you move from job to job and shop to shop, you will begin to realize that different production positions have different levels of responsibility.

Catching on quickly to the nuances of other people's responsibilities is a lot like playing in a band: You have to keep your eyes and ears open at all times, and be a good listener. A video editor will have his or her own preferences for how you deliver media, and it's your responsibility to find out what that method is. Likewise, music editors can make your amazing music choices seem foolish simply by placing them incorrectly in the timeline, so don't give them a reason to make you look bad. Ask them what, if anything, you can do to enhance their workflow, and then be sure to deliver.

Creative Relationships

The relationship you'll have with a composer or artist is a creative relationship, as well as a professional one. You may have to negotiate a fee between the composer/artist and the production company, and then work with the composer/artist to get the music you need for your project. The obvious challenge is to maintain a positive working relationship with the composer/artist through the negotiating phase, so when it comes to the creative process you are in good standing with the composition team and can hurry on to the really important stuff—producing great music for your project.

It is a very delicate situation when you must tell a composer that a song must be changed, or when you must reject bidding composers when, ultimately, you're the one with the checkbook. This can be very painful if executed improperly. The best approach is to be honest and straightforward from the first time you speak with a composer: Always try to communicate directly and in a timely fashion. If you have a project with a healthy budget, you will quickly find that you have thousands of composers beating down your door to get on your good side.

It's important to be nice to all vendors, because you never know where they're going to go in their careers, or when you are going to want to work with them again in the future. If your team has decided not to use a composer, let the composer know as soon as possible, so they are not working on a project they have no chance of landing.

A proper way to handle it is to say, "The decision-makers are going with a different style, but I'm looking forward to working with you in the future." The composer may be disappointed, but he or she should respect your forthright manner. After all, everyone who has experience in this business knows that you win some and you lose some. If an individual can't handle rejection in a professional manner, that's something *you* have a right to remember for the future.

Also, the best creative relationships in a production setting are the ones that have symbiotic creativity between the visual artists (producers, editors, graphic designers, etc.) and music supervisor. When the creative team members feed off of each other's inspirations, the end product is always better. The creative power of many people working together is usually stronger than the power of many individuals working separately.

History shows time and again that the best productions are the ones where everyone has worked together on creating ideas and goals, as opposed to having just one person dictating a concept and deadline. That's why it can be really fun and effective to have a "war room" (otherwise known as a conference room), where the creative team bounces ideas around in order to develop a well-rounded project, musically and otherwise.

How the Role of a Music Supervisor Unfolds

Music supervisors can be brought onto a project in any number of ways. They might have that exact "music supervisor" title and a full-time position at a cable sports network. They may be freelance and move from film to film, or they may be the producer of a TV show on a budget and get thrust into that role, whether they expected it or not.

Meeting Your Colleagues on a Freelance Project

One common scenario for music supervisors is they find themselves in a situation where they are brought on by someone on a project's creative team and begin working without a contract or any real understanding of financial terms. One way this can happen is you show up at a spotting session, or get a VHS copy of the project in the mail, and then you pitch music to the creative team and hope you spark their interest.

A spotting session is usually held in a digital-editing room with proper sound equipment and acoustics; the goal is to audition different songs to visual scenes, toward the ultimate goal of finding the ones that actually work. If your superiors like what you have placed to picture in the edit session, then you'll get asked to start delivering more music along the same creative lines and continue developing relationships with key people on the project. Throughout the project, you'll recognize whom you need to deal with, why you have to deal with them, and when you'll be dealing with them.

Soon you'll find that you are a key part of the team. You have become the music supervisor. (Congratulations!) If you haven't already, this is the point where you negotiate a music services contract for the work that you are doing. (See Chapter 9, Legal Issues, for an example.)

Develop a strategy for each of your projects. Start by brainstorming from a creative perspective. Talk to the creators, writers, director, and producers. Each project has creators. These are the people who conceive of the idea for the project and bring it to fruition. In order for you to understand what they are thinking, you have to talk to them. You have to get a sense of their energy and style. Your goal is to be a positive creative force.

To accomplish this, you must get a lay of the land. Again, who is paying the bills? Who is calling the creative shots? Who is the actual audio engineer who will be doing the design work? Who's mixing down the final product? Who are the main actors/talent? What investment do these players have in music cue decisions? These are questions that you need answers to quickly in order to develop an effective strategy for supervising the sound of a project.

There are different approaches to getting answers to these key questions. If you are vying for a music-supervision gig, then there's a good chance that you are in contact with someone on the production staff who has the ability either to hire you or to refer you to the person who has the authority to hire you. Don't be afraid to ask your contact who the key players are once you're on the team. Always project a confident attitude.

Music Presentations Through the Chain of Command

A very important aspect of the music supervisor's job is successfully presenting music selections to key project decision-makers. There is an art form to how a music supervisor sells a track of music or a concept to a potentially hostile production executive crowd. Trying to accommodate competing agendas with the same piece of music is a true balancing act and a diplomatic art form in and of itself.

The overall success of the project may be crucial, and the jobs of the people you're pitching to could very well be on the line. If a person you pitch to is higher in the executive ladder than your direct report, be very careful of going over your direct report's head. Your boss may find it disrespectful, to say the least, if you have defied his or her authority and gone to a higher-ranking person for consultation. Nevertheless, if you can manage to please the top decision-maker, the rest of the plan often falls into place because your direct report will fall into line on your side.

Unfortunately, as you can see, politics are everywhere…even in music supervision. But, as stated many times in this book, the best music supervisors can remove themselves from the emotions of a project. In order to avoid getting emotionally involved in your creative choices, get to know your audience, and then tailor your clients' sound to the desired audience—not for yourself.

People often get upset in production relationships. They have strong feelings about the creative process, and tempers flair. Relationships get strained. If you maintain a level head and can understand the give-and-take of the creative process, you will find that you will be much more successful in your work. You are hired to navigate the relationships of music placement in a project. Assuming you are not also the writer, director, or producer, remember that those individuals are usually more invested in the total creation of the project, and you are there to fulfill the vision of others. Firmly state your opinion regarding music selections, but accept the creative authority of those on the team who make decisions. State your opinion and move on.

Staying on the Same Page
One of the biggest challenges for the music supervisor is avoiding the communication breakdown. In the production world, it is the language barrier between artists, composers, producers, designers, directors, and music supervisors that often becomes the major hurdle. Finding a common creative language is challenging, but it can be extremely helpful for expediting the project.

For example, a commercial director may say they want music that is uplifting, as opposed to somber. A composer might construe that as meaning motivational or possibly of a New Age style, when in actuality the director really wanted something uptempo in a major key.

The challenge is to understand fully what the decision-makers want by asking questions and citing examples. A good approach would be to ask if they want something that sounds like the famous score to the 1981 film *Chariots of Fire,* or something more like the stirring main theme to the 2000 film *Gladiator.* This eliminates the problem of using descriptive language that can mean one thing to the first person, and something completely different to the other. This is especially true if one or both of them lack formal musical training.

The vast majority of composers speak the language of music performance. They know how to read music; they talk in terms of music theory. But most of the time, the production people don't talk in that language. They use layman terms to talk about music, and you as the music supervisor, have to translate the common person's version of music theory to the composers so they understand what is needed.

Much of the time you are a translator. There is a well-circulated story of how a producer kept complaining that a song was not fast enough, so the composer kept increasing the tempo. Eventually, after a lot of wasted time, the composer realized that what he actually meant was that the song wasn't *loud* enough, and he was simply being asked to boost the master output/gain. The music supervisor has to foster, monitor, interpret, and mediate the communication stream in order to satisfy the musical needs of the project.

Legal and Financial Relations

Music supervisors work inside the production environment to make the best creative decisions possible, while simultaneously acting with an acute awareness of the legal and financial ramifications of using certain pieces of music vs. other pieces of music.

Most often, the music supervisor is the face of the music deals that occur for any given project. When a fee doesn't get paid, you're very likely the one that the artist or their representative will call saying, "Where's my check?" However, usually it's not you, but an accounting person, production-management representative, performance-rights organization, or an independent finance consultant/director who is responsible for paying the bills. You need to know who is facilitating the transaction, and have a clear understanding of the payment schedule from the production team as soon as a creative path is chosen and approved.

Find that information by asking the accounting people pointedly when they will cut checks for music. Be direct in your questioning, and try to get a written or e-mailed confirmation of the discussion. This is important because composers, musicians, labels, and publishers—like anyone else—get upset when they don't get the money they are expecting in a timely fashion. They will confront you about it first because you are the face of the deal. Letting them know how long they can reasonably expect to wait before they receive a check helps head off problems before they begin, but having written documentation as to why a late payment is not your fault will also help direct attention to the appropriate party.

Likewise, ask the project's legal counsel about each and every question with legal ramifications, and don't move forward until you receive clarification from them (See much more about this in Chapter 9, Legal Issues.) If there is a problem with a contract or other legal document that flowed through you, it is vital that you be able to show that the responsible lawyer signed off on it. Along the way, just as with your other internal technical and signed off on it. Along the way, just as with your other internal technical and creative contacts, be sure to find out what the legal counsel needs from you to operate efficiently.

As noted previously, these are the types of situations where it pays off to have taken careful notes of conversations, copied yourself on official e-mail messages, and kept records of everything. You will definitely need access to all of this correspondence during a payment dispute, for example, so it is important to save everything in a safe place with a streamlined system that allows quick access.

Keep Everything in Perspective

Music in most projects is an afterthought. While it is vitally important, it is also the last thing on the minds of the production team most of the time. Usually, the entire project has been shot and basic video edits have been done when the team members finally remember that they need good music and music supervisors. You could easily get hired in the last stage of production, having to quickly get a grip on the decision-makers' preferences, the feasibility of licensing music, and the limitations of the budget. It's intimidating, but it's a part of the profession. If you're passionate, focused, and up for the challenge, the pressure will never be a problem.

PROFILE
Mick Glossop, Film Music Editor
The 51st State

• The role of the music editor
• Relationship with the music supervisor
• Holds the power to "Temp Track Love"

When it comes to placing music in media, the music editor holds a quiet seat of power. Not only is the music editor responsible for cutting the music properly for maximum impact, he or she frequently makes selections for early edits of the project that stick like glue in directors' or producers' minds as work progresses.

U.K.-based producer Mick Glossop enjoys an outstanding reputation as a music engineer, mixer, remixer, and producer, with studio credits including Frank Zappa, Van Morrison, Suede, Lloyd Cole, and many more. Taking those sharp musical instincts into music editing for picture was a natural fit, and he sheds a strong light on the connection to music-

What films are among your recent music-editing projects?
The 51st State, an action/comedy starring Samuel L. Jackson, Robert Carlyle, and Meatloaf. I have also worked on post-production sound design and editing for several independent films in the U.K.

What is the music editor's role in a film?
It covers several areas, and the emphasis varies depending on the role of music in the film, the type of music, and the degree of the director's experience of or interest in music in general. In a film which uses mainly orchestral original score, such as *Titanic* or *Lord of the Rings,* the music editor is the interface between the director and the composer in more ways than one.

This relationship involves some creative functions with respect to the structural and emotional content of the music, and also technical issues—creating cue streamers and markers, click tracks to guide the conductor during the music recording, and of course, actually editing the music, which may be needed when the director gets to hear the music for the first time alongside the film's action. In a film which incorporates a greater proportion of source [CD] tracks, such as *XXX* or *Jackie Brown,* the music editor has to find the best way to utilize a, possibly, short section of a CD track in order to enhance the dramatic effect of a particular scene or even an individual shot.

A lot of directors have very little understanding of the structure of music, and so they rely heavily on the music editor to interpret their designs. The ability to employ intuition and diplomacy in this situation is an advantage.

Who are the people a music editor interfaces with?
The director, the composer of original score, and the music supervisors, during post-production track laying and editing. During the final mix, the re-recording mixers are also involved.

Do you work with the music supervisor? In what capacity?
Yes, they are involved in selecting the source music [existing CD tracks] and negotiating the rights for use in the film. The success or failure of their music selections will depend on the music editor's skills in placing the tracks appropriately.

It has been said that a music editor can be a very powerful type of music supervisor in terms of the selection of music that ends up in the film. Why is that? Was it your experience that you influenced the choice of music in your recent project? Was that an example of what they call "temp track love"?

As with all aspects of filmmaking, the processes are collaborative, in that there is always a lot of interaction between departments and individuals. The degree and type of interaction depend very much on the director and producer(s) and their prioritization of the various aspects of the filmmaking process—the relative importance of music, sound, dialogue, sound design, Foley, and sound effects. The director relies on others to varying degrees to suggest source tracks, and the music editor will be around at those meetings. Therefore, he or she has an opportunity to make suggestions, along with the music supervisors and anyone else for that matter. The director's role in all aspects of the filmmaking process is to solicit advice from everyone and use what they feel is appropriate. As a result, there are always lots of ideas and suggestions flying around. As an involved participant, I was able to influence the choice of certain tracks.

"Temp track love" is inevitable these days. Temp tracks are spotted into the film soundtrack at an early stage of sound post-production in order to create a musical "reference" within which decisions about the other aspects of sound track laying and dialogue editing can be performed. Of course, being "temp," they will eventually be replaced, but by that time, the director, producer(s), and post-production staff will be very familiar with them—at least with the tracks which have worked well with the action up to that point. As a result, choices of tracks for eventual use in the film will always be compared with the temp tracks in terms of their effectiveness.

How did you make your musical suggestion decisions?
Suitability for the scene in terms of atmosphere, dramatic effect, emotional weight, etc. Sometimes a weak scene will need "rescuing" with help from a suitably strong piece of music.

In your opinion, how can artists get their music to the music editor to try to get a piece locked into use for a film?
The music supervisor is probably a better bet for contact with the selection process, but either could be contacted. Another route is via one's music publisher, who will normally spend a lot of time promoting the compositions of their clients within the film world.

Did your experience make you want to do more music editing in the future?

Did your experience make you want to do more music editing in the future?
Yes, I found the whole process very stimulating. Having spent most of my career in commercial music production for albums, I found the different working relationships very interesting. There are a much greater number of individuals working on a film's post-production sound than you will ever see in the production of an album. It's like being part of a small army!

PROFILE
Wendell Hanes, Composer
Style Child

• Composer for TV, films, commercials, video games
• Different music supervisor relationships for different media
• The right way and wrong way to interact

How production relationships unfold depends on more than just the people involved. Music supervisors for different media have different responsibilities and objectives, which can in turn have a big impact on what they need from their colleagues. For composers like Wendell Hanes of Style Child and Bang Music, *www.bangworld.com,* interfacing with music supervisors of all stripes is all in a week's work. His portfolio of rhythmically driven compositions encompasses TV commercials, film, TV shows, and video games, making him well qualified to provide a perspective on how relationships with music supervisors in each field differ.

Highly trained as both a video editor and music producer, Hanes has the enviable ability to apply a finely honed visual perspective to his work. With great visual and musical instincts, he can zero in quickly on the unique demands and expectations of each medium, and pave the way for the most fruitful co-existence possible with his music supervisor on the project.

Commercials: "A composer I know named Michael Montes told me one great piece of advice. He said, 'When you're making music for commercials, always give your clients the outrageous piece.' His reason for saying this was that if you always give your clients' music supervisors something that is so unique—even if they don't like it—they will remember it. And they will remember you for making it. My objective each time I create is to impress myself first. If I can impress myself, chances are I can impress others."

Film: "In film, it's much different. Commercials are thirty seconds.

responsibility to carry the story line. Unlike a commercial, you don't have a chance to do four versions of a complete score and then tell the music supervisor or director to choose one. When you're scoring the entire film, your mental challenge even before you play the first note, is finding the pulse of the film for its duration. I'll be thinking, 'How does what I create in this scene effect what happens in scene twenty?' You always have to be cognizant of the emotional arc or journey of the film.

"I watch a lot of movies and I watch them in two ways. First, I try to watch certain scenes without sound, and then I'll watch it with sound to see how he or she shaped the characters and understand why that particular musical direction was chosen. A great score is exact. It's a perfect marriage. For instance, it's hard to imagine what Sylvester Stallone's *Rocky* films would have been like if Bill Conte had not come up with that famous score during Rocky Balboa's 4:00 A.M. workouts.

"The damage from doing the wrong music can change the meaning of events in the whole movie, causing viewers to dismiss the film as cheap, boring, cliche, etc. Creating just the right excitement, propulsion, richness, or suspense is the single biggest responsibility for the composer. Music, dialogue, character traits, and story lines all have to operate as one unit within the director's vision.

"In films, my work with the music supervisor begins before the first note. The director, sometimes in conjunction with the music supervisor, can also be that force. The first phase is spotting, or determining where the music is going to exist. The music supervisor and the director will say, 'These sections can be scored, but here, why don't we license a Motley Crue song?' A lot of the time, spotting is all about instinct, so they might at one point think, 'This is a great place for underscore,' but then later say, 'Let's take the underscore out and put in a Rolling Stones track.' As a composer for film, I take a step back and I allow the music supervisor and the director to make those decisions."

TV Shows: "One good example is a show I worked on called *World's Sexiest Athletes.* That was a two-hour show filled with interviews of famous sex symbol athletes. The role of the music supervisor was to come up with songs that he and the director liked for every athlete.

"He came to me and said, 'We like this popular song. Can you make a track that sounds like it? Don't get us in trouble. We don't want it to sound so much like it that we get sued. Just give us the same energy and feel. I want to feel the same way I do when I hear the original piece.'

"So, for example, it's the music supervisor's job to say, 'Let's fill this scene with a song by Ozzy, and one by Dr. Dre, and one from Garth Brooks.' I have to have control over all these different genres. I need to know how to make a Garth Brooks track, a Dr. Dre track, a sultry Isley Brothers track, and I'd have to do it in a way that is still credible. So now I'm looking at the music supervisor as the authority figure and I'm saying, 'Okay, I'm taking your lead here.'

"At this point, it's not a completely creative thing for me. Imitation plays a big role. With scoring a film you're still being creative and bringing yourself to the project, but with a TV show where the music supervisor wants you to re-create something that has already been done, less of you is involved."

Video games: "It's not that different from TV shows, in the sense that you still have a framework of, 'We want it to be the latest edgy, hip, popular song.' Video game music supervisors are really consumed with what the latest new sound is out there.

"So, if it's a dirt-bike game, instead of giving them the traditional rock track, now you do some kind of merging of distorted guitar with a hip-hop beat, and the hip-hop beat doesn't have to be 120 bpm. It can be a hip, authentic one that's in the groove at 95 bpm, just like what you would hear on the radio.

"There's a big movement in video games for the track to be done by people who already make radio tracks and have records out. They don't want the video games to sound like video games—no more Pac Man stuff. When the music comes, they want it to sound like a hit record. So they say, 'Can we get DJ Premier and Method Man on the track?' for the menu page. The beats for video games have become more authentic, and more credible than ever. The great mix is not the key necessarily. For TV shows, where networks are steadily upgrading to HD, they want it to sound great. With video games, the mix is not lo-fi, but can be dirty in order to keep it real. It should feel street. A little static on the track? In some cases, that's good.

"The same attitude carries over in the commercial world, too. They also want to stay trendy. If you can find that sound that's a little ahead of the curve, then you're golden. The first time pop culture heard techno was on a BMW commercial, and there's always that chance in commercials to uncover that new sound."

On How Music Supervisors Can Create Negative Production Relationships: "The kind of music supervisor I don't' like to work with are the ones that don't trust you enough to let you experiment. There are some music supervisors that will give you too much information, and too much information can put you in a box where you may feel limited. It's like: 'Here's a box, these are the parameters. Don't' go outside the box. Stay in the lines.'

"I've found that it can also be destructive if you have someone literally right over you. There are situations where I've had to compose in front of the music supervisor—just make it up right there. Music is created in steps, and sometimes people don't' know what you hear in your head when you hit that first chord, It always takes some trial and error before finding the right pulse.

"Once you get all the information from the music supervisor and the director, you then have to harness those ideas into your vision and create a body of work that answers everybody's questions and fulfills all desires. Still, a major part of you must shine through. That's why everyone who does a Marvel Comic film thinks of Danny Elfman, because he's found that magical 'heroic' sound that works. Since he did *The Simpsons* he's mastered the sound of fantasy and imagination, and it's become a strong niche for him."

On How Music Supervisors Can Create Positive Working Relationships: "I like to work with music supervisors that can tell me what they want in such a way that I don't feel like I'm trying to satisfy them only. Once I'm trying too hard to satisfy someone else, a part of me gets lost, because I'm too concerned about doing what they like.

"When they hire you, a positive music supervisor will have confidence in you as a composer. So in the beginning he or she may ask you to experiment, then ask you to pull back a little and say, 'We love this, but can you tweak that?' Good music supervisors can hear what you've already done, and assess it in a way that's not destructive.

"Keep in mind that sometimes when you make music that people don't like, it still can be helpful in the experimentation process for the director and music supervisor. Exploring the direction that's not correct can eliminate a slew of approaches that will save you time in the end as a composer. A great music supervisor will always have interesting solutions and suggestions—that's a key trait that makes them great to work with."

See an expanded version of this Profile at *www.musicsupervisioncentral.com.*

Adam Schlesinger is a man in a band (or two), but he's also a guy who understands the value of media placement for his work. Besides being the founder of two pop bands with good commercial success, Fountains of Wayne and Ivy, he wrote one of the biggest movie songs of the last decade when he created the incredibly catchy "That Thing You Do" for the 1996 Tom Hanks movie of the same name. That song earned him an Oscar nomination for Best Original Song in a Movie, but it's just a part of what makes him a musician who really gets the connection between music and visual media.

How long had you been a rock musician before you got into pairing your music with TV and film?
The funny thing is that when I was a kid, one of my parents' friends was a successful film/TV composer, the late Michael Small. He was sort of my idol when I was a kid—he was one of the few people that had a sustained career in the film and TV worlds, and my parents were actually concerned that it would give me a false impression of how easy or difficult it might be to do that for a living. I assumed that it's just a job that people can have, like being a mailman. I started getting into pop or rock music as I got into middle or high school, but also simultaneously I was interested in all kinds of music. When I got out of college and decided I really wanted to be a musician, I always had the attitude that I should get involved with anything I could. I started getting more professional opportunities at the point that my bands started getting really active and having little hints of success.

How did you get TV opportunities? How can other artists do it?
You have to try to make as many contacts as you can in media, but you have to do it in a non-annoying way. No one likes a musician that comes in and pesters them and appears to be too ambitious. The bottom line is that if you're good and you have a chance to show people your stuff and it's

getting the responses, it may be because the work you're doing is not up to snuff.

What I did was call people up when I got to New York and ask if they knew anybody in those worlds, and I'd ask if I could play them some stuff. I'd usually demo stuff for free, which is where everybody has to start. One guy I called was Steven Gold (see Profile in Chapter 9, Legal Issues), who's now one of my closest friends. He was a friend of a friend, and it was basically a cold call. He was nice enough to say, 'Come on by, give me a tape of the stuff you've worked on.' He was working primarily on TV and advertising. He liked what he heard and was nice enough to give me a shot demoing some stuff.

The other thing that was a huge boon to me was getting involved with PolyGram Music Publishing, which is now Universal. There was a woman there named Holly Greene who heard the seven-inch single "Get Enough" by my band Ivy, the only thing we'd put out at that point. We made two thousand copies of it, she got turned on to it by somebody. It got me and the members of the band into a publishing deal. Once you get involved with that publishing company, then you have a whole team of people looking for opportunities for you.

Publishing is a double-edged sword. You're giving up some rights to your music, but when you're just starting out and need contacts, these are people that are tapped in to markets for your music. I had to write a lot of stuff on spec. My big break was when I got a chance to write for the Tom Hanks movie *That Thing You Do,* and miraculously, my song got accepted.

How did That Thing You Do *come together?*
Basically, they said it was a movie set in 1964 about a band that was American but obviously very influenced by The Beatles; they cited groups like the Knickerbockers, American second-rate British Invasion imitators. They said the title had to be "That Thing You Do," since that was the name of the film and this fictitious band's hit song. At some point, I asked for a contact with somebody from the film production company, Playtone, so I could talk to someone connected with the movie before I started writing the song.

If at all possible, try to talk to the music supervisor or person whose job it is to pick the music and ask as many questions as you can. I find that if I can get the sense of what they're looking for, I can nail it. A lot of times, I lose out on jobs because the information is wrong.

Who did you speak to at That Thing You Do?
I think that the first person I spoke to was the music supervisor on the film, Deva Anderson. I ultimately did speak to Gary Goetzman, who was Tom Hanks' partner, and one of the producers. They were very specific and savvy musically. They gave me the time period and type of bands to reference. It really helps when the people on their end know what they want and have something specific in mind. It's much harder when they don't know what they want.

How long did you have to wait to hear your song won out?
It was quite a few months of them saying, 'You're in the top five, you're one of the front runners, everyone still likes it,' and eventually they just made the decision. The best thing is that once you do get one prominent thing out there like that, then suddenly, you get people looking for you, rather than the other way around. That's when things can change for a writer.

Were you surprised to get the Oscar nomination?
It was beyond my wildest expectations—completely surreal.

How much does an artist learn about licensing, the more they do this?
Legally and financially speaking, it's important to understand the different types of rights that there are. A lot of times, with movies or TV, they'll tell you right up front, "We're going to want the publishing on this." You can see if there's room to move on that; it depends on how much leverage you have to negotiate as to what happens with the copyright to the song. Some TV networks now have a steadfast rule that they have to own the rights, because they know that's where the income comes from.

In terms of getting more work, it comes down to relationships and having people think they can trust you and rely on you. It doesn't matter if you try for a lot of things and don't get the job. It's more about people knowing you can deliver things quickly and understand what they're saying. I'm talking about specifically writing stuff on assignment here.

Then there's the other side, if you're just in a band or you're an artist, and your music is friendly for being used in film or TV. Then it's simpler. Hopefully, people will hear your songs and just want to use them in a TV show. I play in two bands, Ivy and Fountains of Wayne. Fountains of Wayne has sold a lot more records, but Ivy has licensed much more than Fountains of Wayne, because Ivy is much more conducive to that kind of use.

What are some examples of media placements for Ivy?
Ivy has been used in just about every teen TV show that's ever existed! From *Roswell* to *Felicity* to *Melrose Place,* literally dozens of those shows—everything WB has put on the air. The film directors the Farrelly brothers are big fans of Ivy, and they hired us to score [the 2001 feature film] *Shallow Hal.*

Do you regularly work with music supervisors when these placements occur?
There's a couple of parts to that answer. If a music supervisor simply wants to license a song on one of my records, I don't necessarily deal directly with them, because that's mostly a paperwork question. If a music supervisor is looking for suggestions of songs that might work, then I try to deal directly with them whenever possible. My advice is the same for any relationship in life: Be nice, know what you're talking about, and try to develop a relationship with that person that you can maintain over time.

Any last advice for music artists that will be working with music supervisors?
I would say the only thing you want to make sure of is that you don't pester people. I think it's important to maintain and develop relationships, but don't become annoying. It's a fine line, and that just comes down to personalities and general social skills, but I think that everybody in the music business in general is turned off by people that are overly aggressive. The music business is, in large part, about maintaining a casual air, even when it's not really casual!

See an expanded version of this Profile at *www.musicsupervisioncentral.com.*

CHAPTER six

Music Styles and Effective Placement

Picture this movie scene: As the image comes into focus, we see that we're at least ten thousand feet in the air and accelerating at an extremely high speed toward the ground (which appears to be flat with some rocky areas). It's the desert, and as we get closer to the ground, a car speeding down a lone highway becomes visible. A huge cloud of dust trails behind and eventually dissipates in the distance.

The time is early morning, and the sun is barely over the horizon as day breaks. The camera zooms down into the dust cloud picking up pace as it reaches the back of the car. It's a black Chevrolet Monte Carlo with what sounds like a very large engine, and inside are four rough cowboy types with an off-beat Lower East Side Manhattan rocker vibe in their styles as well (good costume designer).

The camera pulls up behind the Monte Carlo and through the back window, between the four passengers, and directly into the stereo control exactly when the driver's finger pushes in a cassette. The camera swiftly flies out and above the car and zooms past it into the clouds as we cross-dissolve to the next scene.

What music would *you* pick for this scene? Don't answer yet! There are many questions that a good music supervisor must ask before getting started. For example:

- How many pieces of music does this scene really need?
- What year is it?

- How old are the people in the car?
- What year is the car?
- What do these people look like?

For this scene, and millions of other possible ones you may be confronted with in your career, you must make your own general analysis of the scene, and then ask the director and/or producer the same set of questions that you asked yourself. Compare and contrast all of the answers, and only then can you begin your search for the perfect music. Soon enough, you'll be ready to present your spotting or song proposals.

Matching Music and Sounds to Media

Effectively choosing and placing a piece of music in a film, TV scene, video game, or other form of media is at the core of every music supervisor's job. The presence of music in all these formats is virtually a given, but what makes picking the right piece of such critical importance? Simply put, the right music or sound effects with the right visual will tell the story. With music, filmmakers can orient the audience to understand exactly what they are trying to get across—even in the absence of dialogue or narration.

How to Select the Right Audio

If you were hoping to find a formula here to accomplish this mission, the fact is that there most definitely is no such thing. In fact, your ability to select and license different—and better—music and sound effects from what other music supervisors would choose is what you'll be counting on to distinguish yourself in the field.

Successfully matching sound to media is a complex assignment. There is simply no substitute for the music supervisor having knowledge of as many musical styles, artists, and works as possible. Imagine being presented with the following music-supervision projects, and think about what music you would choose if you had a very large budget and ample time to obtain your clearances:

1. It's 4:30 A.M. and a classified special operations briefing has just finished aboard the U.S.S. Enterprise (which is in an undisclosed location in the Red Sea). The camera follows two pilots and two navigators as they walk out of the briefing room, through the cold steel hallways of the aircraft carrier, and eventually out on to the hard deck, where their two F-14 Tomcats are waiting. It's very dark outside. The first plane taxis into take-off position, holds for a moment, and launches off the aircraft carrier. The afterburners

produce a blue glow on the sea-face as the Tomcat tears into the night sky. The second plane takes off exactly the same as the first. The only difference is that once it's in the air, the camera view comes into the cockpit of the second plane, as if the navigator were looking back at the U.S.S. Enterprise as it gets smaller and smaller in the distance. What kind of music are you going to pitch for this scene? What genre? What artists? Which song(s)?

2. A very attractive woman in her mid-twenties walks down Madison Avenue in New York City in the afternoon (about 3:00 P.M. on a Thursday). She's wearing a sexy business suit with a mini-skirt and high heels; she's holding a black leather folder filled with papers and other things. Heads are turning left and right as the impressive woman struts down the avenue, when the camera pulls out to an aerial wide shot, showing that a block away around the corner in front of her is a man in a suit walking roughly the same pace. The two approach the same corner from different directions. As they are both obviously in a rush to get where they are going, they each speed up to get around the corner quickly. Reaching the corner, they slam into each other head-on! They both fall down basically on top of each other, and the woman's papers go flying everywhere. The man tries to help gather everything, and the wind kicks up, making it even more challenging. As the wind carries the papers into the air, the camera pulls out into a wide shot and dissolves to black. What kind of music are you going to pitch for this scene? What genre? What artists? Which song(s)?

3. It's the National Football League's most important day of the year: Super Bowl Sunday. It's fourth down on the forty-yard line, and there are four seconds left on the clock. The score is tied, and the team with the ball is looking at a lengthy field goal to win the game. If the kicker misses, the game goes to overtime. In slow motion, the center snaps the ball back to the holder. The holder barely catches the ball as it's snapped very high. Just as the kicker gets into kicking position, the holder gets the ball on the ground and into proper position. The kicker launches the ball with everything he has, and the ball (still in slow motion) crosses over all the players as the linemen try to bat it down to the ground. Everyone misses it, and the ball continues toward the uprights. It appears as if it's going to be a close one because it's heading towards the left post. The ball reaches the

uprights and bangs off the left post and drops into the end zone. It's good! The kicker's team wins the Super Bowl, and everyone in the stadium is wild with excitement. What kind of music are you going to pitch for this scene? What genre? What artists? Which song(s)?

4. The scene opens with a wide shot of the last college graduate of Monmouth University, West Long Branch, N.J., as he receives his diploma behind Woodrow Wilson Hall. The crowd cheers with excitement as all the grads throw their caps high in the air. Cut to close-up of Ben and Jay (two surfer dudes from south Jersey). Ben reminds Jay that there are "head high" sets rolling in at a surf spot just a mile away that locals call "The Pit." Jay gives the nod "okay," and the two sneak away from the crowd, and run to their van. Jay turns on the radio (loud). Cut to the rear tires as they burn rubber and make a loud screech. A few of Ben and Jay's friends laugh as they spot them from the lawn (where the graduation ceremony took place minutes before) as they speed out of the parking lot. Cut to Ben catching and dropping in on a large wave at "The Pit." Ben's still wearing his graduation gown, and in the distance you see Jay also wearing his gown as he floats beyond the breakers in the line-up waiting for the next good wave. What kind of music are you going to pitch for this scene? What genre? What artists? Which song(s)? How many songs?

Now take those same scenarios and place them in less pleasant circumstances that are more like what happens in the real world: Budgets are tight and licensing must be completed within five business days. Does that change what music and sound effects would be best? Not at all. What it *does* change, however, is the music and sound that you are actually going to choose for these projects. For additional practice, you can find more music-placement scenarios at this book's companion Website, *www.musicsupervisioncentral.com*.

The First Steps

Spotting scenes where music should eventually be placed can be an overwhelming task for young and even experienced music supervisors. Relax, take a deep breath, and prepare to focus your thoughts on the dialogue, actions, and motivations of the characters; and always keep in mind that the director/producer could disagree with your ideas at any time. That's all right—the spotting process is, after all, a *process*.

The Spotting Process

The first thing you need to do is read the script and/or view the spot, show, or film. You may or may not do this with the director, editor, and other creative personnel present. While viewing the piece, pause it and replay scenes repeatedly as you sense the need for musical support. Try to decide whether it's a mood or a pacing issue that you're trying to accentuate, eliminate, or support. It could be all of the above.

The music in a scene will almost always directly affect the mood and pacing. Having an accurate understanding of the script and all its parts is the key to making proper judgments. Take the time to study the piece from top to bottom, and make detailed notes including timecode and scene title/descriptions. This will cut down on wasted time when you are bouncing ideas off the production team later. It is perfectly acceptable to make up your own scene titles while spotting. Directors and producers will usually know what you're talking about even if you use a description that they've never used for a scene.

Once you've gone through the piece a few times, and you feel confident with your notes, it's time to set up a meeting with the director and/or producer. Have all your questions about the piece ready, and of course, have your spotting notes ready. Present the director/producer with your spotting thoughts and opinions, and remain totally open to constructive criticism. The goal is to walk out more knowledgeable than when you walked in, so you can do your music-supervision job better. Remember, it's their project, not yours; therefore, your ultimate goal is to spot the piece to *their* liking.

Research Groundwork: Music Genres

One of the great music supervision challenges is to determine what genre or style of music a scene or project needs. It goes without saying that there are many different music styles, and often defining a style is arbitrary. What is the difference between hard rock and heavy metal? Rap and hip-hop? Traditional pop and standards?

Music supervisors must also determine what kind of music the production needs. Is it a popular music cue, a composed piece of music, or a production-music library piece? Knowledge of musical genres can be extremely helpful to music supervisors in communicating with producers and directors throughout the course of a long- or short-form project.

There is a major difference between popular music styles and production music styles. Popular music can be broken down into categories in many different ways. A quick look at the *Billboard* charts provides a dizzying array of categories:

The Billboard Hot 100
Hot R&B/Hip-Hop
Hot Country
Hot Rap
Modern Rock
Mainstream Rock
Hot Latin
Hot Dance Music/Club Play
Adult Contemporary
Dance Radio Airplay
Hot Christian Adult Contemporary
Hot Christian Singles
Top 40
Hot Digital Tracks
Adult Top 40
Top 40 Mainstream

In the production music world, the style categories are equally overwhelming. A quick look at BMG's Production music search engine reveals more than two hundred different musical styles to choose from, such as:

A Cappella
Alternative/Indie
Ancient
Ceremonial
Cheranga
Children
Jig
Jive
Exotic
Fado
Khoomi
Vallenato

The list doesn't stop there, however. BMG also provides musical categories that are named for their application, such as:

Atmospheric
Corporate/Industry
Jazz

Light Contemporary
National/Ethnic
Rock
Sports

The challenge is to determine what style, category, and genre you think would work best for your project, and have the knowledge and skill to find music tracks that fit your preferences. Fortunately, there are some useful resources at your fingertips. The ever-growing All Music Guide *(www.allmusic.com)* allows you to search for popular music by style, song title, artist, and label. Samples of song files can be found for many songs there, as well.

The true value of a site like All Music Guide lies in the depth of information about popular music, artists, and labels, and the fact that the information has been mapped in a very helpful way. For example, when we search for the Rolling Stones, we find basic biographical information on the band, a complete discography, and song highlights. Just as helpful is the way style descriptions are all hotlinked; for example: rock 'n' roll, blues-rock, hard rock, british invasion, pop/rock, british blues, album rock, psychedelic, British psychedelia, England. Clicking on any of these categories will take you to a page with links to bands within the style, as well as a general description of the style as a whole.

itunes *(www.itunes.com),* the revolutionary online record store from Apple allows you to search for music using keywords, including artist and title. This site also includes a styles map that allows you to search within a style. However, their "style mapping" is nowhere near as comprehensive as All Music Guide's. Along with other Websites like *www.rollingstone.com* and even *www.amazon.com,* online resources are very powerful tools for music supervisors, allowing us to do comprehensive research very quickly. Equipped with a healthy knowledge of music in general, we can use these tools to find a track for a project in a matter of hours, not days or weeks as it once would have taken.

Music maps such as these are extremely helpful to the music supervisor who knows he wants a Rolling Stones track, but also knows he must find an alternative due to budget constraints, time restrictions, or both. See where your research takes you. It may lead you to a great-sounding, highly effective, and licensable alternative that you might not have thought of in the heat of the moment.

The next key step is to turn this research into something practical. Find more song options than you think you're going to need for a specific style, and then have them aggregated onto one CD with a printed liner note defining the tracks: Song name, artist, album, and length. Also include in the liner note the title of the popular track that you are trying to approximate (Rolling Stones—"Gimme Shelter," for example).

The liner notes allow you to document your research. We music supervisors often return to tracks that we initially passed on, and the liner notes are a reminder of what is on the CD and in what context the tracks were originally conceived.

However, keep in mind that, when you are spotting music for a project, identifying the appropriate genre to the rest of the team can do more harm than good if everyone involved does not share your familiarity with that genre. It is a music supervisor's responsibility to be sensitive to the fact that other entertainment professionals are not necessarily as knowledgeable about music as a music supervisor must be, and the other members of the creative team may not know what certain genres sound like without a point of reference. For example, if the music supervisor determines that EMO rock is the genre that is most appropriate for a spot, than it is the responsibility of the music supervisor to not only play them the song, but educate his or her colleagues about what EMO rock is.

Developing your knowledge of as many genres and artists as possible is integral to professionalism as a music supervisor; every additional style you can audition mentally while spotting is like another tool in your toolbox. If you're the only candidate for a music-supervision job with a knowledge base so broad that you can successfully recommend, for example, Okinawan trance (yes, there really is such a thing!) for a scene, you may have the edge to get the job and develop a reputation as a highly knowledgeable professional.

Criteria For Selecting the Right Style

Extensive research, study, and knowledge of the project, film, or TV show is one hundred percent necessary to begin the process. The goal is to match the perfect style, instrumentation, arrangements, and composer (if original music will be used) with the project's central plotline, geographic location, time period, and character personalities.

Geography

It is very important to take the geographic locations into consideration so as not to act in a way that conflicts with local culture or history. Here are some questions you may face in a project:

What instrumentation/style is commonly associated with...

the city and urban locations?
rural and farmland locations?
mountain locations?
regions such as Asia, the Middle East, or Antarctica?
the ocean?
outer space?

Determine what music goes with specific geographic locations by researching international music styles on line, at your public library, and/or your local music bookstore—try *www.scotchplainsmusiccenter.com* for example. Outside of specifically researching music and geography, try to find books on foreign civilizations and their cultural histories. Music is important to the history of every nation in the world, whether as entertainment or as a means of communication. Some countries' music sounds unique because of the instrumentation used, and others are unique because of tempo variations, chord phrasings, and style of performance/execution.

Time Period
Musical styles are continually evolving, and it is important to have a working understanding of that process of evolution so you can be historically accurate when your task is to represent styles of past time periods.

What musical styles are commonly associated with...

prehistoric times?
the 1700s?
the 1800s?
1900 to 1910?
the 1920s, 1930s, 1940s, etc.?
What are the signature music styles of today?

Once you have been to the library and the music store, and you've done your research about the sounds and styles of particular regions and time periods, it's time to do some listening. Go back to the music store and buy as much as you can afford. We call this "music studies." The only way to know what something truly sounds like is to listen to it repeatedly. Do a "music study" every time you find a style, sound, or artist that is new to you. The more styles you know, the more you'll be able to add to your spotting sessions. When you're searching for the perfect sound to relate to a specific character with a specific age and background, you're going to want as much knowledge as possible.

Plotline/Character Traits and Motivations

Again, it is crucial for a music supervisor to have a deep understanding of the plotline and characters' personalities and motivations when choosing songs and directing musical composition for film, TV, video games, and other media. Choosing the right key, tempo, style, and instrumentation all come into play. For beginners, experimentation is most often the best way to zero in on the right choice. Challenge yourself to come up with instrumentation and musical styles for some of these common TV and film scenarios, some of which you may recognize:

1. In the 1960s, a fully armed air fleet of military helicopters approach a tropical beach in South Asia overrun with battle, fire, and mayhem.

2. In the late 1960s or early 1970s, a flamboyant African-American boxer enters the ring to box for his third consecutive heavyweight crown, a feat that no man had done before.

3. A quirky and extremely desperate young man with a strong sense of inner-child witnesses his favorite bike being stolen at a shopping mall. He embarks on a nationwide search/adventure to find his bike and seek revenge on those who stole it.

4. A fifty-five-year-old schoolteacher waits to find out if she wins ten million dollars on a popular network game show, and she finds out that she won.

5. In 2003, a popular newscast cuts into regular programming warning viewers that a strong band of thunderstorms are headed in their general direction.

6. In the early 1980s, a young Chicago-based husband and father decides to take his family by car on a vacation across the country with a final destination of a popular theme park in California. Along the way, they're pulled over in Arizona by a highway police officer who accuses them of tying a dog to their car bumper and driving away with it still attached.

7. In the 1950s, a woman undresses herself at night in a highrise apartment-building bedroom as a peeping tom takes pictures of her and hangs them in his bedroom on a daily basis.

8. For the first time in known history, a manned spacecraft breaks Jupiter's atmosphere and approaches the surface for landing, not knowing what they will encounter.

The above scenes are from popular TV shows or movies: 1. *Apocalypse Now* (film), 2. *Ali* (film), 3. *Pee-Wee's Big Adventure* (film), 4. ABC's *Who Wants to be a Millionaire?* 5. ABC Local News (TV show), 6. *National Lampoon's Vacation* (film), 7. *Rear Window* (film), and 8. *2001: A Space Odyssey* (film).

Know Your Context

There is a significant difference between the sounds a music supervisor might pick for different visual media, such as a movie vs. an advertisement. In a movie, you're usually picking music that is tied to a much longer creative concept, and the scene you are scoring is directly affected by the scene before it and the scene after it. Also, in a movie you may have two minutes or more to build music tension. Think of the famous *Jaws* theme: It's nearly a minute before you hear the simple, foreboding strings that create the unforgettable signature of that film.

In an ad, however, you're dealing with just thirty seconds, so the style of the music is going to reflect that temporal limitation. In this arena, you have to deliver the bang much more quickly, which is one reason many advertising agencies look to popular songs that the listener/viewers already know. The ability to determine when to license a track or generate a fresh one is a particularly important skill for music supervisors, and it comes up again and again.

Should I Use Original Music?

Several steps go into choosing and/or producing songs for all onscreen moments. The first, and possibly most important, is the process of determining whether a scene requires original/custom music or commercial/popular music.

Deciding when to use original music vs. licensed music is a fairly simple thing if treated properly. Keep everything in perspective, and know that there is no right answer to this question from a creative standpoint. Commonly, score is used to support everything from serious drama with heavy dialogue to high-intensity action sequences with big explosions. Often, the best thing to do as a music supervisor is to spot the whole film with popular music, just so you're fully prepared. Wait and see what the score composer comes up with, and make a decision with the director and producer as to which songs work better for each scene.

Much of the time, this decision will be made before you ever see a script!

This is because you have to be aware of how large your music-licensing and original-score budgets are. If your executive producer allocated all the music money for original score, then you'll be working with an original composer the whole time, and you won't be worried about licensing popular songs.

On the other hand, you may have a situation where there's a sizable licensing budget, and the producer/director is not interested in original score at all. In this case, you'll be licensing a lot of songs, and some of them could even be custom-made for the film. These types of songs are not considered score, but they are often only available through the purchase of a soundtrack album. With the right artist, this type of positioning could be a good way to sell records and it also makes the soundtrack marketable.

Original music, also sometimes referred to as custom music, is produced from scratch for one sole purpose, such as a promotional branding campaign like T-Mobile Wireless, a TV show like Fox Television's *24,* or Warner Brothers' Oscar-winning feature film series *The Lord of the Rings.* In the film and TV worlds alike, original music is most often also referred to as score. Score is unique to the central plotline and is key in the storytelling and pacing aspects of films, and many television shows ranging from sitcoms and game shows to drama series, news, sports, and more.

Some music supervisors, as well as the composers they hire, are better suited to working in short-form worlds such as TV advertising, where they're dealing with spots that generally range from :15 to :60. Other music supervisors and composers prefer scoring and placing music for long-form projects like feature films, TV movies, and documentaries, which generally range from one hour to three hours or more. Another group falls right in the middle of long and short form, preferring to work in formats ranging from thirty minutes to an hour in duration. Short films, sitcoms, game shows, sporting events, news programming, drama series, action series, and soap operas all fall into the mid-form format.

When working in the world of custom music production for TV, film, video games, and other media, the music supervisor's role is to advise the production team or director regarding the best creative choices for each sequence, and for the project as a whole. These choices often involve tempo, instrumentation, key, and styles/genres. Music supervisors have to listen constantly to as much music as possible in order to draw inspiration from a multitude of options. The challenge of music supervision is to then take that inspiration and create something unique and excellent that enhances the visual content of the project. A clear and original creative statement sets one soundtrack/score apart from all the others, so a music supervisor should strive for originality unless instructed by the production team not to do so.

In film scores, for example, historically speaking, "orchestral" arrangements, instrumentation, and styles have been commonly used. The catalogs of accomplished orchestral composers such as John Williams of *Star Wars, Indiana Jones,* and *Saving Private Ryan* fame; and Bernard Herrmann, whose work graces a number of Hitchcock films, including the memorable *Psycho,* continue to generate revenue. And these talented orchestral composers continue to have extremely successful careers in present-day film and TV. Just because they have been so successful, however, does not mean that their styles of composition must be used for all films and TV shows.

Picking the right style of music should always be determined by the mood, setting, time period, character motivations, character actions, and actual physical location of the piece. Always start with what is logical, and then explore the more "out of the box" possibilities. For example, it's logical to choose Beethoven's Fifth Symphony for a scene that starts with a long shot of an old castle at the top of a dark hill where a well-known vampire hunter lives. That is predictable, though. This could be a good opportunity to have your composer create a new piece of music inspired by Beethoven's Fifth, or you could choose to think more creatively. Try a piece of hard-hitting heavy metal from Black Sabbath's first album, or maybe some dark hip-hop/rap like BLESTENATION *(www.blestenation.com).* There's no wrong answer when you're experimenting. You'll never know if it works if you don't try it.

Hiring the Right Original Music Artist for Your Project

Angelo Badalamenti's scores to pioneering director David Lynch's television show *Twin Peaks* and feature film *Lost Highway* are examples of high accomplishment in the world of drama, suspense, pacing, and mood. Badalamenti is a master of fusing avante garde rock, blues, jazz, and funk rhythms with classically influenced melodies and phrasings, and his music has been sampled by some of the world's leading DJs and bands today. (Check out CD #1 of Kruder and Dorfmeister's G-Stone/Studio !K7 double album release *K&D Sessions* for a beautiful use of a Badalamenti *Twin Peaks* sample on the song "Speechless.")

The style Badalamenti is most known for is unique, and it is often less than successful when attempted by others. If you're an experienced music supervisor and you know how to contact him and secure his specialized talents then your colleagues may call you a hero, if the film project is a murder-thriller feature, for example, with a good script, a marketable cast, and a healthy music budget.

That last point is important. If you're a music supervisor working on a production, whether it be film, TV, or video games, your budget will be proportionate to your level of freedom to employ the services of the people you want. As much as you may believe Angelo Badalamenti is the right composer for your job, your production and licensing budget may not support that decision. Therefore, you will be faced with the job of searching for, and hopefully discovering, an incredibly talented indie composer who has yet to achieve popular success, and whose style is right for the film, is affordable, and is available.

This is why it is an integral part of the music supervisor's role to listen consistently to the demos of composers, bands, and artists that are new and undiscovered. It is equally important to read entertainment and music-industry trade publications, such as *Mix, Hollywood Reporter, Billboard, Remix, Variety, Village Voice, New Music Express, Backstage,* and visit their Websites frequently. It is also important to attend live music performances and concerts of independent, signed, and unsigned artists/bands. By doing so, the music supervisor can study the demographics of show audiences and their response to the music. This really increases the chances of discovering groundbreaking music and furthering your film or TV project, while exposing a new and talented band or composer to the world of multimedia commercial sales and licensing.

Also, just as A&R reps discover and develop musical talent for the purpose of selling records, music supervisors are searching for, placing, and producing music for the purpose of branding and selling a film or TV show, and possibly selling a soundtrack album. There are any number of musical marketing and promotion possibilities that the music supervisor can employ to simultaneously raise the profile of a project, and increase its overall profitability.

In the process, music supervisors make it possible for artists to collect licensing and performance fees in ways other than from radio play and album sales, not to mention the fact that, for an artist, licensing a piece of music for a film, soundtrack album, or TV show is paid promotion. In this way, music supervisors have the power to strengthen the artistic community and actually help create more music-selection choices that will be available to them later down the line. Make no mistake: Music supervisors are today's A&R executives.

Evolving Music Styles

Just like all other facets of culture, music styles for visual media have evolved over the years. As a music supervisor, it's important to be familiar with the music of all eras so you can not only know what's current for a project set in the present, but what's historically accurate for a project set in the past.

In the 1940s and 1950s, for example, the predominant style for film scores was straight orchestral masterworks from composers such as Miklos Rozsa and Elmer Bernstein. The late 1960s and early 1970s, on the other hand, were a time of great diversity in film and film music, with syrupy strains like *Love Story*, and the sublime "Waltz" and "Love Theme" from *The Godfather*. In the 1980s, composer Jerry Goldsmith's triumphant *Star Trek: The Motion Picture* fanfare and John Williams' unforgettable *Raiders of the Lost Ark* ushered in the post-*Star Wars* blockbuster sound.

Synthesizer-based, pop-influenced music, such as Harold Faltermeyer's "Axel F." from Beverly Hills Cop, threatened to take over film soundtracks in the mid-1980s, while composer Maurice Jarre brought an orchestral sensibility to the all-electronic score in his brilliant "Building the Barn" from *Witness*. By the 1990s, symphonic sounds, rock rhythms, and synthesizers began to blend, while composers utilized a full palette to really open up their orchestrations. In the "Aughties," styles as extremely disparate as electronica and classical have blended seamlessly in scores like *The Matrix* (see the profile on Jason Bentley in Chapter 2, Theory and Application).

There are many different and talented composers in the world, and they all have individual specialties. It's the music supervisor's role to be aware of the broad spectrum of talent, including composers nobody else knows about yet, and it all starts with styles of music. Does the project require orchestral, jazz piano, country guitar, funk, electronica, soul, or some fusion of a variety of styles that is completely innovative and groundbreaking? Once that is determined, you need to find the best composers available in the genre that are affordable for the project, and secure their services.

Crossover Success

Breaking through to pop radio and MTV is a rare and outstanding accomplishment in original music composition, especially when the music was originally created for the primary purpose of branding a television show. This can be considered a particularly successful piece of music supervision.

A great example of hit original music composed to brand an hour-long action/drama TV series is the theme song from the popular 1980s action drama series *Miami Vice*. In 1985, Jan Hammer's highly charged "Miami Vice" theme broke through to successful soundtrack album sales and regular Top Forty radio play, and nabbed two Grammy awards, making it the first TV show theme to do so in nearly a decade. The show's successful soundtrack album features more than just Hammer's original theme; it showcases classic songs by some of America's favorite rock musicians at that time, like Phil Collins and Glenn Frey. More than a decade later, the song "I'll Be There for You" by the Rembrandts served as the theme to the NBC sitcom *Friends* and became another radio-friendly hit.

When an original song from the score of a movie or TV series receives extensive mainstream exposure, it's likely that it will end up being licensed for some kind of compilation album or DJ album. This is a perfect way to further the incoming revenue generated from the TV or film project's original budget, and it is a prospect that would be of interest to an industry executive.

In the long-form world of feature film, Thomas Newman's piano melody and main theme "Any Other Name" from the score of the Oscar-award-winning 1999 movie *American Beauty* was licensed and remixed many times after the original release. Surprisingly, remixes of Newman's masterpiece film score made their way into the world of clubs and dance music for years after *American Beauty* hit theaters and went to DVD/video. Listen to the 2002 Virgin Records release *Pure Chillout* or the 2001 Universal International compilation release *Sunset Ibiza* for appearances by both Thomas Newman and Jan Hammer, among other film and TV composers.

Putting It Together

Taking all this information and these processes, and then relating them to visual imagery, is the next step. Imagine you're working as a music supervisor on a film that has multiple scenes at a house party, with different people at different locations, yet it's all happening at the exact same time. What factors determine the genres of music that should be considered?

In social scenes such as a party, it is first important to consider the demographic of the people at the party. For example, which character is throwing the party, and what kind of music do they like? Also, what kind of people have been invited to the party, and what kind of music would these people commonly enjoy or listen to under the given circumstances? Collaboration with the director is key in answering questions like this, because the director has the most intimate connection to the characters (and the director has creative authority).

In this scene, once you have a clear understanding of the character throwing the party and their motivations, you can focus in on the right genres. This is because the guests at this character's party were, presumably, invited by the character, so they are, in turn, a direct reflection of who this person is as an individual.

Furthermore, at a party, the person throwing it usually has control of the music. These obvious facts, with their subtle psychological underpinnings, are worth considering for the hypothetical party scene described above, and are present in some form or another for most scenes you will ever place music for, either in fictional or non-fiction settings.

Matching a Personal Profile to Music

One of the most important dynamics in music supervision is the character's personal profile. Many times the selection of genre can be derived solely from a character's intellectual makeup and what drives him or her. Other criteria to examine include environmental surroundings and circumstantial factors. For example, what kind of music would be appropriate for a scene in which a woman just found out the man she was engaged to is homosexual? One could predict that the female character would be confused, sad, or enraged upon learning of such news.

But first we need to consider the question: If she were to listen to music, what kind of music would it be? It depends on who she is. If she's a party girl, she may choose to listen to party music such as hip-hop, dance, house, or techno artists like The Crystal Method, Fatboy Slim, Outkast, Kelis, or Sasha & Digweed, to name a few. However, our character might be someone who's emotionally sensitive, from a small town in the Midwest, and who just moved to New York City and fell in love for the first time in her life. In that case, it's likely that her farm-based upbringing would associate her with country, blues, or folk music, and it would make sense to look into artists like James Taylor, Tom Waits, Johnny Cash, Stevie Ray Vaughan, and Dwight Yoakam. Once you know your characters, the songs that work for their scenes will come.

Whether the format is a TV scene, video game, film, or other form of media, the right music is critical to balancing the mood and pacing properly. Music supervisors make it their business to comprehend the wealth of musical possibilities that might be appropriate. If you love music, you don't have to be a rock or rap star to have a successful career in the entertainment business. Music supervisors interact with all the stars in Hollywood *and* the music biz. Music supervision is one of the only careers out there that truly bridges the gap between sights and sounds.

music supervising for a weekly TV series. "The unique part of TV is mostly in the volume of work," says the L.A.-based music supervisor for the long-running Fox comedy series *Malcolm* (formerly known as *Malcolm in the Middle*). "For *Malcolm* I will find somewhere in the neighborhood of one hundred-twenty-five to one hundred-fifty pieces of music per year, whereas with a movie you might find twenty-five to thirty pieces, and that's a very busy one.

"I think Linwood Boomer, creator of *Malcolm,* chose me to do the show just because he likes my taste in music. He told me what he was looking for on the pilot, I brought him a CD, and it made him laugh! He's not so interested in what's hip and happening; it's mostly about what's funny to him."

Houlihan started out as a trained opera singer who eventually moved to L.A. to expand on her experience in TV news production. After scoring a gig as an assistant to a New Line Cinema music executive, Houlihan moved to Universal Music Publishing, where she was pitching to music supervisors. Next, she got the chance to music-supervise the 1997 movie *Eve's Bayou,* and Houlihan was hooked. Two indie films, then a pair of TV pilots, including *Malcolm,* followed, and she had a steady music-supervision gig.

Houlihan starts the selection process by watching the onscreen talent carefully. "My favorite part of it is watching the scene and tapping into the actors' emotions," she explains. "When I see a movie for the first time, I'm more into the actors. The second time, I focus on the music. I try to feel what they're feeling and translate that into the music."

A show's theme song is a crucial part of the sonic branding for every show, and Houlihan executed that task to perfection when she lined up "Boss of Me" by They Might Be Giants—a selection that netted the show a Grammy Award for best original theme song. "Linwood was a fan of They Might Be Giants," she recalls. "They were approached with a script and then sent a demo. It was like 'That Thing You Do.' The Giants updated the sound sent a demo. It was like 'That Thing You Do.' The Giants updated the sound of the demo when they heard the other music in the pilot. It's much more contemporary rock—it's *bratty* rock."

Within the twenty-two episodes per year, Houlihan will be responsible for finding anywhere from two to twelve pieces of music per twenty-two-minute episode, with some interesting music placement opportunities and challenges along the way. "We'll use artists like the Dub Pistols, Soul Coughing, or an instrumental by Junior Senior," she says.

During the season, her typical month is hectic, to say the least. "In general, we mix three episodes a month," says Houlihan. "As you can imagine, there's always episodes in different forms of production. I might have one show with an on-camera shot on Tuesday. I'll spot another show which has been edited on Wednesday—there's a cut they're happy with, and we'll watch and say, 'We want music right here, and in order to help the action, we'll look for something fun and bouncy. Make it really big here, but out by the time she says that line.' Then three days after the music spotting, I'll come back and we'll do a viewing. At that point, composer Charlie Sydnor has written a score, and I have found other source music, which is something we have to license. We'll present our ideas, and at the end of the session we're usually eighty percent done. I'll do clearances based on what Linwood wants cleared, and Charlie will do anything needed to his mixes."

Based on her budget, Houlihan has different levels of artists that she seeks out for her weekly soundtracks. "If they're unsigned, I know I can get them for a better price, and that's always a factor, especially on the hour-long shows, because the hour-longs tend to have the same budget as the half-hour shows. For the network series *Wonderfalls,* for instance, I had three categories of music I was looking for: two recognizable songs per episode from Universal or whatever, and those are top dollar. Even the mid-level heard-of-'em-before-but-not-so-hot-right-now kind of major-label song will cost right now, in this market, about $17,000 for an all-TV-in-perpetuity quote for the world, which is $8,500 for publishing and the same for master rights. The next tier down is $6,000 to $10,000 all-in, mid-level of artist from something like the Minty Fresh label, and then there's the 'cheap and cheery,' as we like to call them—completely indie, no representation—for $1,000 to $1,500 all in, with video buyout. I also use TAXI *(www.taxi.com)* for a lot for their stuff. You just call them and tell them what you're looking for, they give you the number and you work directly with the artist."

The most challenging aspect of Houlihan's job comes when it's time for downfall of TV music supervision: A lot of paperwork. Clearances are not easy: They require a lot of research and follow up, and somebody who really has a mind like a steel trap.

More and more TV shows are putting multiple seasons out on DVD, and *Malcolm* is no exception. Along with the added distribution, however, come additional licensing complications for Houlihan, who will have to renegotiate licenses for each piece of music used during the season, and inevitably be forced to replace some of them.

According to Houlihan, her field of music supervision for TV is in a period of fast growth. "TV used to be an August-to-May job," she says, "but now it's really an all-year job, because there's no TV season anymore. Fox is debuting five shows in June, and it will be a constantly revolving door. I think that music has been recognized as a key element in shows, especially with the younger demographic, and there are and more music supervisors doing TV."

See an expanded version of this Profile at *www.musicsupervisioncentral.com.*

PROFILE
Doug Wood, President
Omni Music

• The power of the music supervisor
• For matching, pacing is key
• Producing music libraries

If anyone should be passionate about proper music placement, it's Doug Wood, President of Omni Music *(www.omnimusic.com)*. His company pioneered the use of compact discs for library music in 1985, and has been a major player in providing licensed music for visual media ever since.

To Wood, the role that the music supervisor can take—boosting a project by selecting the right music—is downright heroic. "As a music supervisor, you have the opportunity to make the project better than it would otherwise be," he states. "You have the opportunity to lift a film up, for example, and really deliver it to the audience in the way that the director wants it done. You can also ruin it if you're not careful. Every music supervisor has a 'eureka' moment like I had for so many years, where I was matching up music to the video. You spend a lot of time looking, trying it again, moving it, and when it's right it creates its own path, and the whole thing just takes off like a giant airplane and flies. It's fun to sit there, watch it, and think, 'That's the piece.'"

Wood knows what it takes to get going in the right musical direction. "I think one of the important criteria for someone selecting music is to separate out, 'These are my tastes and what I love,' from 'but this is what the film needs.' Sometimes they're the same and sometimes not.

"I often see shows or movies where the music is okay, but it's not propelling the film along much either. Somebody can say, 'Here's a montage where I want to use my favorite song,' but it's not doing anything. Then there are cases where the music can have the opposite effect of what's intended; I often see that in corporate communications. It's fine for Company X to think their widget is the best ever, but when playing Strauss' '2001,' it's a bit much. Often, the music is really a little over the top for the subject at hand."

When matching music to a scene, Wood pays attention to the pacing, first and foremost. "Tempo is one of the first things you want to look at," he says. "When you audition music for people, they say it's too fast or too slow; that's one of the easiest things for them to identify. I also think you have to look at your picture and ask, 'What kind of scene is this? What kind of frame of mind are the actors in?'"

Wood points to the evolution of sports highlight music to demonstrate how music placement tastes can change, and how vastly different musical styles can be applied to fit the same purpose: "Sports highlights have really seen an interesting metamorphosis over the past fifteen years," he notes. "Fifteen years ago, it was trumpets, French horns, timpani, the-king-is-coming regal power, because we'd all been taught that's what that music meant.

"Now it's all rock. You hear a little trumpet and trombones, but pretty much the electric guitar has replaced those instruments and come to be perceived as powerful. That's a really cool thing, and it cuts across virtually every demographic in this country. It shows you the power of music and the collective consciousness we all share, and it's worth thinking about how society hears music and what we perceive as powerful."

The fast-exploding musical world has given music supervisors a mind-boggling number of genre choices for their projects. "I have about three- to four hundred key words to describe music—it's getting more and more difficult every day. We have a lot of cross-pollenization between music styles. You have Latin music and jazz and techno all coming together, rap influences, traditional rock 'n' roll. In the case of sports music, you have heavy rock mixed up with trumpets and brass, along with a heroic, triumphant thing, which is not rock 'n' roll's roots. There's music that blends four or five different styles."

As one of the people who selects what music Omni provides to time-strapped media producers and music supervisors, Wood has clear ideas of what can work fast. "Especially in the library business, we need to be aware of how people listen to music and what they associate with it, because we're trying to package it for our clients to use," he points out. "A perfect piece captures a universal feeling that my clients will really latch onto, such as a great piece of drama music they can use for a variety of scenes, but it captures that feeling perfectly and does it very quickly. With library music especially, we don't have the luxury of a 16-bar intro because we have to orient that audience to where the director wants them to be and then get out of the way, so setting that mood is critical. With the right piece of music, you can transport an audience to the year 1650 in two seconds, or transport them ahead fifty years; make them laugh or cry in a few seconds. I challenge anyone to show me any other medium that can act that fast."

PROFILE
Ron Burman, Senior VP of A&R
Roadrunner Records

With their ability to bestow national exposure and commercial success on an artist by selecting their music for a project, music supervisors are increasingly being called "the new A&R." But before jumping to this conclusion, it's a healthy idea to examine the way a true A&R (Artists and Repertoire) professional goes about his high-profile—and high-stakes—job.

As the man who signed the multi-Platinum hard-rock act Nickelback to Roadrunner Records, as well as up-and-coming acts such as Thornley and Theory of a Deadman, Ron Burman understands what it takes to make a winning music selection. Burman rose to his much-coveted position after years in the trenches, managing indie bands and booking music festivals, all the while gaining a sharp sense of how to match an artist to his record label, and identify a hit song in the process.

Based out of Roadrunner's New York City office, Burman's job is a whirlwind of activity that involves constantly evaluating new music, forging and nurturing relationships, and making artistic and commercial decisions about the acts already under his care. "Basically, my responsibilities are to find and identify new, talented artists that I think could be huge," he explains. "Once I've done that, sell it to my bosses (the owner and the president), and convince them that this is someone we should invest in because we believe we can sell a lot of records. We're like a bank, and this is like venture capital. That sounds cold, but the more I do it, ultimately I realize that's what it's like, and if I can't convince my bosses this could be huge and has a big upside, then it won't get signed to my label."

Signing an act to the label is just the tip of the iceberg, however. "Most A&R people don't get involved in everything—but the good ones do," Burman says. "In addition to locating artists, I'm trying to cultivate relationships with people that are going to feed me bands. That's hard, getting good gatekeepers from all over the world. Once I find an act, have the contact, and get people to allow me to sign it, then I have to convince everyone internally to get excited about it.

"That's the 'A,' but it's A&R, so what's the repertoire? If the act has twenty-five songs, but you know there will only be ten to twelve on the record, you're going to have to go through the material with them, and ask what they want and what will make the record most commercially viable."

As the Senior VP of A&R for Roadrunner, Burman is like a music supervisor in that he needs to execute all of these tasks in support of reinforcing the label's unique, identifiable, and coherent sound. "Roadrunner does everything from rock to heavy metal, and historically it's been known as a heavy metal label. It encompasses every niche within the rock/metal spectrum, from hardcore, EMO, punk, straight-ahead metal, retro metal, extreme agro—within that scope. There has always been commercial rock, and there has been a specific edict as to what we can or cannot do.

"A Roadrunner band has to rock. They have to be a live act; they have to be able to pull it off live. At their core, I think they need some aggression. Every band on the label has a guitar. That's not a mandate, but it is a thread. I think we have a brand, unlike other labels in the spectrum, and we've expanded the brand with bands like Nickelback, Theory of a Deadman, and Thornley.

"I'm like a music supervisor here because I'm the gatekeeper. I'm the one who has to be immensely discerning, saying, 'Is this going to fit in the puzzle? Will this be a worthwhile placement for the label?' Like they'd put music in a film and really try to be honest about it. It's really being able to discern the good from the bad, what does and doesn't fit, and what creatively makes sense."

Likewise, the work of music supervisors for TV, film, and video games can be an enormous boost to Burman's work. "It's paramount," he confirms. "An example would be how Lea Vollack of Sony was doing *Spider Man*, something that was appropriate for Nickelback came up, and Nickelback's Chad Kroeger wrote this song 'Hero.' We thought this was the perfect opportunity to introduce the face of Nickelback with this blockbuster: People might have heard of Nickelback, but not known who Chad Kroeger, the singer, was. Now people know, 'Oh that's the guy from Nickelback,' and they might not be able to do that with the contemporaries of Nickelback.

"We have someone here at Roadrunner, Michelle Van Arendonk, who does that for our own soundtracks, like *Resident Evil, Freddy vs. Jason, MTV Headbanger's Ball,* and *Road Rules.*

"Getting one of your artists' songs selected by a music supervisor could be the vehicle that opens the door to a whole other level of exposure. You can achieve a lot by being on the radio, but you're usually pandering to your specific demographic. Sometimes when you're on a soundtrack, you're often exposed to different demographics that might not have otherwise been exposed to your music—it can be a wider swath."

Although Burman sees the parallels between people in his position and music supervisors, he sees important differences as well. "I personally don't agree that music supervisors are 'the new A&R,'" he states. "It's definitely another vehicle for A&R; it's definitely a complement, but it's not the new A&R. It's a whole different thing. Picking a song to be on a soundtrack is a lot easier than picking an artist you want to invest a sizable sum of money in and develop their career. A soundtrack can have a couple unmemorable songs and that might not kill it, but you can have a crappy record and the artist—and their A&R person—could be toast."

CHAPTER seven

Cue Sheets

Music supervisors must keep an up-to-date and accurate log of all the music placed in films, television shows, and ads, and submit that log to the performing-rights organizations: ASCAP, BMI, SESAC, etc. As a music supervisor, you should understand that this is a taxing and formidable task, and as a result, it must be built into your music services contract and/or budget proposal for work to be delivered. It's also important to realize how important the generation of cue sheets is to the composers and publishers of the songs used in the projects you work on. For many professional composers in film and TV, it's literally their paycheck.

The Importance of Cue Sheets

Cue sheet generation and maintenance are possibly the most important tasks in a music supervisor's job, because this is the way the music supervisor ensures that the writers and publishers of the songs that are used receive their performance royalties. BMI, ASCAP, and SESAC (which are PROs, or performing-rights organizations) maintain vast computer databases that log music composed for film and television. These databases are updated continuously. However, this system is not complete unless music supervisors like you log and submit cue sheets regularly that display exactly what music is used in a production, how and why it is used, for what duration, and who gets paid (and how much) performance royalties as a result.

Is it possible to use music you've licensed without subsequently filling out the cue sheets? Yes, it is possible, and unfortunately many time-starved music supervisors do just that so they can move on to the next project. You should make sure that this is a bad habit you never develop. Remember that accurate cue-sheet reporting is an important part of follow-through in your relationship with the composer/artist whose work you are licensing. If you are under-reporting your usages, composers and artists will be far less inclined to work with you in the future, and they may ensnare you or your production entity in legal action to claim their royalties.

At this time in the entertainment business, there is no standard or master "template" for a cue sheet. Although that may sound ridiculously inefficient, it is true. However, the music supervisor represents the musical choices and interests of the companies for which they work, and sometimes these companies will offer their own custom template for cue sheets. Be ready to adapt to new formats as you get new jobs, but always know the core elements that make up a complete cue sheet.

Cue Sheet Elements
A cue sheet that is filled out correctly includes the following critical information:

- The Series Name or Film Title
- Episode Title
- Episode Number
- Air Date
- Show Length
- Music Length
- Production Company Information
- Song Title /Album Title/Record Label
- Composer
- Publisher
- Performing Rights Society
- Timing
- Usage

When there are multiple writers involved in the composition of one individual piece of music, this must be indicated on the cue sheet for the program. When writers and publishers split royalties in any way other than a 50/50 basis (such as a 33/33/33 percentage split for three equal partners in composition), this must also be indicated on the cue sheet for the program. This type of detail is critical to performing-rights organizations' accounting, and more importantly, payment calculations.

As more and more independent producers and cable operators distribute product to the marketplace, it becomes increasingly important for music supervisors to file accurate cue sheets if all parties involved are to benefit from their talent, connections, and hard work.

The Cue Sheet Process

Artists, composers, and their management teams will often prepare rough-draft cue sheets for music supervisors to review for comparison purposes. They might also ask to see those "final" cue sheets filled out by the production company before they're submitted to the performing-rights organizations, to make absolutely sure they've been filled out correctly.

The production company is not obliged to show these final cue sheets to anyone other than "in-house" team members, but you can if the team members want to, for artist approval. Letting composers and writers check the cue sheets can help create positive relations and ensure that all parties involved will receive accurate compensation. This is also the kind of option that can be written into a music-services contract between a composer and music supervisor, or between a composer and a production company, before the project goes into the production or post-production phase. Be sure, however, never to show a cue sheet to anyone outside the organization that hired you unless you have the approval of your in-house legal team or direct report.

Once the cue sheet has been filled out, it goes to the artist's PRO, either by e-mail, through a proprietary system designed to wire cue sheets instantaneously, or by hard copy if necessary.

Again, please don't forget that the songs you use in your productions directly impact people's careers and livelihoods. It's no wonder artists and composers take their royalties so seriously, and you should too.

Sample Cue Sheet

Below is a "moldable" cue-sheet template that should suffice for most, if not all, of your production needs when it comes to a generic TV or film program. Remember, many of the templates provided in this book are for you to use, edit, and change per your specific needs. You can find a downloadable version of this cue sheet, and others, at this book's companion Website, *www.musicsupervisioncentral.com*.

Sample Cue Sheet

Series/Film Name: Weekly World of Music
AKA: World of Music
Episode Name: Rock 'n' roll Episode
AKA: Rock 'n' roll
Prod. #:   WWM 101
Episode #:   101
Show Duration: 30:00
Original Airdate: May 12, 1997
Total Music Length: 5:28
Production Co./Contact Name:
Music Music Music Productions
Ms. Ima Worker
3422 Music Place
This City, CA 31234-1768

BI: Background Instrumental VI: Visual Instrumental
EE: Logo
BV: Background Vocal VV: Visual Vocal
TO: Theme Open TC: Theme Close

Cue # Title % Society Usage Timing
Composer
Publisher

---

001 Weekly World Opening Theme TO :32
  W   Sam Writer 50% BMI
  W   Joe Lyric 50% ASCAP
   P   My Publishing Co. 50% BMI
   P   JoLyr Music 50% ASCAP

002 Weekly World Bumper BI :15
  W   Sam Writer 50% BMI
  W   Joe Lyric 50% ASCAP
   P   My Publishing Co. 50% BMI
   P   JoLyr Music 50% ASCAP

003 Pop Song VV 3:43
  W   Swen Composer 60% PRS
  W   Galen Lyricist 40% PRS
   P   SwenSongs Inc. 0% PRS
   P   SwenSongs USA 100% BMI*

004 Weekly World Bumper BI :18
  W   Sam Writer 50% BMI
  W   Joe Lyric 50% ASCAP
   P   My Publishing Co. 50% BMI
   P   JoLyr Music 50% ASCAP

005 Weekly World Closing Theme TC :35
  W   Sam Writer 50% BMI
  W   Joe Lyric 25% ASCAP
  W   Sara Artist 25% SESAC
   P   My Publishing Co. 50% BMI
   P   JoLyr Music 25% ASCAP
   P   Sara's Music 25% SESAC

006 Music Music Music Productions Logo EE :05
  W   Sally Logo Writer 100% BMI
   P   Music Music Music Publishing 100% BMI

When is a non-music supervisor a music supervisor? All the time! As soon as Boom Pictures *(www.boompictures.tv)* principals Matt Ginsburg and David Leepson won the bid to produce and direct the thirteen-episode History Channel series *Extreme History with Roger Daltrey,* they knew that music-supervision skills would be important to their mission.

"Our job title was executive producer, line producer, runner, production assistant, music supervisor, janitor—and sometimes Roger's roadies," Ginsburg laughs, recalling their time in the field with the famed lead singer of The Who. "Wherever there wasn't civilization, that's where we went: The nine most difficult places to do production in the United States!" While they were shooting footage for their no-holds-barred look at historical tales of survival, Ginsburg and Leepson were also doubling as music supervisors on the road. The pair stayed in constant contact with composers Glenn Schloss and Erik Blicker of G&E Music, directing them regarding the show's theme, as well as demonstration and mood music. The team completed music for fifteen minutes per twenty-one minutes of show, or more than two hundred original total tracks. By FTP'ing or FedEx'ing audio files from their studio in New York City, G&E were able to supply Ginsburg and Leepson with music for approval at any time, anywhere.

"We started thinking about the music right away," says Ginsburg. "The music is the pulse. David and I are all about the pacing and vibe, and that's what makes a show's style."

"You've got to think about music from the beginning," Leepson adds. "It changes the way we shoot the show. After we shot some stuff, we would show it to Glenn and Erik; that spurs even more ideas, and it goes back and forth in a collaborative process."

The composition that got the chemistry going was G&E's opening theme, a rootsy techno song that mixed Western acoustic guitars with beats from a Korg Electribe groovebox (listen at *www.gemusic.com/portfolio/portfolio.html).* "I wanted to do something different for the show than what's on the History Channel," Ginsburg says. "We wanted to shoot it on a grainy stock of film and come up with a cool brand for it. They nailed it: Once we listened to the music, we were able to visualize even more what we were doing. We were like, 'We'll shoot this on Super-8, and put Roger in different places.' So we knew the music before we even shot the open. For us, it was a tremendous blend of attitude and the Daltrey vibe, but it wasn't Who-ish. There was something nostalgic and familiar about it."

For Boom, one of the keys to selecting G&E was a past working relationship, and the knowledge that they could get into a groove. "A good relationship is the key thing, because this is very collaborative," says Ginsburg. "You want to be with people who obviously share your sensibility to some extent. They know when we get enthusiastic about something, we mean it, or we'll say it's the other way: 'Dude, it's not working.'"

Although Boom often needed the tracks as fast as possible, that didn't mean they simply expected the music house to work quickly. "When it comes to expectations, it's not, 'These guys should be turning these cuts out faster,'" Ginsburg explains. "It's our responsibility to be as articulate as possible and use language these guys can understand, and say, 'We want a Beck-meets-Daniel Lanois type of thing,' and talk to them in a language they all share. It's a common thing to hear, 'We want it to be sexier,' but what does that mean? So to say, 'Hey, can you give us a little more distortion? Or kick the rhythm up and make it more staccato?' and speak in music terms, helps."

As the music supervisors as well as the budget managers on the project, Boom could have chosen to go with library music and save a bundle of money, but they decided not to. "Stock music sounds like stock music," says Leepson. "For a show like that, we couldn't find the vibe we needed in a CD library."

Once the music was wrapped and edited in with the shows—at about fifty to seventy cues per show—Boom had no licensing to clear, since they used all original music. There was paperwork, however, to ensure that G&E gets their performance royalties. "We have to submit 'rights bibles' for every show," Leepson says. "They include rights for everything from footage to music, with scripts and transcripts for the show. The History Channel will honor them and handle reporting of the music cues to the performance societies."

Ginsburg and Leepson are film and video guys, not music pros. Still, they realize that being able to act as music supervisors on their own projects is an important skill. "It's so much a part of the process," says

Ginsburg. "The music and the story are all intertwined, and it's not something we would want to defer to someone else."

The final result was a series that made Boom Pictures' client, The History Channel, happy. "We had final say on the music, but they ultimately signed off on everything," Leepson states. "They love the music. It was a big thing for them because it was different."

For visual artists like those at Boom Pictures, wearing the music supervisor hat is often a necessary, welcome responsibility for fulfilling their vision. "The music is the show," Ginsburg concludes. "It's as much of the show as the narrative and the pictures. We're ravenous when it comes to having the opportunity to create with music. That's such a key element in our sensibility, and how we approach production. I think there are lot of producers and directors that are the exact same way."

CHAPTER eight

Licensing

As much as we'd like to be able to use whatever songs we want for our projects, getting the required permissions often requires negotiation. The standard way to facilitate a negotiation is by issuing license requests and interpreting licenses. This chapter will outline the many different types of licenses used in the business today.

Licensing and the Music Supervisor

If the sole responsibility of a music supervisor were simply to audition and choose great songs, from Bach to the Blues, that work perfectly for every project, there wouldn't be much need for a whole book on the profession. However, the reality is that picking the right music is just a small component of the music supervisor's job. Securing the rights to the desired music and/or sound effects is a totally different beast.

Licensing represents approximately fifty percent of the responsibility that any given music supervisor has on any given project, at any given time. Having an understanding of the licensing process and all the necessary types of licenses is critical to becoming a successful music supervisor.

In certain situations, however, it is entirely possible that you could work on a job that only requires that you select and place music in visual scenarios. When this is the case, there is most likely a "rights and clearances" department in the company that hired you, but you would still be responsible for providing cue sheets and detailed song usage information to the rights and clearances division on a regular basis, so that songs can be cleared and proper licenses negotiated with composers, publishers, production-music libraries, and record labels.

On most projects, however, the music supervisor is responsible for coordinating all the music permissions. Therefore, every music supervisor must have a thorough understanding of rights and permissions. If music that is used in a project is not properly cleared, the project is potentially liable for damages to the composer/songwriter, publisher, and record label. Improperly cleared music could cost the production a fortune in legal fees and re-edits, as well as damages awarded by the courts. If you are the music supervisor when a music-related lawsuit hits the CEO's desk, you won't necessarily be held liable in a court of law, but you could most definitely lose your job and credibility. Therefore it is absolutely essential that music used in any project, big or small, is cleared through the proper channels. Additionally, consider it your responsibility to stay abreast of legal changes that can—and do—affect music supervisors.

The Basics of Licensing

Music supervisors must be fluent with many legal and semi-legal terms. Let's start with the basics of licensing.

Composer: The author(s) of a musical work. Upon conception of the musical work, the composer(s) owns the song entirely. Having ownership of a song in its entirety means that one entity owns both the publisher's and writer's shares. Upon a work's inception, a composer owns one hundred percent of the writer's share and one hundred percent of the publisher's share.

Publisher: An entity that buys or leases the publisher's share of the copyright, eventually building a catalog of music to be licensed and sold within the terms of the publishing deal.

Song: A copyrighted musical work. A song is made up of two equal shares: The writer's share and the publisher's share of music and/or lyrics.

Writer's Share: Owned by the composer or composers, this represents fifty percent of the song's copyright. Although the composer or composers always have authorship, this does not automatically translate into a guarantee of royalty rates, since this share can be sold, left to heirs, etc.

Publisher's Share: This represents the other fifty percent of the copyright. The composer has the option to sell any percentage up to one hundred percent of the publisher's share, either to a publisher or other entity like a manager.

Library Music: Music published for the specific purpose of being licensed to film, broadcast, and other media uses.

Licensing Libraries

Using music from less-celebrated sources, such as pre-existing music libraries like Killer Tracks, Video Helper, Omni Music, Sonomic, and Meet Your Beat *(www.meetyourbeat.com)* is not as complicated as trying to license popular music. The music libraries have developed efficient licensing-request processes that make it quicker and easier than using music from other sources, and many libraries are fully licensed once they are purchased.

With libraries, music supervisors can dramatically streamline the licensing process because music libraries are specifically set up to deal with the different needs of diverse projects. You could, for example, purchase music from a library and only purchase the performance rights, without sync. Further, these tracks can be licensed in a matter of minutes, instead of weeks.

Music libraries also offer the option of executing a *needle/laser drop,* rather than purchasing a *blanket* license.

Needle/Laser Drop: One-off uses that are individually paid for in the absence of a "blanket" license.

Blanket License: A more expensive license that clears use of all the samples in that library for one price.

In order to determine whether it is more cost-effective to purchase a blanket license or a needle/laser drop, you must evaluate how much library music you are going to use on the project. If you will be using multiple tracks, it may be cheaper to purchase a blanket license. If, however, you will only use one or two pieces of music, a needle drop would be better. Once you have determined the amount of music you are going to use from a single library, you should contact the library company's sales representative to discuss what the best license arrangement would be for your project.

Licensing Production Music From a Composer

Production music created by a composer whom you hire specifically for the project comes with its own varying levels of complexity. Often, the music supervisor will negotiate the publishing rights from the composer. A music house supplying a theme to a TV producer for a company with its own publishing unit (such as ABC, which is under the same corporate umbrella as Disney Publishing), for example, can expect to give one hundred percent of the publisher's share to the producer's publishing designee. For a music supervisor, the advantages to this arrangement are twofold:

- Your employer—the producer—will make money back through the performance-rights societies every time the theme is played.

- It ensures that the song can't be turned around and placed elsewhere by the composers. Because your network owns the publishing rights, it alone controls where the music gets used.

This dynamic may very well change in an indie movie scenario, however. In this case, you can probably get the composer's services for less money up front in exchange for allowing them to keep all their publishing rights.

From a licensing perspective, in situations where the budget allows you to choose between, say, a newly composed piece of music or a minor hit by the hip-hop group The Roots, which is the easier path for the music supervisor?

If you're dealing with the composer, you should be able to "direct license" their music through them, since they probably own the writer's share, publisher's share, and master recording. Licensing-wise, this is faster and less risky than trying to clear rights for a popular song. However, keep in mind this route requires a lengthier creative process, and may place more pressure on you to convince your producers that this is better than going with The Roots track they had in mind all along. As always, there's no right or wrong approach. You have to be aware of the politics and time constraints of each particular situation.

If you go the popular-music route, the process becomes much more complicated, but it can also be worth it. Each medium—TV, film, video games, new media—presents its own challenges when it comes to acquiring the proper license(s) for popular music, whether the tune you want to use is by Miles Davis, Paul Oakenfold, or U2.

Master, Sync Performances, and Mechanical Licenses
There are four types of music-usage licenses that music supervisors must understand. They are:

Master License: Once executed, affords you the right to use the "master recording" of a song, which is usually owned by the record label, producer, or original artist.

Synchronization License: Once executed, affords you the right to synchronize a song—usually owned by the publisher or songwriter/composer—with a visual under the specific terms of the agreement. Commonly referred to as a "sync" license.

Performance License: In the United States, ASCAP, BMI, and SESAC exist to protect the rights of composers and publishers and specifically to manage the distribution of performance royalties generated from radio, television, live, and Web usages 365 days a year. Music supervisors are responsible for collating the information for producers and/or broadcasters to keep the societies informed about the use of their members' music by filling out cue sheets (see Chapter 7, Cue Sheets) and submitting them to the society and/or publisher.

Mechanical License: If one mechanically reproduces a piece of prerecorded music to be distributed and sold on any format (CD, DVD, VHS, digital downloads, etc.), a mechanical license must be negotiated with the publisher. These licenses can be expedited through the Harry Fox agency *(www.harryfox.com)*, which represents more than 27,000 music publishers, and is the foremost licensing resource for the mechanical reproduction of music.

A Licensing Scenario for Broadcast TV

Every licensing situation is as different as the medium, people, and music/sound effects involved; giving an example of every potential situation would be impossible. Nonetheless, examining a hypothetical scenario is helpful for illustrating what a music supervisor routinely faces. Let's look at a scenario in broadcast TV first.

Imagine that you're working as a music supervisor at NBC and you choose to use "True Nature" by Jane's Addiction off of the album *Strays* for an episode of a weekly drama that will air anywhere from two to five times a week over a one-year period.

Is a complicated licensing process necessary for master and sync rights? Not necessarily. If this episode were only to air one time in a six-month period and the song was used only once in the whole show, NBC would have the right under the "Ephemeral Rule" to use the song.

Ephemeral Rule: Under the condition that an Annual Blanket License has been negotiated with one of the three performing-rights societies, a cable or network TV station may air as "background vocal or instrumental" any piece of popular music one time in one complete show within a six-month period.

Properly executed, annual blanket licenses between networks like NBC and the performing-rights societies ASCAP and BMI allow music supervisors to work with popular songs like this rather easily.

Annual Blanket License: A license negotiated between a broadcast network or affiliated TV station and one or more of the three performing-rights societies (ASCAP, BMI, and SESAC) granting the network the right of single-performance usages under the Ephemeral Rule with the condition that the song usages are logged and reported according to their standard form.

In the cases of sync and master licenses, what you are working for is "clearance":

Clearance: Obtaining approval from the person or organization that has the authority to grant permission to a third party to use a piece of music or sound effect in combination with another medium. This is what licensing is all about.

The clearance a music supervisor is after in the NBC/Jane's Addiction example here is for two licenses. First is the synchronization license, which, as you'll recall, affords you the right to synchronize a song with a visual under the specific terms of the agreement. It will most often be negotiated directly with the publisher of the song and is often referred to as a "sync license." To find the publisher of virtually any specific song, you can do a quick search at *www.ascap.com, www.bmi.com,* and/or *www.sesac.com.* Depending on the site, you can keyword-search by song title, writer, and/or artist to find the publisher. Each of these sites provides phone, fax, e-mail contact name, and mailing address information for all of their affiliated publishers.

The second license needed is the much more expensive master license, which is usually negotiated with the record label, but a master recording can also be owned by the producer, original composer, or another entity.

The Role of the Performing-Rights Societies

Once a song is cleared, the music supervisor needs to submit a cue sheet to the performance-rights society responsible for that song and artist. In addition to requiring a cue sheet, the performing-rights societies are your gateway to locating a tremendous amount of music. ASCAP represents more than 170,000 United States composers, songwriters, lyricists, and music publishers, ranging from Duke Ellington to Beck to Madonna; BMI represents approximately 4.5-million musical works by more than 300,000 artists; SESAC's numbers are comparatively smaller, although it is gradually gaining in membership.

There are also a number of performing-rights societies in foreign markets to be aware of when dealing with distribution performance outside of the United States

County	Society	Website
Australia	APRA	www.apra.com.au
Canada	SOCAN	www.socan.ca
France	SACEM	www.sacem.fr
Germany	GEMA	www.gema.de
Italy	SIAE	www.siae.it
Japan	JASRAC	www.jasrac.or
Mexico	SACM	www.sacm.org.mx
Spain	SGAE	www.sgae.es
United Kingdom	PRS	www.prs.co.uk

There is also a consortium called FastTrack *(www.fasttrackdcn.net)*, which is a global alliance of music copyright societies, including BMI and ASCAP. In addition, there are dozens more performance-rights societies in the countries around the world. Canada's SOCAN has links to many more at *www.socan.ca/jsp/en/resources/around_world.jsp* in case you need to reach them.

Note that if you are at a TV station, when working with ASCAP and BMI you also have the option of choosing a Per Program license. In this case, the station would use its allocated blanket fee as a part of the calculation of a monthly per-program fee. In this case, each per-program licensee would report the music content and the advertising revenue associated with each of its local and syndicated programs on a monthly basis. The station's monthly per-program fee is then determined in part by the amount of ASCAP music in those programs, as well as the amount of revenue generated by those programs for the station. The per-program fee also includes an "incidental use" component, which is fifteen percent of the station's allocated blanket fee. ASCAP only accepts monthly Per Program reports electronically.

At SESAC, the only alternative to obtaining a blanket license is to negotiate a separate license agreement directly with the copyright owner of that song.

The performance-rights societies are aggressively using the Web to make it easier for broadcasters and TV stations to use their music. BMI, for example, offers a service on their site called BMI TV Select that streamlines the process. SESAC's license agreements are also easily requested and downloaded from their Website.

Now that you have chosen the specific song you want to use for that NBC dramatic episode, you need a sync license from the publisher and a master license from the record company. Finding out who owns all those rights can be a challenge, but searching the database of the performing-rights societies is usually an excellent way to start.

Once you have tracked down the publisher and record company, contact them to determine how they prefer their license requests to be formatted and submitted. Generally, each entity will want the same information to be stated in the request form (see below), but it is important to deal with each and every publisher and record company as an individual entity with individual needs. Once you have determined what is required, you fill out and/or create (since oftentimes you end up customizing your requests to your recipient and project) the forms completely. None of the requested information is optional.

Before you send any formal request to the publisher and record company to begin the negotiation process, have your direct supervisor approve the documentation. That person may be a creative director, director, producer, or even legal counsel. This is especially important because by getting "senior approval" for the paperwork, you indemnify yourself from possible blame or liability in case the deal goes bad.

Here's an example of a license request that was designed to administer and negotiate a sync license for Tom Petty's 1989 hit "Running Down a Dream." This agreement was negotiated on the preferred terms of the publishing company, EMI April, which owns the publishing rights to the track. The detailed rundown was obtained by researching EMI April Music's contact information at *ASCAP.com,* which then led to their general-assistance automated phone service. Take note of each field and the descriptions in [brackets], provided as a guide to you in your information search and creation of a License Request Form. This sample license request form could be used to attain synchronization, master, and/or mechanical rights. More specifically, the record label would receive this in the form of a request for the master license, and the publisher would receive it as a sync-license request. See additional license request templates at this book's companion Website, *www.musicsuperivisoncentral.com.*

A Sample License Request

[your production company's or broadcast company's name]
[street address]
[city, state and zip code]
[phone:]
[fax:]
[cell:] (not required depending how accessible you'd like to make yourself)
[your e-mail]
[your name and title]

mm/dd/yy

Attn: [contact name] *or* [type of media i.e., broadcast or film] Licensing Division
EMI April Music, Inc.
c/o EMI Music Publishing
Fax*: 212 000–0000*

Re: A Synchronization License for Tom Petty's recording of "Running Down a Dream" from his MCA Records' Greatest Hits album as background music for [name of the project title, production company, and broadcasting company].

Terms:

   Song Title: Running Down a Dream
   Writers: Michael W. Campbell, Jeffrey Lynne, Thomas Earl Petty
   Performer: Tom Petty & The Heartbreakers

Publishers:

   EMI APRIL MUSIC INC.
   C/O EMI MUSIC PUBLISHING

ATTN: JENNIFER INSOGNA
000 SEVENTH AVENUE
NEW YORK, NY 10019
Tel. (212) 000–0000

GONE GATOR MUSIC
C/O WIXEN MUSIC PUB INC.
ATTN: RANDALL WIXEN
00000 PARK SORRENTO
SUITE130
CALABASAS, CA 91302
Tel. (818) 000–0000

WILD GATOR MUSIC
C/O GUDVI, CHAPNICK & CO
SUMITOMO BANK BUILDING
00000 VENTURA BLVD.
SUITE 00
SHERMAN OAKS, CA 91403
Tel. (818) 000–0000

Type of Media: [Cable, Television, DVD, Network, Broadcast, DVD, Internet, VHS, etc.]

Video / Program Title: [Whatever the title is.]

Video Summary: [A one-line overall project-encompassing description of the images that will be associated with the song usage, but not necessarily married to the song itself. It's a summary of the production script and its general message.]

Scene Description: [A one- or two-line description of the actual scene in which that the song will be used.]

Length of Song Uses: [Give the actual timings of the cues.]

Number of Usages: [How many times was the song used?]

Use: [Vocal or instrumental]

Usage Type: [Background, visual, open theme, etc.]

Number of Copies: [If the license is for DVD, VHS, CD, or some other mechanical format, this information will most likely be requested by the publisher.]

Wholesale Price:
Retail Price:

Length of Production:
License Duration: [example: One Year/Twelve Months]
Territory: [example: Worldwide, Domestic, Canada, Japan, etc.]

Company Name: [The production company creating the project.]
Producer: [The producer's name]

Note:
Please respond with a price quote and sync license for the above usage of this song at your earliest convenience. Our target air date is (xx/xx/xx). Thank you for your time and assistance, and we look forward to doing business with you.

Sincerely,
David Hnatiuk
Music Supervisor

AUTONATIC Productions
autonatic.com

Master Licenses and More

Let's return to our hypothetical NBC/Jane's Addiction scenario, where you have chosen to use "True Nature" by Jane's Addiction for a weekly drama episode that will air two to five times per week over a one-year period.

Be aware that when licensing for the broadcasting world, certain pieces of airtime "real estate" are more valuable than others. If the rights holder sees that the song will be used for an NBC prime-time series, they will charge more than they would for a 4:00 A.M. news report on a local station outside of Omaha, Nebraska. The reason so much information is needed is because all of these details will affect not only the asking price but whether or not permission will be given at all.

Now that you have contacted and provided necessary information to the song's publisher or publishers—there could be more than one—you must contact the rights and clearances division of the associated record label (in the case of "True Nature" by Jane's Addiction, you would contact Capitol Records). The reason you are doing this is to gain rights to the master license of the song's recording.

Remember that the master license, once executed, affords you the right to use the "master recording" of a song, which is usually owned by the record label, producer, or original composer. Often, sync and master rights can be negotiated simultaneously in one license, especially if the original composer owns the recording being licensed. Record labels will often offer to act as liaison between you and the publisher, if you have not already contacted the publisher on your own. It is in your interest to license directly with the publisher and cut out the record-label "middleman," but negotiating with the record label could end up working in your favor if you've got a tight deadline. If you have a solid contact at the label, their muscle can be applied to negotiate the sync licenses through the publisher, which can help you save time, if not necessarily money.

Licensing Cover Songs

Note that if master rights are not affordable, you can choose to re-record the song with a different performer, therefore alleviating the cost of clearing the popular version of the song. In this case, an *arranger* may become involved in the process. In the event that you do not wish to use the popular master recording of a given song, an arranger can re-record the song and potentially create a new arrangement of the song.

If an alternate arrangement of the song is to be recorded, the record label, composer, and publisher will most definitely request to approve the final product before it goes to air. In order to record a cover version of a major song title like "New York, New York" written by John Kander and Fred Ebb and most famously performed by Frank Sinatra, for example, you need first to license the sync rights from the publisher. Alternatively, you may try to obtain the rights to use a cover version that has already been recorded by another artist besides Sinatra, which may be more affordable. In that case, you would locate Kander/Ebb's publisher to obtain the song's sync rights, find out which cover versions are available, and then get in touch with the record company of the artist of your choice to negotiate master rights.

Let's take our NBC/Jane's Addiction scenario one step further and say the drama in which you placed your song ends up going to DVD because it had become extremely popular. In this case, you're asking for the license to reproduce mechanically the format in which the song was originally delivered/sold/distributed.

If you have a question about executing the mechanical license, don't hesitate to contact Harry Fox. They'll be happy to work with you throughout the process. Working with Harry Fox is the most efficient way to obtain mechanical licenses for film and TV soundtracks that are manufactured and distributed in the United States As the music supervisor in charge of obtaining the mechanical rights for a soundtrack, it's your responsibility not only to get those rights, but to make your producers aware of the royalty rates that must be paid to the artists included on the soundtrack.

In the case of our hypothetical NBC dramatic series episode, if you as the music supervisor executed all of the above licenses by the time the show went to air, then you did your job. No matter what form of media you're working in, the best time to start trying to obtain your licenses is as soon as every required bullet point on the request form can be answered by your client/employer. This is because it's reasonable to expect the negotiation of a license with a major publisher to take one to four weeks.

Keep in mind that, at any point in that process, it may become clear that it is impossible to use your desired piece of music. The sync, master, and/or mechanical license simply may not come through, and depending on your production, not having all three will be unworkable.

If, for some reason, you did not execute the above licenses but still went ahead and inserted the song into the production, you would risk shouldering the blame for a potentially large copyright infringement lawsuit with Jane's Addiction's estate of publishers, label representatives, and legal cooperative teams. You will not be held liable for the actual money at stake, which could be a $25,000-to-multimillion-dollar lawsuit. However, you will be at risk of losing your job and respectability, which in this business is virtually your lifeblood.

Licensing for Film

While many of the same basic principles apply to TV and film, several aspects of licensing are particular to the film realm. Sync and master rights for our Jane's Addiction song will still be needed, and it will also be your responsibility to anticipate whether or not a soundtrack may be released. If so, mechanical rights must be cleared, as well, for every song in the movie that subsequently goes onto the soundtrack, either by going through the Harry Fox Agency or directly to the publisher.

One advantage music supervisors have when dealing with films, indie films in particular, is the ability to negotiate a back-end deal if finances are limited. This can give you and the licensors some flexibility that makes it possible for a potentially expensive song to be licensed at a low rate at first, with that rate increasing as the film clears certain financial hurdles. A back-end deal can be part of the sync and master licenses, and can be structured like this, for example:

Festival Rights:	$ 500
Broad Rights:	$3,000
Bonus at $3-Million Box Office:	$3,000
Bonus at $4-Million Box Office:	$3,000
Bonus at $6-Million Box Office:	$3,000
Bonus at $10-Million Box Office:	$3,000

(From the *Indie Guidebook to Music Supervision for Films*.)

Broad Rights: This term is also referred to as "All Media," and it covers a lot. When you negotiate for broad rights, this is a summary of rights that include: Festival rights, theatrical, free television, pay, cable and subscription TV, CATV, closed-circuit into homes TV, airlines, ships, ancillary rights in connection with the film, in-context TV, DVD and video cassette trailers, and a Universalwide videogram and DVD buyout. There are also many other separate agreements, which could involve future and emerging technologies, soundtrack album rights, and advertising campaigns using trailers, radio spots, TV advertising, and more.

(From the *Indie Guidebook to Music Supervision for Films*.)

Licensing for Digital Media

While licensing practices have been firmly in place for quite a while in the fields of TV and film, in the field of digital rights (which refers to transmission over the Internet), the rules continue to change rapidly. The ease of file sharing over the Internet has made that medium an area of grave concern to songwriters and publishers.

The Internet may continue to have a "Wild West" feel to it for some time to come, but this doesn't diminish the responsibility of the music supervisor to obtain the proper master, performance, and sync licenses when working with this medium. If you're working with a broadcaster and you're not asking for digital rights to a song, then your rights will be cheaper. The more formats that you use to broadcast a song, the more expensive the master rights will be.

Fortunately, acquiring the correct performance licenses for music represented by the performance-rights societies is relatively simple. Not surprisingly, they're readily available on their Websites.

ASCAP: www.ascap.com/weblicense/
BMI: https://dlc.bmi.com/dlcmenu.asp
SESAC: www.sesac.com/licensing/internet_licensing1.asp

The Harry Fox Agency is also heavily involved in the evolution of digital rights. Although mechanical licensing may not factor heavily into your duties as a music supervisor right now, the fast-changing digital landscape demands your constant attention. If you find yourself working with digital downloads, visit *www.harryfox.com*.

Licensing for Video Games

In the video game world, the clearances you'll need come in the form of sync, master, and mechanical licenses. Sync from the publisher comes into play because the song is being synchronized to on-screen action. The master license is owned by the record label, so you'll need to secure those rights from that entity. Finally, since the game is going to be reproduced, either as a physical package or in download form, a mechanical license is also in order.

Licensing for Advertising

In advertising, the trick is to obtain the necessary sync licenses from a song's writers and publishers, and master rights from the record label. If, for example, you were at an ad agency and had a budget of $150,000 to license a Korn song for Chrysler, you would issue your license request to each of those entities. Once you get the okay and the cost, as a representative of the production company, you cut each entity a check and you're ready to air. Submitting cue sheets for performance royalties is also part of the equation.

International Licensing Considerations

International rights must be a standard part of the request form. Be sure to add anything that you think needs to be considered in executing the licenses for your particular project. If you don't expect the project to be distributed outside of the United States, don't negotiate worldwide rights; your budget could take a hit for covering unnecessary bases. These rights can always be renegotiated at a later date if the project proves popular and international distribution comes into the picture.

Simple Licensing Solutions

There will be a lot of times when you want or need to minimize the time and effort you expend on licensing. Time may be too short to deal with the skilled negotiators that come with writers and publishers of more desirable music, and the money may not be there either.

What are your options? Again, that's what music (and sound effect) libraries are there for—to streamline this process. They're able to do this because, when they purchase music from a composer, they also purchase the master and/or publishing rights, and those rights can be administered straight to you, along with the music.

Another choice is to work with independent or unsigned artists who will appreciate the exposure of having their music in your production. It's still essential to do paperwork, but in this case you'll likely be dealing with much less bureaucracy. Your negotiations will be with a much smaller record label (or no label at all), the artist, and/or the management. Because an independent artist may not even have a publisher or a label, simple letters of agreement will suffice.

Remember...

Having a firm grasp on the concepts of licensing is key to starting a career in music supervision. Your expertise will grow quickly as you develop a true working knowledge. When it comes to rights and clearances, keep your job, impress your peers, and strengthen your reputation with every move you make.

THE MUSIC SUPERVISION BUSINESS
SCHEDULE A
STANDARD TERMS & CONDITIONS

1. SERVICES: THE MUSIC SUPERVISION BUSINESS shall provide music supervision services to Client for the Picture designated in the Agreement. THE MUSIC SUPERVISION BUSINESS shall consult with Client to suggest music that is suitable for the Picture and shall perform all other customary music supervisory services as may be reasonably required by Client, including without limitation:

 (i) Assisting Producer in preparing a budget for all services to be rendered in connection with the selection of and recording of the "Music" defined below;

 (ii) assisting Producer in the selection of all musical materials to be included in the soundtrack ("Soundtrack") of the Picture ("Music"), and all composers, songwriters, audio producers, and musical performers for the Soundtrack;

 (iii) Supervising, as requested by Producer, the recording and synchronization of the Soundtrack;

 (iv) Assisting the director of the Picture in connection with the supervision and coordination of all recording and dubbing sessions for the Soundtrack;

 (v) Supervising the selection of Music for, and/or the recording of, an MTV-type video, if any;

 (vi) Assisting the music editor in the preparation of music cue sheets where required; and

 (vii) Performing all other customary music supervisory services as may be reasonably required by Producer.

Unless otherwise agreed to in a separate writing signed by both parties, Client shall be responsible for selection of all final music for the Picture. Client is responsible for all license fees, performance fees and the like, charged by third parties (i.e., record labels, music publishers, etc.) for use of the musical compositions and/or masters embodying the musical compositions that are used in the Picture. THE MUSIC SUPERVISION BUSINESS will work in conjunction with clients designated business affairs person(s) to make every reasonable effort to secure all necessary use licenses for the Picture music on terms and conditions most favorable to Client but makes no guarantee as to the amount or cost of such music license fees.

2. MUSIC SERVICES FEE: The Music Services Fee (the "Fee") to be paid to THE MUSIC SUPERVISION BUSINESS by Client shall be the Fee designated in the Agreement. The Fee is based upon a maximum of _____ musical tracks selected by Client and covers only the professional services THE MUSIC SUPERVISION BUSINESS. No portion of the Fee shall cover or be applied to any licensing fees, performance fees, guild payments and the like charged by third parties (i.e., record labels, music publishers, etc.) for use of the musical compositions and/or masters embodying the musical compositions used in the Picture. The Fee does not include overnight delivery, messenger, shipping charges and/or out-of-pocket travel costs incurred in connection with the Services provided by THE MUSIC SUPERVISION BUSINESS and Client agrees to pay all such costs pursuant to the terms herein.

3. PAYMENT TERMS: 50% of the Fee is due upon execution of the Agreement with the remaining 50% of the Fee due upon the completion of Services by THE MUSIC SUPERVISION BUSINESS. All additional charges and any duly authorized changes to the Fee shall be accounted for and applied to the second 50% payment. No credit shall be extended to Client unless provided for by a separate written instrument duly executed by the parties hereto. All claims for adjustments must be made in writing within 15 calendar days of invoice date. A late payment charge of 1.5% per month will be charged on all past due invoices. If an invoice remains unpaid, Client shall be liable for all collection costs, including reasonable attorneys' fees and court costs, incurred by THE MUSIC SUPERVISION BUSINESS pertaining to the Agreement.

4. REPRESENTATIONS & WARRANTIES: Client represents and warrants: (i) that it has the ability to perform its obligations under the Agreement; (ii) that it does not have and will not make or authorize any obligations, commitments or grants to any other person, company or entity that will impair or prevent the performance of its obligations and undertakings contained herein; (iii) that its performance of the Agreement will not violate any existing agreement or duty, including, but not limited to, any confidentiality agreement or restrictive covenant with any third party; and (iv) that it shall honor and fully comply with any and all licenses obtained with respect to the music contained in the Picture.

THE MUSIC SUPERVISION BUSINESS represents and warrants: (i) that it has the ability to perform the Music Supervision Services; (ii) that it does not have and will not make or authorize any obligations, commitments or grants to any other person, company or entity that will impair or prevent the performance of its obligations and undertakings contained herein; (iii) that its performance of the Agreement will not violate any existing agreement or duty, including, but not limited to, any confidentiality agreement or restrictive covenant with any third party; (iv) that its services will be performed in a professional and workmanlike manner in accordance with applicable professional standards; and (v) to the best of THE MUSIC SUPERVISION BUSINESS's knowledge, Client's use of the musical compositions and masters embodying the musical compositions secured by THE MUSIC SUPERVISION BUSINESS on behalf of Client shall not infringe on any proprietary right of any third party or violate any law, statute, ordinance or other governmental rule or regulation.

5. INDEMNITY: Client agrees to indemnify and hold harmless THE MUSIC SUPERVISION BUSINESS, its officers, directors, employees, shareholders and agents from and against any and all claims, actions, suits, liabilities, damages, costs, losses, expenses, reasonable legal fees and court costs that may arise from (i) any breach or alleged breach of Client's representations, warranties or covenants under the Agreement; or (ii) any claims or violations of any proprietary rights arising from the Picture that are not the result of any breach of THE MUSIC SUPERVISION BUSINESS's representations, warranties or covenants under the Agreement.

THE MUSIC SUPERVISION BUSINESS agrees to indemnify and hold harmless Client, its officers, directors, employees, shareholders and agents from and against any and all claims, actions, suits, liabilities, damages, costs, losses, expenses, reasonable legal fees and court costs that arise from any breach of THE MUSIC SUPERVISION BUSINESS's representations, warranties or covenants under the Agreement.

6. ARTIST CREDIT: For each track secured by THE MUSIC SUPERVISION BUSINESS used in the Picture, Client shall provide in the end credits of the Picture, in the size and type afforded to all other credited artists, on-screen credit to the performing artist, the song title of the master, and the record label that owns the master used in the Picture.

7. CREDIT: Client agrees to afford THE MUSIC SUPERVISION BUSINESS all of the following credit designations: Provided Supervisor fully performs all material obligations hereunder and is not in material default of this agreement, and subject to applicable union requirements and approvals, Client agrees to accord Supervisor credit in the end titles of the Picture and Soundtrack Album, if any, in substantially the form: "Music Supervision Services provided by: YOUR NAME for THE MUSIC SUPERVISION BUSINESS". In all other respects, the style, nature and placement of Supervisor's credit shall be determined by Client in its sole discretion. Neither casual or inadvertent failure, nor any failure by any third party, to comply with the provisions of this paragraph shall be deemed a breach of this Agreement.

a. **THE MUSIC SUPERVISION BUSINESS Packaging Credit:** Client shall place THE MUSIC SUPERVISION BUSINESS's standard logo (provided to Client by THE MUSIC SUPERVISION BUSINESS) on the exterior product packaging in a suitable size and location.

8. DUE DATES: The Due Date for All Picture Music referenced in the Agreement is an estimated date established by Client. THE MUSIC SUPERVISION BUSINESS's ability to complete the music supervision services by such Due Date is subject to THE MUSIC SUPERVISION BUSINESS's timely receipt of all Client approvals and are exclusive of any Client changes and/or final music licenses from third parties. Client shall be timely informed of all license fee requests secured by THE MUSIC SUPERVISION BUSINESS from third parties. THE MUSIC SUPERVISION BUSINESS makes no representation or warranty as to the availability or timeframe of availability of any particular musical composition or masters embodying the musical compositions for use in the Picture.

9. CONFIDENTIALITY: Neither party to the Agreement shall disclose any terms or conditions of the Agreement to any third parties unless necessary to effectuate the purpose of the Agreement.

10. TERMINATION OF AGREEMENT: In the event of material breach of the Agreement, including but not limited to, a breach of any representation or warranty contained herein, the Agreement may be terminated by either party upon Fourteen (14) Days written notice, unless the defaulting party shall have cured the breach within that 14-Day period to the non-defaulting party's satisfaction. All payments received by THE MUSIC SUPERVISION BUSINESS are non-refundable in the event the Agreement is terminated by Client for any reason. All sums due and owing to THE MUSIC SUPERVISION BUSINESS, but not yet paid, at the time of either party's termination of the Agreement shall remain due and payable and shall survive any such termination of the Agreement.

11. CONFLICTS/CHOICE OF LAW: If there is any conflict between any provision of the Agreement and any present or future statute, law, ordinance, regulation or collective bargaining agreement, the latter shall prevail; provided that the provision hereof so affected shall be limited only to the extent necessary and no other provision of the Agreement shall be affected. The Agreement shall be governed and construed in accordance with the laws of the State of XXXX applicable to contracts entered into and fully performed therein, without regard to any principles of conflict of laws. Only the State of XXXX courts shall have jurisdiction over controversies regarding this Agreement; any proceeding involving a controversy shall be brought in those courts.

12. MODIFICATIONS: This Agreement cannot be amended, modified or changed except by a written instrument duly executed by the parties hereto. This Agreement cancels and supersedes all prior negotiations and understandings between the parties relating to the Services.

13. SOUNDTRACK ALBUM SERVICES: If Client causes music from the Soundtrack to be recorded or re-recorded for a possible single record or long-playing record album or comparable audiotape or cassette, and if Client requests Supervisor's services for such recording or re-recording, Supervisor shall render such services as are customarily rendered by supervisors of Soundtrack Albums, including, without limitation:

   (i)   Supervising the recording and mixing of the Soundtrack Album;

  (ii) Assisting Client in the selection of a Soundtrack Album distributor; and

 (iii) Performing all other music supervisor services as may be reasonably required by Client in connection with the Soundtrack Album.

Notwithstanding the foregoing, (1) Client shall be solely responsible for negotiating and documenting all agreements (including clearance agreements for all music) relating to the Music and the Soundtrack (it being agreed that Supervisor shall research and provide contact information for all music to be cleared for Picture); and (ii) Client shall have all creative and financial controls with regard to the Picture, the Music and Soundtrack. In addition, Supervisor shall use best efforts to adhere to the approved Music budget for the Picture. Supervisor shall not incur any costs not in accordance with the approved Music budget without Client's prior, written consent. Also, Supervisor shall not have the right to enter into any written soundtrack album agreements or publishing agreements without Client's prior, written approval.

Any and all agreements with respect to the distribution and exploitation of phonorecords of the Soundtrack (the "Soundtrack Records" or "Soundtrack Album(s)") shall be entered into between Client and the distributor of the Soundtrack Records ("Record Company"). Client and Supervisor acknowledge that, as between Client on one hand, and Supervisor on the other, Client is and shall be considered for all purposes the owner of the copyright in the Soundtrack.

What *is* the Harry Fox Agency, anyway? In a world full of licensing entities marked by official-sounding acronyms like ASCAP, the name of this mechanical and digital licensing powerhouse causes some initial confusion. Music supervisors only need to understand the services of HFA on select occasions—such as when the plans for a movie soundtrack include an accompanying CD release—but when that time arrives, knowledge of the NYC-based agency can prove extremely valuable.

Founded in 1927, HFA represents the mechanical licensing rights of more than 27,000 music publishers, who in turn represent the interests of more than160,000 songwriters. A mechanical license grants the rights to reproduce and distribute copyrighted musical compositions (songs) on CDs, records, tapes, and certain digital configurations. In short, if you want to put a song on a CD soundtrack you're selling, or make it available as an Internet download to promote the movie, you will need to obtain a mechanical license from the music publisher, and the publisher will probably be represented by HFA.

"Legally, we are an 'agent for a disclosed principal,' and are fairly constrained under the copyright statute regarding what we do," says Michael Simon, Senior Vice President of Licensing and Chief of Strategic Development and Marketing for HFA. "In English, that means we represent music publishers for a very specific purpose: Issuing mechanical licenses and collecting and distributing the royalties from those releases. This is unlike the traditional role of a Hollywood agent that goes in, cuts the deal, has broad discretion, and effectively advises the client on a deal that they found for them. We receive offers to use our clients' work, and we bring that offer to our client for consideration. Unless a music supervisor is dealing with songs that will ultimately be mechanically reproduced on a CD or other medium, they may not need to work with us, but they should be aware that the ability to obtain mechanical licenses, in addition to master rights, may be a gating factor for a soundtrack release."

Simon points out that music supervisors working in the world of sync licensing usually aren't involved in CD production, although overlap is definitely possible. A forward-thinking music supervisor should bear in mind whether or not a particular song could be included in a subsequent CD or DVD release when he or she is assembling the music for a movie or TV soundtrack.

"How can a music supervisor benefit by knowing about us in their career?" Simon asks. "It's not necessarily in working with us to create a particular soundtrack. It's having information about the songs so that they can inform the film company about possibilities for auxiliary product, such as a commercial CD release. It would be unfortunate if the key song in the film can't be included in a soundtrack release, but at least you would know that at the outset, rather than leaving it as an unhappy surprise for the film company to discover. In general, if the music supervisor renders their service to the film company in a way that produces a product that is more easy to exploit, they will have a happy employer who says, 'This person knows music, but just as important understands the infrastructure of the business. I don't get sued, everything is clean, and this music supervisor understands rights profiles so that we have an easier time of exploiting soundtracks. I want to work with them again.'"

Using HFA's *www.songfile.com* site is one quick way to research and find a song's profile for mechanical licensing. "When a music supervisor calls about rights, we have tools available and we encourage a music supervisor to investigate and understand the publishing rights that are implicated by their intended use," says Simon. "Keep in mind that the music supervisor wouldn't be the one to actually obtain the mechanical rights; the contract parties for an album release are the soundtrack manufacturer/ distributor and the song's rights holder. For a music supervisor, it's about delivering a package that *can* be licensed, not one that *is* licensed."

So although you could go your entire career without personally obtaining a mechanical or digital license with HFA, your employers will appreciate that you kept the role of the agency firmly in mind as you lined up music for their project. "I probably get sixteen calls a week from music supervisors who don't understand the rights that they need for the initial film production are sync rights, which HFA does not handle," says Simon. "However, I can send them in the right direction to get those rights, and I also try to educate people on the difference between sync and mechanical rights, in the hope that in a year when the project comes out as a CD soundtrack, they will advise the record company releasing the album to come to us for those rights."

In the meantime, keep an eye on HFA. As distribution models become more complex, the agency with the funny name may very well be the first to arrive on the licensing scene. "We are currently facing an increased complication of the industry, in part because of digital distribution," Simon observes. "It used to be a CD, cassette, eight-track—now there's a dozen configurations. Instead of performing-rights societies to whom you pay a fee and get a blanket license for their repertoire, in the mechanical world we license a song at a time. We've got so many more configurations that we track at a usage level: How many CDs, plus downloads, streams, tethered downloads. In twenty years, no one will look back at this time as a major disruption in the arts due to technology; people will say that was the beginning of the next boom for business."

PROFILE
Chuck Doud
Music Director
Sony Computer Entertainment America

- Trends in video game music
- Licensing music for the format
- Fees

Music supervision for video games comes with its own set of trends and issues. *Mix* magazine's senior editor, Blair Jackson, offered a sharp look inside the latest rules concerning video game music and sound effects in this informative article, "How Video Games Can Save the Music Industry: Licensing":

One fairly recent development in game audio is the steady increase in the licensing of songs by both established and up-and-coming rock and hip-hop artists, usually not at the exclusion of a conventional music score, but in addition. *NBA Live* has wall-to-wall hip-hop; Snoop Dog contributed three new songs to *True Crime: Streets of L.A.*; Peter Gabriel has a song on the soundtrack of *Uru: Ages of Myst*; *Grand Theft Auto: Vice City* is loaded with "classic" and more modern rock tunes; gamers can mix their own version of a P.O.D. song on *Amplitude*; and the list goes on and gets longer every day.

It's a good marriage: The games get some hip cache, and the artists and their record companies reach millions of listeners (potentially) and pocket some serious change. In some cases, DVD soundtracks from the games have been sold separately and done very well; in other games, there might be a separate music CD included in the package. It's definitely been pushing up the expense of making games, but it's been good for a record industry that's still very much on the ropes.

"With the advent of PlayStation and console games actually appearing on a CD[-ROM], you finally had enough storage capacity to have real music on the game created by real composers," comments Chuck Doud, music director of Sony Computer Entertainment America. "The turning point in the industry was probably *Wipeout,* which came from our London studios. That was the game that pretty much set the standard for including licensed music in video games. It was primarily electronica, which perfectly matched the feel of the game."

Formerly based in Boston but now working in Sony's Foster City, Calif., game production facility, Doud used to write music for games himself—including a number of PlayStation titles—before moving into his current executive capacity. "Now, I spend half my time working with the record industry to secure artists for our games, and the other half of my job is finding composers or producers to create original content for our games, essentially like a movie score. Increasingly, the line between those two roles is starting to blur.

"Three years ago, when we first started licensing a lot of music, there was this great fear among the composers that we were going to be taking work away from them," Doud continues, "but in fact, the way things have fleshed out now, there's actually more work. There are more games, more music, and it's all being used more creatively within the game. Also, we're more likely now to have multiple people working on the music—we might have someone working on the score and other people taking the multitracks and adapting them to the game. All that, in addition to licensed content. Right now is a good time to be doing music for video games."

When it comes to licensing, Doud and his counterparts throughout the gaming community have found the record labels—and most artists—to be extremely receptive to fitting tracks into video games. "While we like to put a few 'name' bands on each of our titles that incorporate licensed tracks, our focus is really identifying emerging artists that have a good chance of blowing up in the near future. When done right, video games are a good place to showcase emerging artists and mid-tier bands, or established artists who want to reach a different demographic. It's almost like it's becoming the next MTV. People are hearing about bands and being exposed to them for the first time through video games.

"A lot of times we end up hearing songs before the record labels do," Doud adds with a laugh. "Typically, we start working on a soundtrack from eight months to a year before a game is released, so we're out there talking to [artist] management and looking to coordinate games with their own album releases to maximize promotional opportunities. In addition, as long as the production quality is on par with something we would get from the major labels, we also always save a few slots for artists who don't have the support of a record label, but whose music we feel fits the game play and delivers something new to the player that, chances are, they would not have otherwise been exposed to."

The fees for licensing tracks vary wildly, just as they do in feature films. A David Bowie track is probably going to cost a lot more than a Papa Roach track, to name two artists Doud has licensed. Newly commissioned tracks will usually cost more than licensed ones. Increasingly, too, game producers are asking for, and receiving, multitrack tapes of both licensed and original music that they can massage or even remix to fit songs into the games. As Doud notes, "If we have a song that's actually going *into* a racing game, instead of just appearing over the credits, we might need to make some adjustments to the mix because it has to compete with the sound of the engines. We want to make sure the mix comes through, so it might not be the same mix you hear on the radio."

Custom mixes and exclusive content—that's the direction licensed music is headed in the world of video games.

By Blair Jackson, March, 2004, reprinted by permission from Mix *magazine.*

PROFILE
Sarah Fluegel
VP of Operations
MIDIRingTones

• Enterprising business models in music and technology
• Ringtone licensing

If personalized music supervision has a nice ring to it, then check out ring tones. The ability to pick out custom chimes, songs, and sound effects is one of the most appealing features of cell phones, and it takes sharp music supervision skills to make it happen.

At MIDIRingTones *(www.midiringtones.com),* the sounds of cell phones have proven to be big business. Started as a side project in 2002 by a trio of web developers, the company soon blossomed into a venture big enough to be acquired by greeting-card-industry giant American Greetings. What's the connection? "Greeting cards are all about self expression," observes Sarah Fluegel, VP of Operations for MIDIRingTones. "It's telling others who you are. I think it was a natural progression; American Greetings moved from hard paper cards to the online aspect of it."

During the company's rapid rise, Fluegel and her co-founders got a crash course in the complexities of licensing for ringtones. "We quickly learned how much work licensing ringtones was in the U.S.," she says. "For polyphonic or monophonic ringtones, there are two types of rights you have to obtain: Performance rights, which is ASCAP, BMI, and SESAC; and you also have to get rights from the publisher. For master tones where you need the actual source with the lyrics and the singer singing it, then you need to go to the record labels and get a master-use license. Originally, we were supposed to be able to just get a license from the Harry Fox Agency, and they would go to the publishers for us. However, Harry Fox was not ready to start signing ringtone licenses, and we had to start going to publishers independently.

"The five major ones were Warner Chappell, BMG, EMI, Sony, and Universal, so we started with those. Then we discovered that a lot of the hit songs, especially hip-hop and rap, the Number One sellers typically have more than one publisher that own more than one song. We had access to a lot, but not a lot of what we needed, so we started going to the next level of publishers like Famous Music, Fox Music, and just kept going. Today, we have over eighty ringtone agreements in place with different publishers. It's rare when a song is one-hundred percent owned by a publisher. We have songs owned by six or seven publishers—you have cases where a publisher owns two percent of a song, and you can't put it out until you have one-hundred percent."

A fast scan of MIDIRingTones' list of available tones at any particular time will reveal Top Ten hits, never-die classics like Peter Frampton's "Baby, I Love Your Way," and seasonal best bets like "The NFL on Fox Theme" and "Notre Dame Victory March—Fight Song" in September. Major categories include urban, pop, rock, themes, decades ('60s, '70s, '80s, '90s), country, classics, originals, sports, holidays, genres (big band, jazz/blues, classical), regional, and religious.

Knowing which new tones to go after is a relatively straightforward process. "A lot of it, we follow *Billboard* and we try to get the *Billboard* Top 100," Fluegel states. "Typically, what's tops at *Billboard* is going to be a top-seller for us. Then next is internal request, where our content team suggests things to make, and we take a lot of user requests. A lot of other ringtones, like songs by the Beach Boys, just come from internal requests, whatever our content team sees fit. We obviously try to put out the hot sellers right away. It follows the eighty-twenty rule: Eighty percent of sales come from twenty percent of our catalog, but we need that depth there so, for the people looking for that obscure song, they find it and keep coming back."

The growing number of publishers issuing "pre-approved" lists of ringtone licenses has also made music supervision more convenient in some ways. "Typically how it works with most of the publishers is that whenever you want to create a ringtone of the song, you have to request permission for that specific song," Fluegel explains. "Now there are some publishers with pre-approved lists, so, for example, whoever has licenses with EMI, they send out updates with a pre-approved list for ringtones. There's not a lot of exclusive content, so a lot of providers have the same ringtones. If you want an exclusive, it all depends on the publishers. It usually involves money: Advances, higher royalties, or other incentives you can offer."

The licensing process can move relatively quickly, if need be. "It depends," Fluegel says. "If it's an EMI song, we can submit it to EMI for approval and hear back the same day. If it's a hot song, we'll start our content team with the creation side right away and, if we do get the license, we can get it out the same day. But it can go to the publisher, then go to legal, etc. That all depends on the publisher, too—they'll look at it, sign it, and sometimes it can take a month.

"The royalty rate is set: Ten cents or ten percent of the sale price, whichever is greater. We have to negotiate on advance and on territory. A lot of licenses cover U.S. only, but we try to cover the world whenever we can."

Fluegel points out that there are some specific hazards of ringtone licensing that music supervisors should know about. "The big one is to be aware that there are a lot of writers that don't allow it. You can have three writers; two will okay it, and one won't—that means we cannot use it. It's always a big day when a writer that used to not allow ringtones changes their minds. The monophonic tones, they're right, they didn't do the songs any justice, but then when we started moving into polyphonic, the writers started seeing what a big market it is.

"Other than that, it's a lot of work in the U.S. when you have to go to a lot of publishers independently, as opposed to other countries where there's a central agency. Harry Fox has a ringtone license now, but it's not as comprehensive. You sign it, so Harry Fox goes out and gets it. We do it ourselves, because we know what we're doing and we don't feel we should pay people outside, although you will find a publisher that will only go through Harry Fox. On the other hand, not all publishers will go through Harry Fox."

Although MidiRingTones took off rapidly, Sarah Fluegel isn't surprised by the fast growth of her music-supervision-driven field. "Music has been a way of expressing yourself forever," she says. "People want to show who they are, and that's what personalized ringtones are all about."

CHAPTER nine

Legal Issues

Music supervisors must be aware at all times of the legal issues at the core of their creative choices and subsequent business dealings. Furthermore, a music supervisor must be comfortable with his or her own level of professional legal representation and protection before beginning any new project or even exploring the possibilities of strategic alliances or partnerships.

Having the right legal documentation ready to submit to your new clients at the right time is crucial, and the key is often held in the hands of a highly qualified entertainment lawyer. Entertainment lawyers are part of every business aspect of music, television, film, the Internet, and live events. Your clients need them, and you need them. Consult them whenever you have a question with legal ramifications.

License Agreements

License agreements are struck between production companies and music providers every single day. Music supervisors are responsible for providing accurate song-usage information (in the form of a license request) to the music provider, so the provider can turn around and send the production company a license agreement detailing the exact usage and price.

When going through the process of executing a license request, receiving an actual license, and finally submitting it for payment, the music supervisor is not personally entering into an agreement with the music provider (which may be a record label, production music library, independent producer/

composer, or publisher) but rather is doing so for the production entity that the provider represents. However, as mentioned in the Chapter 7, Cue Sheets, the music supervisor is responsible for providing accurate music usage details, as logged in the cue sheets that were previously created for the relevant program or film.

The music supervisor will be held accountable if inaccurate information has been given to a music provider, and a music supervisor may even lose his or her job as a result. It's important to know that the music supervisor will not be held directly liable for infringement in a court of law. The production company who has hired the music supervisor could be sued, and the production company may then choose to reprimand or fire the music supervisor for questionable decisions or lack of accuracy in logging cue sheets and/or executing license requests, or even bring suit to name the music supervisor as a third-party defendant on grounds of negligence.

Even though the music supervisor is not necessarily the one who could be sued for a copyright infringement, he or she is still responsible for license negotiation in many cases. That means you must have a working knowledge of the music budget of the production on which you are working. The process of negotiating with a music provider puts you in the "driver's seat," so to speak, because you are making high-level decisions that directly effect how much money will be spent by your employer on song usages.

This can be a very sensitive area, because there's money involved, and most importantly, it's probably not your money. Unless you are also the producer of an indie production, it's your employer's money, and you have been entrusted with it. One mistake on your part could result in a copyright infringement lawsuit for the production company. This could easily cost you your reputation and your job, because your employer is going to be irate, to say the least. The only hope you will have is that, if you were smart during the negotiation process, you took the time to share your notes with producers and directors. This way, if the production is faced with a lawsuit, you could rally the support of those you consulted during the initial license negotiation process with the licensor. Approvals in writing all along the way are a great weapon against any subsequent legal claims.

Copyrights

Always remember this about copyrights: A copyrighted sound recording is made up of two separate yet united bodies:

Musical Work: The copyright of the song itself.

Sound recording: The copyright of the actual recording of the song. As mentioned earlier, music supervisors may choose to try re-recording a song, which would alleviate the need to clear the rights for the original sound recording. If you do not plan to re-record the song, then you will need to clear both the "musical work" and the "sound recording" aspects of the copyright.

Public Domain

When dealing with older works of music, even a standard like "Happy Birthday," music supervisors need to use extreme caution. Songs like this seem to have been around since the beginning of time, and you might assume they are available for anyone to use without needing clearance from anybody— existing in a state known as *public domain.* But "Happy Birthday," and a great deal many songs like it, are *not* in the public domain, and it's critical for a music supervisor to know that before approving, for example, a scene with a group of people gathered around a cake, singing.

Public Domain: Any and all compositions that are not protected by copyright law.

Determining which works are in the public domain and which are not can be extremely complicated, and should never be left to chance. In general, however, works published in the United States and copyrighted in the year 1922 or earlier are considered to be in the public domain—in the United States. These rules vary from country to country, and just because something is considered to be in the public domain in the United States does not mean it has that same status in other countries. If your media is going to be released internationally, you need to double-check that old song's status in each country.

Music supervisors who use nothing but their intuition to assume that a very old standard, or a particular one of its arrangements, is no longer protected and need not be cleared are leaving their employers open to an extremely costly lawsuit. Rights holders of iconic works such as this make it part of their business to discover unauthorized uses and to seek compensation.

How can you determine for sure if a work is in the public domain? If at all possible, consult a *musicologist,* a person with an academic background in music history who has the knowledge and resources to confirm that the work in question is, in fact, public domain. (See Music Profile: Irwin Coster, later in this chapter.)

Another way, although more complicated and less bulletproof, is to determine proof of public domain yourself by getting it from a certifiable source. Sites like *www.pdinfo.com* have a database, reference to other sources, and a wealth of information about public domain. These can be excellent, but be sure to read their disclaimers. Working in the public-domain gray area without one-hundred percent confidence may be a chance that just isn't worth it. If your production company wants to use a golden oldie that they assume is free for the taking, and you can't confirm it and get your legal department's blessing, strongly advise an alternative.

Trying to get around the issue by commissioning a new "sound alike" recording from a composer who supposedly differs just enough from the original is also a risk and an invitation for a copyright infringement lawsuit. (See Music Profile: Steven Gold in this chapter.) By the way, you should not be held liable in the event that you've commissioned an original piece of music—with no intention on your part of it being a sound-alike—and it is later believed by a copyright holder to be too similar to their older, pre-existing piece of music. It is the implicit responsibility of the composer or music department that supplied you with the music to guarantee that their "original" music was copyrightable. Using a sound-alike piece may get you around the license for the actual sound recording, but will leave the door open for the publisher to sue or demand compensation.

Fair Use

The concept of fair use of a musical arrangement often comes up in comedic situations where a parody song is used. For example, cable channels like Comedy Central love to put a scene from the 1980s over the top with a riff on tunes by icons like Robert Palmer. The general rule of thumb here is that if commentary that is political or social in nature is being made on a piece of music, then the underlying structure of that song can be used as a basis for the new piece you may be commissioning from a composer. As always, be sure to keep your production's legal team in the loop.

Examples of Legal Pitfalls

A typical lawsuit in the world of license agreements and television would occur if the music supervisor documented four background song usages at thirty seconds each in a program that's airing one time, but the music provider later finds out that what was actually used was six background usages at two minutes each in a show that actually airs once a week. Make sure your notes show the actual direction you received for this project.

In film, it's a little different. In the United States, there are no performance royalties generated by performances in movie theaters. However, in many countries overseas, the composer/artist *can* make performance royalties from their movie music being played in theaters. If you want to avoid a serious lawsuit with all fingers pointing at you as the person in charge, you need to be aware of the performance licensing situation in each and every country where that film is going to be released, and report accordingly. To avoid legal problems down the road, do not use a song that cannot be cleared within the constraints of your film's music budget. That budget may be anywhere from two to fifteen percent of the entire film budget. In a major film release with a total budget of $30 to $80 million, that figure will most likely be around four or six percent.

What About Samples?

What if you want to use a song that includes multiple samples of other songs. For example, suppose you're considering the DJ/artist Coldcut, and one of his releases on Journeys by DJ Records *(www.journeysbydj.com)*. His music is amazing, but some of it has samples, so realize that in order to use one of his pieces with samples in a film or TV show, you must not only clear the core "musical work" and "sound recording," but you must also clear the rights to each and every sample used in the recording/song. If you do not, than your production company could be sued for copyright infringement.

For example, a film that the authors of this book recently supervised called *Heights,* starring Glenn Close, included an Underworld song from the album *Beaucoup Fish* called "Shudder/King of Snake," which uses a sample from Donna Summer's hit song "I Feel Love." In this case, we had to clear rights for both songs, and there's no way around it.

The use of samples in songs is more common than it used to be. Keep sample use in mind when you are working with any artists' songs, no matter how original they sound to you. In other words, you should always take into consideration the possibility that a song submitted to you could have a sample in it, and you must inform the rights holder that you require every detail regarding samples in a submitted song. It's not a bad idea to ask your lawyer to add a line to the licensing agreement that certifies that all parts of the recording to be licensed are one-hundred percent original and that the owners assume all liability if it is later proved otherwise. Typically, standard licenses will certify this for works that are said to be one-hundred percent original, and most if not all licensors and licensees' lawyers should not have a problem including this language.

Do your homework on ASCAP and BMI's Websites for accurate data on who owns rights to which songs, and don't always rely on album inserts or credits to tell you the whole story. In the scenario described above about the Underworld tune "Shudder/King of Snake," the album insert didn't credit Donna Summer. We only found out that the bass line in the song was Summer's by performing detailed searches through the performing-rights societies' Websites. Then, we had to deal with her label and publisher in addition to the label and publishers associated with Underworld to clear all the rights to the song. It's a lot of work, but it's got to be done if the song is right for the scene and soundtrack.

Always double-check your resources when obtaining music clearances, and never rely on just one source for information, even if that source is the album credits! Every decision you make in this business could be your last if you're hasty. You're better off being considered picky than lazy and careless.

Union Issues

In addition, if you are attempting to license a piece of music that was created under the jurisdiction of a music union, such as the American Federation of Musicians (AFM), then your production company will most definitely be subject to additional fees, or *residuals,* for the musicians who performed on the original studio recordings. This scenario is most common when a music supervisor is re-licensing film scores. They are often union jobs. A disclaimer that such fees have been paid is standard in agreements for this type of music.

What's the Worst Thing That Can Happen?

In the worst-case, most outlaw scenario, if a production company openly violates copyright laws and distributes a media work with music in it that is not cleared, the company risks being hit with an injunction prohibiting the release of the film, and a lengthy court battle. Do your homework, and you'll never be a party to something like this.

Music Supervisor Agreements

The type of contract a music supervisor works under depends first and foremost on the job situation. Often, the contract known as a *music supervisor agreement* or *music services agreement* will not be necessary if you are being hired for an on-staff music supervision position. In this case, the company hiring you will probably have a standard employee agreement, which you should review in detail before signing. A well-organized independent or major TV/film production company that is hiring you for a contracted position for a determined period of time may also ask you to sign an employee agreement.

When you are hired for a job as a freelance music supervisor, whether it is for TV, film, a live event, or any type of interactive media, you must be ready to submit a music-supervisor agreement or a music-services agreement. This is basically a production deal tailored to the world of a music supervisor, and it's an important contract to have in hand.

Terms of the Agreement

Among other things, the music-supervisor agreement for a freelancer clearly states such key terms as:

- what services you will provide for the client
- what and when you will be paid
- the duration of the agreement

Otherwise commonly known as a "deal memo," your contract specifically outlines the services that you, as the music supervisor, will provide for an agreed-upon project and/or length of time or term. This contract will also include the music supervisor's monetary compensation for the project.

Furthermore, it will tell you exactly *when* you will be paid. It is typical to be paid fifty percent up front at the time of being hired, and the remaining fifty percent upon completion of the project. This contract will also outline how the music supervisor will be reimbursed for expenses related to the production.

It is also common, when your services are to include the music supervision/production of a soundtrack album, that you will receive more pay and/or percentage points (known throughout the industry simply as "points.") In this case, you will be paid for the third-party record advance, as well as retail sales.

Points: The percentage of the gross sales of the SLRP (suggested list retail price) that you get in return for your music-supervision services on any given music-supervision project.

Points can be extremely valuable, and should be negotiated for whenever possible; having even a portion of a point on a high-profile soundtrack that is expected to sell well can be worth far more than a flat fee. If the party with whom you are negotiating refuses to give you points, you may very well decide you don't want to be involved. It's a judgment call that you need to evaluate on a case-by-case basis.

When points are part of a contract, the music supervisor usually will start with receiving one percent of the gross list retail sales SLRP, and that amount will rise to one-and-a-half percent at 500,000 USNRC (United States Net Sales Through Normal Retail Channels), and rise to two percent of SLRP at 1,000,000 USNRC net sales. (This information is courtesy of the authors of *The Independent Film Producer's Survival Guide,* Schirmer Trade Books.)

This contract will also list the type of on-screen credit you will get, including your title, how big your name appears, and at what point in the credits it is listed.

Your Lawyer Should Take a Look

Whenever possible, as a music supervisor, you should retain a respected, trustworthy entertainment lawyer to review contracts for employment before you sign them.

Also, it's important to realize the difference between working as a freelance/contracted music supervisor and working as an on-staff music supervisor. Simply put, if you're "on-staff" then you're working under the blanket terms and conditions of the company that hired you. If you are "contracted or freelance" then you're working under the terms that you and your lawyer have specified—terms that will subsequently be negotiated with your future client/employer.

In both of these scenarios, you should have a lawyer helping you to negotiate with your client or the company who is offering you a staff position.

It is also important to realize that you will have to pay a lawyer, not only to look your agreement over once it's been tendered, but to draw up an initial music-services "template" agreement that you can tailor to suit each individual job, throughout your career. You should only have to pay a lawyer once to create a template music services agreement for your business dealings, but it is common to have a lawyer review and approve changes and updates you've made to a template agreement that you plan to submit to a new client.

If possible, the lawyer who reviews your edited music services template should be the one who originally designed it. He or she will be more familiar with the language and will, therefore, spend less time on it, meaning they won't have to bill you as much.

The bottom line is, unless you're a lawyer yourself, do not overlook any details. Never assume that a word and a handshake are sufficient to start a freelance job.

Keep Your Legal Team in the Loop

Depending on the production, a lawyer's services will be needed not simply for a contract, but for varying degrees of consultation throughout. The legal team may be your employer's in-house attorneys (whether you're on staff or freelance), or a lawyer who is paid either on a case-by-case basis or on retainer. The production company is responsible for paying these legal fees.

In the world of short-form production, like television, you will usually find that your client has an attorney on retainer. In the film world, movies take much longer to produce, so lawyers will usually be needed mainly at the beginning of the project when the music supervisor gets hired and the deal parameters are being determined.

The other side of the concept of keeping your lawyer "in the loop" is that, if you choose to leave them "out of the loop" for some reason, you could be risking valuable time in the future. A lot of the work music supervisors do with lawyers is in preparation for future jobs. We music supervisors must be prepared at all times, and if we want our legal teams to be prepared as well, we must keep them up-to-date as to the details of our business dealings.

Keeping your lawyers up to date about your business doesn't mean you have to call them every day or even every week. Once or twice every two weeks, send your entertainment lawyer a detailed e-mail profiling everything that happened to you in the course of your current projects, and describing jobs that may be developing for you in the future. This way, your lawyer is already familiar with what you're doing before the time when he or she must take an active role in your business again.

SAMPLE MUSIC SERVICES AGREEMENT

THIS AGREEMENT and the attached Schedule A Standard Terms & Conditions (collectively referred to as the "Agreement") are made effective as of (month) _____, (year) by and between YOUR MUSIC SUPERVISION BUSINESS ("THE MUSIC SUPERVISION BUSINESS") located at _____ and the undersigned ("Client") in connection with the below referenced information.

WHEREAS, THE MUSIC SUPERVISION BUSINESS provides music supervision and soundtrack production services to Clients of film, television and multi-media products and Client desires to retain the professional services of THE MUSIC SUPERVISION BUSINESS as an independent contractor under the terms and conditions set forth herein:

Picture Name:

Estimated Picture Release Date:

Picture Format (Vhs/Dvd/Tv/Internet):

Estimated Number Of Picture Units To Be Manufactured:

Total Music Budget Available For Licensing:

Due Date For All Picture Music:

Client Name & Address:

Client Telephone & Fax:

Client Representative:

Client Email Address:

Music Services Fee: **$Dollar Amount**

Soundtrack Compensation: **# of Points (%) SLRP**

In consideration of the promises and mutual covenants contained in the Agreement, the parties hereby mutually accept and agree to all terms and conditions of the Agreement on the date above first written:

_____   The Music Supervision Business

By: _____   By_____
Its: Authorized Signatory   Its: Authorized Signatory

Other Types of Agreements and Contracts

Whether you're in the entertainment business or any other field, even the best of friends should have contractual agreements when planning to do business with each other. Some other types of contracts that you might encounter in your business dealings are *partnership agreements* and *joint ventures.*

In your travels as music supervisor, you probably will run into other music supervisors or entertainment professionals whom you feel complement your talents and weaknesses in ways that are extremely beneficial and productive for all of you. If this is the case, than you may want to consider entering into one of the following types of strategic alliances:

Joint Venture: This is when two or more entities come together to work on a specific project. These two entities are not creating a new company. They are agreeing to join forces to complete a specifically outlined project over an agreed-upon term or time period. It is common that two companies will decide to enter in to a joint venture it is believed that both companies' services and expertise are needed to accomplish the job at hand. It is up to the two (or more) entities to decide who gets what percentage of the total pie. Other important issues this agreement might cover include: Whether equal credit is given, whether the rights to a work are owned jointly, how expenses are split up, and what happens if one of the collaborators is disabled or dies while the work is in progress.

If you wish to start a new company, that usually will happen in one of two ways. The first way involves you acting alone as one music supervisor creating a company that functions to provide specific music services to various entities. The second way is the same, except it involves you having a partner or partners. In this case, you will have to ask your lawyer to prepare an operating agreement.

Operating Agreement: An operating agreement is a contract designed by your lawyer that clearly defines what the roles of each partner are and how each partner will be compensated in return for his or her efforts. Generally, each partner will be paid a mutually agreed-upon percentage of the net income of the company.

If business is going very well, you and your partners (if you have any) may want to elevate yourselves above freelance status and form an S Corporation or LLC (Limited Liability Company.)

S Corporation: An operating structure where business income is passed through the corporate entity, and then taxed only to its owners via their individual tax returns.

LLC: A structure of legal ownership that allows the owners to pay business taxes on their individual income tax returns like partners or a sole proprietorship, but also affords the owners the legal protection of personal limited liability for business debts and judgments, exactly as if they had formed a corporation.

Laws governing S Corporations and LLC's vary from state to state, so be sure to check how it is regulated in the state where you are setting up your business. If you have partners, LLCs can be divided up between the principle owners with an operating agreement to define who owns what percentage of the company.

Why the Paperwork Is Important

You never want to be misunderstood when it comes to services to be rendered, whether it's related to a job you're being hired for or a partnership you're considering. The bottom line is that all parties involved must be explicitly aware of what their roles are. You do what you are hired to do, and nothing more or less unless you renegotiate your contract.

Contract renegotiation is a sensitive topic, but sometimes it is a necessity.

As a music supervisor, your services and time are extremely valuable, and you deserve the same consideration as others in the company who hired you. If you feel that someone is trying to take advantage of you or your time, then you must address it. You should call your lawyer to action only after you have made a concerted effort to address the matter yourself first.

No matter what the legal area, keep in mind that the nature of licensing can be as fluid as the laws that govern it. For example, a 2004 ruling by the Sixth Circuit U.S. Court of Appeals made a landmark ruling in the case *Bridgeport Music et al vs. Dimension Films* that any use of a digital sample of a recording without a license violates copyright, no matter what the sample's size or significance in a song. If it holds, this decision will have widespread impact on the production of sampled music—and its subsequent licensing. Rulings such as this underscore the importance of keeping on top of laws as they change. It also serves as a reminder that music supervisors must get in writing the fact that the song facilitated for their production is either one-hundred percent original work, or that any samples have been completely cleared. If they don't take that step, their production company could be liable.

Music supervision may be a field with a lot of creativity, but the music supervisor should always have one eye on the legal aspects of the job. The more you are aware of the complex laws that govern the way you operate and the choices you make, the better.

PROFILE
Tom Swift
Entertainment Attorney and Producer
Tom Swift Associates

• Entertainment attorney with music and visual media clients
• The importance of sync licenses
• Music supervisor liability
• Negotiating tips

No doubt, music supervision is a creative profession, but its legal underpinnings run deep. The key to staying on top of the laws that govern the licenses and contracts music supervisors deal with is having a clear idea of when you can handle it yourself, and when to call the lawyers. Tom Swift *(www.tomswift.com)* went from being a Top-40 charting rock singer to a highly successful entertainment attorney, representing the likes of Billy

Squier, Steven Tyler and Joe Perry, and Ginger Baker, as well as movie executive Lorenzo DiBonneventura.

Swift believes that music supervisors who try to master all the legal aspects of their job may be biting off more than they can chew. "People who think they know the law can get themselves into a lot of trouble," Swift says. "A little legal knowledge is a dangerous thing. You can't afford to make a mistake—if you do, you're out of the business. So, find a good attorney, and have him investigate the production entity to be sure they are solvent and can pay their bills. If you've got a competent attorney, she will watch out for the pitfalls and landmines, go through it with you, and tell you how to avoid them.

"What will happen is a process of osmosis. If you're a college student and take on the role of music supervisor for a picture, the first time out you're going to learn the hard way, and you'll need someone to consult with—someone with whom you can build a relationship. Later on, if you're a pro music supervisor, when you have supplied forty hours of music for film and TV, you may not need to rely on your attorney nearly as frequently because you will have come to know the issues—but you'll still use a lawyer to do many of your documents.

"Most of the pros I know hire attorneys to, first of all, elicit the relationship between production entities and themselves, making sure that they have enough money to pay you and all artists and the third parties you work with. This due diligence is important, especially for the neophyte."

According to Swift, the legal document that many music supervisors, especially those working in TV and film, can expect to encounter the most is the synchronization, or "sync" license. "That's the primary mechanism by which the rights to associate music to electronic visual imagery is granted. It is a critical legal document. In the entertainment business, the sync license is an inherently legal and sophisticated document and not to be trifled with. It is a grant of rights, and these are the rights that songwriters and publishers have with which to make their living. It's interesting because it combines the business and legal aspects of the transfer of rights for intellectual property. This is the essence and meat of entertainment law: The transfer of rights, either personal service rights or intellectual property rights."

Sync licenses can be as different as the songs they represent. "I've seen them be from two to twenty-four pages," Swift observes. "The form of the document has a great deal to do with the nature of the production entity. A studio that has lawyers on staff and is expecting to resell their product and re-license their product immediately is much more likely to have an exceptionally deep, redundant, particularly onerous document, than is an independent film whose budget doesn't allow for lengthy negotiations."

There are other crucial legal documents that music supervisors deal with regularly. "The most important contract that a music supervisor sees is the one between the production entity and the music supervisor. Those can be onerous, and depending on how sophisticated the producer is, very, very specific. Music supervisors should watch out for production entities attempting to shift the liability of faulty or failed licenses and all the damages associated with that problem onto the music supervisor.

"Therefore, what they really need to do is protect themselves from issues where, by no fault of their own, they deal with people involved in fraud. For example, someone could say they own rights to a particular song and they don't, you pay the wrong guy, and then the true rights holder comes forward. At least you have a good defense to a criminal copyright action because you didn't do it intentionally, but the damages can be six figures in a heartbeat. This raises another important issue: Be sure that the production entity has insurance, and that the music supervisor is named in the E and O [Errors and Omissions] insurance."

Remember that there's a big wide world out there, and the international aspects of sync licenses can keep things fluid. "In terms of the grant of rights, that's covered under the 'territory' in the sync license," Swift states. "A quick example is that you might get a limited license and say, 'We're not on final music yet, but we need to get this production out to the festivals. You get a festival license, and that's the territory—festivals in the United States. On the final contract it will say the world, or the universe, or even the galaxy, which I find to be a tad pretentious. The grant of rights will cover the international broadcast of the final product, and the financial aspects are controlled by performing-rights agencies internationally, which the studios physically contact. Warner Brothers, for example, will have people in London, as well as in Los Angeles, who will assist in handling all of their European royalties, or someone who does their Asian royalties, although the Asian markets are famous for piracy."

At the heart of it, getting legal contracts signed is all about negotiation, and Swift recommends that music supervisors apply smart bargaining skills and a diligent work ethic to the personal relationships that put those negotiations over the top. "The music supervisor's job is to deliver a creative, thoughtful presentation, and to make sure the rights granted are sufficient and accurate," he concludes. "There's no substitute for finesse when that's what's called for. You can read about music supervision all you want, but if you're excited about it and you need to get started, you'll find a production and offer to music-supervise for cost."

"You'll meet the producer, hopefully they're happening and they'll do another movie, and they'll remember you because you did a great job. That's what it's all about: Sending follow-up letters, thank-you cards, remembering birthdays, and sometimes forcing yourself to go to places you don't want to go. Being thorough is what it is."

Tom Swift is available to help in this business if you have a project with "real legs." "Good luck and don't be afraid to try. Ask yourself what you would attempt if you knew that you could not fail."

PROFILE
Irwin Coster
Musicologist
Coster Music Research

• When to call a musicologist
• Public domain
• Fair use

You may not have met a musicologist yet, but as a music supervisor, you better start making friends with one. Scholarly experts with a deep, academic knowledge of musical history, theory, cognition, and philosophy, musicologists are an important resource to turn to when the legal usage status of a piece of music is in doubt.

As the film and TV world's leading musicologist, Irwin Coster, President of Coster Music Research, has been making judgment calls on public domain and fair use for decades, helping music supervisors head off nasty lawsuits—or serving as an expert witness in unauthorized usage cases when he wasn't contacted in time. Besides being a soundtrack consultant for the top studios, including Paramount, Disney, Fox, Universal, New Line, Tristar, and Miramax, he is also the creator of a massive database that incorporates musical phrases of published, copyrighted music and public-domain music, covering multiple genres. With more than 100,000 titles and more than one million song phrases, that database is as comprehensive as it gets.

Coster regularly fields questions from music supervisors who want to know if an older piece of music has passed into the public domain, or if a similar version qualifies as fair use. (See explanations of both public domain and fair use earlier in this chapter.) Think your film's director can shoot a scene with everybody singing "Happy Birthday" without licensing it? Think again, because they can't. Think your TV show needs clearance from Ritchie Valens' people before the lead singer can perform "La Bamba"? Not necessarily, because it's just his bass line that's copyrighted—the rest of the song is in the public domain.

Get the picture? These things get complicated quickly, and smart music supervisors should have no compunctions about getting an expert opinion if they have a shadow of doubt regarding a piece of music. "Nothing can be taken for granted anymore," says Coster. "For instance, go on a kids' show set: If they sing 'I'm a Little Teapot,' that's protected! The music supervisor needs to know about the piece they're performing: What is the status of it? That's the primary thing. If it's supposed to be a public domain song, how do they know that it is, both in the lyrics and music? That would apply to the copyright status if it's a copyrighted work, whether it's public domain in the United States and not the rest of the world, or in Canada and not in the rest of the world, that type of thing. When dealing with older songs, you need to know its entire history. To find that out, they can call me or another musicologist for the copyright or public-domain status of the work."

The question of public domain comes into play each and every time a new song is recorded for any type of media production. Trying to skirt the issue with a "sound alike" that has a few melodic changes to avoid legal action by the copyright holder is an outdated concept that should be avoided. "Then you get into copyright issues," says Coster. "The particular piece of music may have been applied for as a usage, and finding the cost, the music supervisor's company decides not to use it. Now you have the double-edged sword of using a substitute that has no bearing on the source they originally wanted. If a sound-alike is recorded, the music supervisor has to be careful that the company they work for hasn't applied for a license on it. Sound-alikes are almost out now, there are so many suits. These are dangerous usages. It's absolutely better not to bother with doing a sound alike, and instead come up with an original piece of music—as much as they can."

If you're in a situation where a musical parody is in order, you may be on slightly firmer legal ground. "If you make a political or social comment on a piece of music, you can use the underlying structure as a basis on that particular piece," Coster allows. "The famous example is 'Pretty Woman' that [infamous 1950s cover group] The Crew Cuts did and got away with it, and there are many others. It's very edgy to decide at what point it's not fair use, so that becomes a legal aspect, really."

Depending on your status with your employer, you may not get personally sued for a mistake. But your production company certainly might, and that's just not good. To avoid a serious mess, advance communication with the production's legal people is essential. "The music supervisor won't get sued; they're just a party to it," says Coster. "But the company will get sued for unauthorized usage of a public song, and it becomes a very costly thing. In the instance of fair use, the music supervisor should ascertain before then that it's gone through the legal department of the studio, and that the song's use is a 'yes' or 'no.'

"If they're going to do a thing like that, there have to be discussions with legal and decide whether they'll go ahead or not, so legal has to be involved in advance on fair use. In my dealings with studios, they're very aware of this issue, and there is coordination between music and legal departments. If you're going to commission a parody with a composer, or shoot a performance on site, there needs to be coordination."

Because music supervisors regularly work with music departments or hire outside composers to create and record completely original music for their productions, Coster maintains that the hiring music supervisor should not be compelled to then turn to a musicologist to make sure that the new piece of music doesn't bear an overwhelming resemblance to a preexisting but obscure composition. "If it's a piece of music written, the responsibility lies with the music department. Those composers are claiming that their new composition is a copyrightable work, and the music supervisor has to take the word of the music department that it is copyrightable. So in that case, the responsibility of not running afoul of public domain or fair use laws lies with the music department, not with the music supervisor."

All of this adds up to a simple fact: In an era where music supervisors expect to be able to get all their answers on line, there are some questions that they should definitely take to their friendly neighborhood musicologist or music attorney. The result is not only protection for the music supervisor and his or her reputation, but protection for the people who hire them with the justifiable expectation that their music supervisor can keep their production out of the courtroom. "Every music supervisor should have a musicologist that they can call," Coster agrees. "It's very dangerous to go out unless you know all the facts on a song, and hopefully, before they go out on the shoot, all questions have been brought up to the music and legal departments. Everything should be honest and fair, with nothing hidden from the producer or director on the shoot, because they can be the innocent victim."

PROFILE
Steven Gold
Composer, Compositions Inc.
Chappelle's Show, The Man Show, Saturday Night Live

• Music supervising and composing for comedy
• Feel-alikes
• Sound-alikes

Music is serious business to most people in the industry, but to Steven Gold of Compositions Inc. *(www.compositions-inc.com)*, it's purely a laughing matter. Here's a look at a highly professional composer who can do double-duty as a music supervisor, handling the high-pressure needs of weekly TV series music supervision on a moment's notice.

As the man behind the music that drives home the humor for TV programs such as *Saturday Night Live, The Man Show, Crank Yankers, Chapelle's Show, Howard Stern on E!* and more, Gold is a guy who fully understands the value of finding a niche. "In the past five years, everybody has been able to get access to a method of recording quality music," says Gold, in his downtown New York City studio. "Whether it's digital audio, computers, sequencers, something like Reason, everybody can produce the tracks and everybody wants to. Who's getting the jobs are the people specializing in their niche market, and their talent shines through. So it's not a matter of having the capacity to record; it's knowing what you're doing musically or creatively."

So what is it about Gold's music, no matter how classically classical or Eighties-cop-show-accurate, that still has a giant giggle lurking behind it? According to Gold, it's all about the context the song will be placed in, and the ability to keep a straight face when you're composing it. "It's almost like not being funny—taking itself seriously," he explains. "Only about ten percent of the time do you have to make the music sound funny. Because it's underscoring a comedic moment, it has to support it—not really be invisible, like a film score might be, but over the top in its obviousness. As if you were saying, 'This is supposed to be a serious action cartoon, not comedy.'"

When it's called for, Gold is ready to extend his services beyond composition to include music supervision. "All of the shows that I work on require a certain amount of music supervision, because not everything I do needs to be original. When they hire a company like ours to provide all the music for an episode, under the time constraints, we have to prioritize what is done as an original piece and what is done using libraries. I have a music supervisor on staff to maintain and utilize my music libraries, which currently number about three thousand CDs. However, my music supervisor isn't there to obtain master or sync licenses—that's not the type of music supervision we do.

"On a typical network show, for example, the show's music supervisor would spot the show, then say, 'This scene needs an original composition, this scene needs a licensed song, this scene needs a piece of library music…' In my case, since I'm often hired by cable shows without an official music supervisor, my company does the whole thing. So Comedy Central's *Chappelle's Show,* for example, hires me to do music supervision and composing, but for licensing they might hire an independent contractor. (See Music Profile: Evan Greenspan). The show's producer may also try to do it themselves, but it's harder for them because they don't have the contacts with the record companies."

Besides great ears, arranging abilities, and fast thinking, Gold's comedic niche calls for other specific skill sets. Knowing the ins and outs of the networks' Standards and Practices censors may mean recording four different versions of a song about a dog that licks his own, uh, anatomy. Another important thing Gold has to know is what legally constitutes parody, and what doesn't.

"Sometimes you are asked to do a 'feel-alike,' and sometimes a 'sound-alike,'" he says. "For the feel-alike, no license has been obtained; you have the real song as a reference, and your composition is really close, but it's changed enough by the letter of the law not to constitute copyright infringement. Guys like me have to know how far you can take it. In the realm of comedy or parody, the lines are a little softer.

"With a 'sound-alike,' you can make it sound just like the song, because a sync license has been obtained from the publishing company. This is much cheaper than trying to also obtain the master license to sync the original recording, because that master license can be ten or twenty times more expensive than the sync. It is also much easier to get the publishing company to grant the sync license—they feel there is much more value to having the actual artist's recording heard on the show.

"For one recent show, we needed a Hall & Oates type thing, so I did this," Gold says, as something quite "Maneater"-like comes through the speakers. "Arrangements aren't really copyrightable unless it's an arrangement of a public-domain piece, and also my melody is different. Plus, the scene parodies Hall & Oates; it mentions them. I know all the laws, and I have copyright infringement insurance that I pay every year because I do so many feel-alikes. There are tricks of the trade to doing the closest feel, ways of duplicating the arrangement without copying it, or changing the melody by reversing the melody line."

Steven Gold is living the life he dreamed of since he first stepped into a recording facility, only better. He's constantly working on his studio tan as he works with some of the funniest people in the world, making their stuff even funnier through an ever-expanding understanding of music. The better he gets, the more he realizes that having skills is the number one way to stay alive as a composer in the Twenty-first Century.

"Everyone has a project studio set up in their house, and the studios that survive are going to be the ones that provide a talent, whether it's a great TV mixer or a great record producer," he says, in all seriousness. "The composers will survive if they're good composers."

By David Weiss. Reprinted with permission from *Audio Media*. See an expanded version of this profile at *www.musicsupervisioncentral.com*.

CHAPTER ten

Getting the Job

If you don't "get the job," all of the music-supervision training in the world won't help you. It's critical to understand the art and business of music supervision before entering into a real job situation, but it's also important to know when you've had enough schooling and how to find and pursue potential jobs in the field.

What You Need

All aspiring music supervisors must have on hand the following self-promotional and branding tools at all times:

- biography
- résumé
- video reel
- business cards
- Website

Once you have these tools, it's all about a quick phrase called "You, Who, and How" which you'll read about throughout this chapter. Just remember, without the "you," there is no "who and how." The key is confidence.

Possibly the most important thing to remember is that there is not one foolproof way to get a job in any business, whether it's entertainment or gourmet cooking. You will hear different stories from every successful person you ever come in contact with about how they achieved their positions. It is important to listen closely to experiential accounts from people who are willing to offer them (there are plenty in this book), but it will ultimately be *you* who makes it happen. The responsibility of searching for, seeking out, and achieving the right position falls directly on your shoulders.

Confidence Is Key

Confidence may be an intangible factor, but it's one of the most important assets anyone can have in order to compete in music supervision. Once you get the job, it's your responsibility to make superiors and executives feel confident about what you are doing for them. But before that happens, you must first find confidence in yourself.

Without self-confidence, you will have a much tougher time convincing an executive producer, producer, and/or director that your creative musical decisions are sound. If you're going to recommend a song for a scene, it's essential to deliver your pitch with strength and conviction, because no film or TV executive has the time to question the confidence of their creative staff's decisions.

Once you have confidence in your skills, you have to have confidence in communication. You can have all the music-supervision knowledge and skill in the world, but without a strong verbal pitch, it will be of very little use. Anyone who wishes to enter the entertainment industry should strongly consider taking classes in topics such as public speaking, voice and diction, and/or oral interpretation of scripts/poetry. This type of training will give you a huge edge in self-assuredness—extremely necessary for addressing a room of entertainment executives about your particular expertise, which in this case is music supervision.

Use the tools in this book to help build your self-confidence on all levels. Also, use the scenarios and business models set up in this book to construct new models and exercises to train with. Once you've gained enough confidence through hypothetical training and practice, it's time to start building your self-promotional kit/media kit.

Brand Yourself

First, you must think "out of the box" as far as your own professional branding and promotion. When it comes to image, being "safe" is *boring*. Don't be like everyone else who's been successful—being "out of the box" means you're not adhering one-hundred percent to any one method of designing a résumé, biography, or reel. (See the Music Profile on Walter Werzowa in Chapter 4, Sound Design, for an example of how a reel done "wrong" can land you a job.)

Remember, these promotional/branding tools are representative of you and your skill set. If you are trying to brand yourself as an original and talented new music supervisor, there's no point in appearing just like everyone else that decision-makers in the entertainment business have seen many times before.

In developing your bio, résumé, reel, and Website, it is essential to decide how you are going to express your personality through your art and business. Being able to brand yourself as a music supervisor with a personality and a vision is challenging, but if you start right away, you will be able to accomplish it. For example, don't use the same text font for your résumé that everybody else uses because it's worked in the past. Move on, and take a step in a direction that could CATCH SOME ATTENTION.

Your main goal in putting together your media kit is to CATCH the ATTENTION of your potential client/employer. Take some risks in developing your résumé: Blow the font size up on your name, maybe throw some color into it, and come up with an artistic treatment/layout that's totally new and different but reads well. Don't go too far, however. One common mistake is making your résumé so artistically "out there" that a conservative human resources manager will have a hard time understanding the actual contents of the document. Be sure to pass it around to your teachers, friends, and family, and get some feedback before you send it out.

Building Your Résumé

What does a potential employer—whether it's for a video-game internship, TV music supervision slot, multimedia Website, or indie film—look for on a résumé? In most cases, they're looking for some kind of relevant experience, meaning they will want to know if you've ever done anything in the realm of marrying sound or music to any kind of visual medium (live or pre-produced). Although you may think you're in the classic Catch-22 situation (i.e., "If I've never done music supervision before, how can I put something on my résumé that gives me any kind of music supervision credibility?") the answer is this: If you're meant to be a music supervisor, you've probably been doing it in some form or another for your entire life.

Have you ever:

- DJ'd a party or event? (If so, then you've done music supervision in a live venue.)
- worked for your college radio station, or been part of the music for a play?

- worked at a hotel, restaurant, store, or bar where you'd regularly pop CDs into the stereo to contribute to the ambience?
- played in a school band in support of a team sport?
- made a mix tape/CD/iPod playlist for a friend, loved one, or family member? Have you made one for your fraternity or sorority?

These are all music-supervision activities that, if you are creative enough, can be articulated into quantifiable experience. Bottom line: If you took the time to do it at some point in your life, it's real experience. Discover new ways to articulate in words the experience that you previously didn't even realize you could use. Websites like *www.employ.com* can help you develop this kind of technique.

Building Your Bio

Writing your bio is often easier than writing your résumé. It's your opportunity to describe yourself and your experience beyond bullet points or sterile text résumés. A bio is basically the story of your life, as related to your particular trade—in this case, music supervision. Sometimes you'll choose to send your bio before your résumé.

Your bio should be no more than one page and no less than three short paragraphs. Most executives don't have the time to read through a lot of text, so if something looks too long to read, it may never be read at all. Use your best judgment to keep thoughts to-the-point and brief, yet colorful and interesting. Again, refer to sites like *www.employ.com, www.thevelvetrope.com, www.tvjobs.com,* and *www.entertainmentcareers.net* to begin and maintain this thought process.

The following is an example of the bio for one of the co-authors of this book:

David Weiss is a New York City-based writer with deep experience covering technology, professional audio, and music. He is the founder of D Media Inc. and *www.dwords.com,* a successful communications-consulting firm for the technology sector. Industries he has worked with include HDTV/SDTV lens and camera manufacturing, audio manufacturing, fiber optics, free-space optics, software, recording studios, and audio post.

Mr. Weiss is also the New York City editor of *Mix* magazine. His work has appeared regularly in a wide range of media outlets including, *Audio Media, Pro Sound News, Live Sound International, Remix, Digital Television, TV Technology, Systems Contractor News, Time Out New York, Drum! magazine, Archi-Tech,* and more.

A drummer for twenty years, Weiss studied audio engineering at The New

School. He was sound designer/music supervisor for the critically acclaimed off-Broadway play *Syndrome,* and is the producer of the multimedia music library *www.meetyourbeat.com.* A native of Detroit, Weiss holds a BA in Communications from the University of Michigan. He lives in Manhattan.

Realizing Your Reel

What about your reel? The same question that might have come up while you were putting together your first music-supervision résumé may very well resurface when it comes to putting together your first reel: "How can I build a reel if I don't have any audio- or video-editing skills, or music-supervision experience?"

1. Make friends with people who do know how to edit audio and/or video.

2. Hard-record broadcast and cable-television shows, ads, and movies, strip out the music already there and put in your new and better music. (If you do so, be sure to indicate "for demonstration purposes only" in the opening sequence.)

3. Do Internet searches for pre-digitized movies of the same that are downloadable for "personal use," and add music with a program like Vegas, Acid, or Final Cut Pro. (Personal use means that you're not reproducing the content for the purpose of organized distribution or sales of any kind.)

We'll delve deeper into how to make those editing contacts in the ensuing pages, but first, let's talk about finding the right content for your first reel. The best way to organize a high-impact reel is to focus on your strengths, and avoid applying for projects that play to your weaknesses. For example, you don't want a music-supervision job that focuses on classical music if you know nothing about the genre. You should definitely make it your business to learn classical and work on it for the future, but it's not necessary to market yourself for something that you cannot act on at a competitive level.

If your strength and confidence lie in specific musical genres, like hip-hop or folk, focus on marketing yourself in those directions. Furthermore, find the visual content that effectively supports those musical genres. For example, if your strength is in electronica, seek out quick-cutting, psychedelic visuals that merge well with that music.

A broadcast television or film reel, for example, should be no shorter than three minutes and no longer than five minutes when you are focusing on short-form spots like advertisements and promotions. If you're working on a reel that focused more on scenes, then you should choose scenes that start and resolve in a matter of moments (one to three minutes each), and your total reel could range from eight to twelve minutes.

Finally, on what format should you provide your reel to your perspective clients? DVD? VHS? Highspeed on line? The answer is "on whatever format you find out they can use." How do you find out? Ask. If you cannot ask, give your reel to your perspective client/employer on the easiest format there is to view: VHS, DVD, or QuickTime movie on CD-ROM are generally the most user-friendly. Many times, a client may want reels submitted on Beta, Digi-Beta, or other related formats. If that's the case, do what you have to in order to make it happen for them, because if you give them something in a format that's inconvenient for them to view, they're likely to toss it aside and move on to the next. Make it easy for your prospective client to hire you.

There are sample music-supervisor résumés, bios, and reels on this book's companion Website, *www.musicsupervisioncentral.com.*

Working Your Website

This is where your Website comes in. No matter what hard formats you're using to put your reel on (VHS, CD-ROM, DVD), always make sure you have your reel posted on line for anyone to view at any time. You never know where you'll be when you need to show someone your reel, and you may not have the resources in a short-notice situation to get someone a reel on a hard format. This won't be a problem if you can send them directly to your personal Website, where your reel can be viewed in QuickTime, Real Player, or Windows Media Player 24/7, worldwide.

Having a strong Web presence is becoming more and more important in music supervision. As production teams do more and more of their work on line, they are also looking for more content on the Internet. When they need a service, like digitizing content, new fonts, new software, and music supervision the first stop is usually Google.

Therefore, you want to make sure that you are positioned on the Internet to be found by people who would want and need your services. Take inventory, determine your strengths as a music supervisor, and highlight them on your Website. Consult with a Web expert on ways to improve your standings in music-supervision searches. There are multiple techniques for moving your name closer to the top, some of which are free and some of which are costly. For example, if you are from Baton Rouge and have an ear for Cajun music and have relationships with Cajun artists, then you should be sure when someone searches for "music supervisor Baton Rouge Cajun" they see your name first.

Creative Self-Marketing Methods

Just as there are no limits to how TV shows, films, and video games are now marketed, there are also no limits to marketing yourself as a music supervisor. The key is to commit time to doing it. Making custom reels whenever possible is a good idea.

Taking the time to customize your reel, résumé, and bio for clients is undoubtedly the single most effective way to get the job. It shows a prospective client or employer that you are the man or woman with the specific and necessary tools and talents for their very specific needs.

Volunteer Your Time

If you need to get started, one very effective thing to try is to volunteer to music-supervise a project in order to get some experience, build your reel, and meet people who produce media. Go to the local colleges and universities to find out what professors teach media content creation, and then talk to them about providing music-supervision services for their students' projects. You might end up working with the next Steven Spielberg, but even if you don't, the point is to get experience and meet people.

Internships in any and all fields related to music supervision can frequently be obtained with persistence and that snazzy résumé. There are many angles, but landing a spot in a broadcast news or film studio music department, publisher, record-company licensing division, music-management firm, entertainment law office, composition house, or music-supervision firm are just a few of the places to start. Besides providing invaluable experience in the field, internships often yield incredible connections (David Weiss, one of the co-writers of this book, kicked off his illustrious career with a summer-long internship at the now-defunct IRS Records.)

A lot of people have misgivings about "giving away" their time for free, but the true way to view internships is as an investment of your time, instead of your money. Work hard, prove your mettle, and decision-makers will want to work with you on the next job—and they'll find a budget for your services. There are many music supervisors working today who made just such an investment, and cashed it in later for a full-fledged career in the field.

Build Your Own Licensing Database

Other new music supervisors will take the step of negotiating licensing agreements with bands and artists in order to create a database or portfolio of licensable music that they can then pitch to production teams. The result is a mix CD/DVD/tape of bands with whom they have relationships, allowing the aspiring music supervisor to create a promotional package that can be distributed to people making movies, ads, games, and all the other media that requires music.

This is a new approach to music supervision, because instead of looking at the needs of a specific production and then trying to find the right music, the music supervisor is trying to aggregate music that might work in any number of productions, and supplying it to production teams along with "music supervision services," e.g. licensing, talent relationships, and legal agreements.

Networking

Getting that music-supervision job also requires a commitment to personal networking. In order to develop a personal network, you must create and continually update a contact list. Develop a means of communication in order to remind people of what you are doing. Perhaps it is a monthly newsletter, blog, mass e-mail, or even phone calls. People in the production field tend to forget who and what people do, so it's your job to remind them of you and your services. Don't be annoying, however—it can be a fine line to walk. Being overly aggressive is not recommended (although it does sometimes work).

Making friends in the business goes along with the "Who" in the phrase "You, Who, and How" introduced in the first paragraph of this chapter. Go where the entertainment and music people hang out, and hang out with them. It's that simple.

Start by committing some funds to visiting some of the major annual music and entertainment-related conferences, such as MIDEM, the *Billboard* Film & TV Conference, CMJ, South by Southwest, the Miami Winter Music Festival and Conference, BDA, NAB, Promax, the Tribeca Film Awards, the Cannes Film Festival, Sundance Film Festival, Marco Island Film Festival, and more. Thousands of key connections are made every year at these events— that's really why they're put on in the first place. If you don't go to at least one or two of them every year, you will be missing a lot.

Go to live shows at local clubs in your area, and go to as many concerts as you can afford (or get yourself on the guest list). These are the places where music and entertainment professionals go to discover new talent, and the bands performing are new talent that you may want to work with one day. Many successful music producers, for example, have found hit acts that put them on the map by going to clubs and handing their card to bands that they liked (producer/engineer Gordon Raphael did just that to lure the New York City band The Strokes into his modest Lower East Side studio, and the result was 2001's critically acclaimed album, *Is This It?*).

Also, don't forget your friends from school—elementary to Master's degree. Many successful people in any industry will say, "It's not what you know, it's who you know." The truth is that it's both. Be good at what you do, but make an effort to be around those who do what you want to do, or those who hold the key to the door that will bring you to the place you want to go.

Do Great Work!

Quality control is extremely important to getting the job, keeping the job, and then getting rehired for the next project. You want to make sure your product is top-notch. The formula is simple: A music supervisor provides great music for a project, and is hired to work on another project with the expectations that the music will be similarly great.

The opposite can happen, as well. The music supervisor who did a great job is hired again, and when it comes time to deliver the tracks they are poorly performed and produced. It could be that this time, the music supervisor just didn't have access to more quality content, had promised something he couldn't deliver, or got lazy. Whatever the reason, the end result is that this music supervisor has lost credibility. Will this person get called a third time? Probably not.

Your reputation is everything. From your first music-supervision job to your last, try to provide the best content you possibly can given the constraints of the project. Stay committed to high quality, maintain your "first-time" enthusiasm, and chances are good that you'll earn respect and continued employment. Remember, the media universe is exploding, and loads of new content is going to be needed. Once you get your foot in the door, there's no excuse for being shown the way out.

Stay on Top of Developments

Due in large part to the non-stop advances in digital technology, the world of music supervision is constantly changing—fast. To stay in the game, you must keep abreast of changes, advances, and even setbacks in the business.

The well-known story of Napster is a good example. Napster was a file-sharing service that revolutionized the way digital content was distributed, and music supervisors were as excited about it as anybody. With Napster, they could search anybody else's hard drive—that was on the network—for music and download it for free, giving them access to a world of audio they could only have dreamed about before 1999.

only have dreamed about before 1999.

Music supervisors were logging into Napster and searching far and wide for music—already digitized—and dumping songs into media projects to see how they fit. If the result was right, then all they had to do was contact the license-holders and negotiate an agreement. Then United States courts determined that file sharing in this way was illegal, and that using this method of auditioning music for projects constituted copyright theft. Even though, in the case of music supervisors, the music would subsequently be licensed legally, the method they utilized to obtain the content was deemed criminal. You can imagine how many music supervisors were frantically deleting their Napster libraries as a result of that ruling.

In its place we now have iTunes and other legal online music services, where music supervisors now have the ability to spot-check digitized commercial songs for a small fee.

The bottom line: Keep on top of technology. You must understand the general capabilities and implications of new editing tools like Pro Tools, Final Cut Pro, and iMovie, even if you can't actually edit in them. You need to know what file formats they use, as well as how they are imported and exported. This knowledge will help make you an invaluable member of a production team and keep you working.

Finally, go to seminars and lectures, take classes, and read articles. There will be regular updates on relevant events at this book's Website, *www.musicsupervisioncentral.com*. Keep yourself educated about music supervision and keep meeting people. Music supervision as a profession is growing rapidly because of all the developments in new media. Get yourself a solid footing now, and you will be make a living in no time as you make media come to life through music.

Good luck!

PROFILE
Evan Greenspan, President
Evan M. Greenspan Inc. Music Clearance

• Business enterprise in music supervision
• Customer service for clearances
• Building relationships

While the employment picture of music supervision often entails freelancing, or working for large studios or broadcasters, Evan Greenspan is his own company, Evan M. Greenspan Inc. *(www.clearance.com)*, in 1987, Greenspan has become the go-to guy in music clearance for a huge list of clients, including feature films, HBO, ABC, CBC, NBC, and more, and he has done it on his own terms.

"Most music supervisors are in entrepreneurial mode," Greenspan observes, "meaning it's basically them, or maybe them and an assistant. EMG has grown to the point to where we've got staff who do nothing but handle clearance requests and negotiations, and others who do nothing but license administration."

Nice work if you can find it, but Greenspan is the first to admit that it was a long road to building an enterprise. Educated as a composer and playwright, his career began with 1970s and 1980s mega-producer Alan Landsburg, when Greenspan was the only person on staff who found the licensing of production and library music interesting. He seized on the niche, and spent the next few years learning on the job to become an expert at the ins and outs of music publishing, licensing, and clearance.

In the mid-Eighties, he was one of the first to employ new personal computer software to automate the clearance process, ultimately developing EMG's own music-clearance software, which today stands as a patented database/music-rights business process. "That's one of the biggest assets of the company, and we are constantly evolving it," he says. "Basically, we automated the flow of information before a lot of publishers had their own computers. Our data goes back to 1985. What's so useful about that is you can look back over the years and say, 'Here's our experience in clearing a particular song, here's how long it took, here's what it cost.' Our experience can now serve as a predictor."

Greenspan has found success by paying close attention to what his clients—who range from large networks and studios to small in-house corporate departments and independent producers—really need from him. "This is a service business, and any good service business is focused on meeting the needs of its customers. So we tried to listen to people, and say, 'What are they asking about music clearance?' Here's what they want to know:

> Is this use feasible at the terms I have in mind?

> What resources will it take to get cleared?

> How long will it take to get?

At what terms can I realistically license this?

"If you can get those answers on a consistent basis, you'll be successful in the business of music clearance. The problem is that the answers to that are in the hands of other people: The publishers, the record labels, or the artist."

In addition, to his database, Greenspan relies on the excellent relationships he's nurtured with copyright holders over the years, as well as his understanding of what the art of music clearance is all about. "You are asking somebody for the use of their private property for some other purpose," he states. "This is a process that is never going to be automated: You'll never have an eBay of popular songs. It's no different from walking into an art gallery and saying, 'Hi, I'd like to borrow your Monet masterpiece to impress the guests at my party. How much?'

"Some producers don't understand that it doesn't work to call up a copyright owner of some well-known music and say, 'I only have ten dollars for your song. It's ten dollars more than you have now, so take it!' Pretend you own that Monet. You'd be asking, 'Who are you? What will you do with it? Where will it be hung? How long? Will I get it back? Will it be damaged?' Copyright owners are most concerned with protecting the long-term value of their property. You might have the greatest low-budget film in the world, but don't assume that publishers will give gratis licenses based on the merits of the film alone. It often takes a lot of convincing, and then some money, to get permission."

EMG's long-term track record for clearance is a lofty ninety-four percent, made less-than-perfect in many cases by the songs and artists that are perennially unavailable. "Van Morrison, for example, is well known for not responding to film and TV requests," says Greenspan. "So is Neil Young. Part of being an expert is knowing where the problems lie, and we have found it best to communicate the potential difficulties to the client up-front. There's always a potential for trouble when people say, 'It has to be this song and this song only.' Sometimes it's just unavailable. When Tom Cruise took over the 'Mission Impossible' franchise, that theme song *became* impossible—the studio simply would not grant licenses for it. Make yourself aware, and then say to your clients, 'Here's what I believe your experience will be, and if you trust me, I'll guide you through this.'"

For Greenspan, the incredible amount of consolidation in music copyright ownership has forever transformed the industry. "When I started in the early Eighties, there were thirty major publishing companies," he notes. "That number is now five: Warner/Chappell, Universal, EMI, Sony, and BMG. If you take any ten popular songs, the odds are very good that half of them will have something to do with those companies. It's harder in the sense that a lot of traffic is being directed through a limited number of doors. Inexperienced producers may say to you, 'Don't they know this request is for a prime-time network show?' You have to say, 'Of course they do, but they're also dealing with all the other networks, a forty-million-dollar movie, and a ten-million-dollar commercial, so we have to get in line.'

"There are not a lot of levels of authority in music rights. There's usually a publisher who represents their own interest and that of the songwriter, and a record label who communicates with the artist's manager or the artist themselves. If you get a 'no,' it's usually from the artist or the songwriter. You're usually very close to the source."

There's no question that being self-employed in this tricky field pays off in the end. "There is a wonderful art to pairing music with picture, and when you're involved in the choice, then see it on the screen and say, 'I got the rights to that,' it's extremely gratifying," Greenspan concludes. "When you watch the results, you derive a great deal of satisfaction having played a part in the creation of a production. When it's over, the feeling is always, 'Wow, it was worth it.'"

PROFILE
Gene Sandbloom, Assistant Program Director
KROQ Los Angeles

• Radio program director as music supervisor
• Picking hit songs
• Getting an extremely desirable job

If rock radio has a headquarters, it's at KROQ in Los Angeles, a station that can make or break an artist by putting their song into the rotation. As the first commercial station to take a chance on hugely influential bands such as Coldplay, Nirvana, Portishead, and countless others, KROQ has been a top tastemaker since the late 1970s.

Behind that big cultural impact at KROQ are the program directors (PDs), radiocentric music supervisors who match up their music, not with movies or video games, but with the ultra-edgy whirlwind that is Los

Angeles. "L.A. is not a normal city," points out Gene Sandbloom, Assistant Program Director for KROQ. "We represent ourselves as a true Top 40 station for L.A. KROQ is a unique radio station in that it is treated much as an A&R department. It's not a station that follows trends—it's a station that breaks new ideas."

A lifelong music devotee, Sandbloom went from college radio to an A&R position at MCA Records, to heading up a radio industry trade publication, and then to KROQ in 1992. When he and Program Director Kevin Weatherly arrived at the station, they decided it was time to give its cutting-edge philosophy a shot in the arm. "It had become stagnant—they were playing music associated with the eighties like The Cure, The Smiths, and Depeche Mode," he recalls. "We felt that the station in the early days had committed to breaking new bands. We decided we didn't care what it was, but we wanted to be the next big thing, and it was grunge. No one was playing Pearl Jam or Nirvana on the radio, and when we did, that took KROQ to the next generation. Since then, we've always been committed to keeping KROQ on the forefront, just two steps ahead of music."

Like the best music supervisors, Sandbloom juggles multiple working relationships and is fiercely committed to keeping his ear at street level. "We've kept the programming pure," he says. "We meet with all the record companies every week, and they bring us their priorities, so to speak, the projects they're most excited about that have the biggest potential. But we go beyond that. We hop on the Internet, poll record stores, go to indie record accounts all over Southern California, and find out things not on major labels that are breaking, and that people are just plain talking about.

"We take the best of that, and once a week on Tuesday we listen to music for three hours nonstop. Sometimes it's just the program director, music director Matt Smith, and myself. Or we might invite phone operators, van drivers, artists, managers, or record-company reps to sit in and listen to the music. We vote on it, and at the end of the meeting, the stuff that does the best on a consistent basis gets added to the rotation."

Sandbloom sees multiple parallels between his job and that of music supervisors for visual media. "We're like an A&R department," he says. "I consider A&R to be a central cog in the wheel. We're a spoke, and the people that do music supervision for TV and film are another spoke. The great A&R people of the world are not being force-fed, they're out there looking. A great music supervisor would go out and have a vast knowledge of music, so they could draw from a vast number of sources. Music tends to come out in clumps, and you might have a lot of similar-sounding bands, and you can't play them all at the same time. So two or three years go by, things settle down, and you can go back and draw something off those past records.

"We're constantly looking for things that fit your individual needs. A music supervisor is looking for a song for an action film, we're looking for rock records—and you have to beat down the walls for a rock record you think is going to work for you."

While the songs that Sandbloom and Weatherly greenlight for airplay on KROQ will quickly end up on music supervisors' most-coveted lists, the choices music supervisors make can likewise influence the way Sandbloom works. "It affects us," he agrees. "We keep an eye on what's selling, and that can make us want to put records on the air. I remember a Pepsi commercial with a very unique song that stood out, and we said, 'Pepsi is doing a billion-dollar campaign. It's everywhere.' So we put the song on the air, and we started getting complaints that we were playing a TV commercial! It no longer was hip, it was a sellout."

When it comes to picking music for a living, being a radio PD can put you in a hugely influential position, but you'd better come prepared. "You have to be extremely organized," Sandbloom says. "You have to have a great ear, not be adverse to change, always looking ahead, be able to find great talent in its raw state and then nurture it. You always have to rewrite the book—you can't just follow what's already been done."

PROFILE
Murray Allen, VP of post production
Electronic Arts

• Video game music supervision
• An audio expert's perspective

In the multi-billion-dollar video game world of Playstation, Nintendo, X-Box and on line, the only constant for music supervisors is change. An industry that was operating with the most basic of sounds a dozen years ago has now become hit-record territory, backing up the action with great music that has to satisfy its young and very demanding audience.

When Murray Allen, VP of post-production for Electronic Arts *(www.ea.com),* joined the leading game developer in 1993, they got a musical heavy hitter. An audio pioneer, Murray had previously been president of Universal Recording, one of the largest studios in the United

States At Universal, he oversaw the development of many of today's post-production systems, including the use of digital technology and DAWs for television. More than 250 films and TV soundtracks—many of them EMMY- and GRAMMY-nominated—were produced under his watch.

At EA, Allen has witnessed a rapid increase in the technical capacity of video games—improvements that have made a major impact on how today's video game music supervisors, also known as audio directors, attack their jobs. "I joined the company in August of 1993— those were the days of the Sega Genesis, and use of the CD on the machines was just starting," Allen recalls. "With the Sega Genesis, we had only five voices to work with. It was like writing for string quartet, so my first directive to composers was, 'Keep things simple, keep thinking of the rhythm of the game, so the rhythm of the music will coincide with the action of the game. Make it click—not artistic or esoteric.'

"Fast-forward to today, and music for video games is still a challenge. It's a computerized medium, and you have to make it work interactively. A movie is ninety minutes long and you have a storyboard, but here you have to make it so that, no matter how the player plays the game, the audio track tells the story. The player is the mixer, the final editor, and you have to out-guess everything they do."

As music supervisor for EA's popular *NCAA March Madness* and *Wing Commander* series, among others, Allen sees important similarities and differences between doing the job for video games and other media. "I think in one way it's all the same, because basically you have to choose the type of music and composers for the type of story you're trying to tell artistically. But in a feature film or commercial, it's more linear and you can take more liberties. Say there's a movie scene where a car is going up the mountain, so the director says, 'I need forty-five seconds to get the emotion I want.' You have that luxury in a linear medium.

"In video games, all of a sudden the player will press a button and they're somewhere else, so from an editing point of view, or a storyboard layout, things are very different. For example, on our *Lord of the Rings* series, with Howard Shore's music, they had to re-edit it to get the big fight scene to match up. You have to pick the music that furthers the excitement of the story that you're trying to tell."

Assembling music is a healthy mix of licensed tracks and composers. "Licensing in video game music today," Murray says, "you might pick bands that you think will break when the game comes out in four or five months, and you might give the game a boost. Sometimes it has something to do with the game, sometimes it doesn't, but if it's really hip or cool, demographically it's good for the age levels you're trying to get. If you're doing a game like *Madden NFL Football,* an original orchestral score has no meaning, vs. a dozen licensed popular rock songs that have meaning to the people playing it.

According to Allen, today's video game music supervisors have to be up for the fast-evolving technical challenges of their field. "It's a very heavy job relative to normal music supervision. Working in the digital domain, you only have so much area on the disc that you'll be able to use effectively. Whether it's licensed or newly recorded music, you have to deal with lots of sound effects, dialogue, etc.

"A good music supervisor should be able to understand the problems of implementing all the audio, including the music, into the game. You don't have to be incredibly technical, but you should have a little bit of a mathematical mind, and have people working for you that understand the full technicalities."

The video game music supervisor also has an interesting group to work with, that's different from the talent in a cable TV unit. "A team can have a hundred people on it easily," Allen confirms. "You have to understand that in video games, the sound effects are looked at as lead instruments: The explosion for a gunshot is the lead instrument. It's an entire soundstage, and they all have to work together.

"Then the director and music supervisor decide what music to use and what not to use. If you're just a straight music supervisor, you're still at the mercy of the producers and editors who are telling the story. On the other hand, if the music supervisor is in a position to control things, then the game will sound better. In most cases, the music supervisor is also the audio director. They should be one and the same. If they license it, then the audio director decides where to put it and when to use it. The audio director meets with executive producers, and even the chief executive gets involved."

It all calls for keeping in touch with the ultimate executive decision-makers on the sound mix: The players themselves. "It's an interactive sport, not passive," Allen points out. "It's not just watching videos. It's an active thing, and the point is to get video game players so they're in the game. The more exciting you make it, the better it is."

See an expanded version of this Profile on *www.musicsupervisioncentral.com.*

In the world of TV, there is an often overlooked musical option that goes beyond licensing tracks or hiring composers to make new ones: Live bands. Read on to find out what goes into making a live group part of the musical mix, and how the musicians themselves can fulfill many of the music supervisory functions themselves.

On the menu of career options available to a musician, nothing is more mouth-watering then a steady gig. Mix in a high-profile factor, like daily appearances on national television, and that regular job is even more luscious. It's an exceptionally rare delicacy, and it's the one that percussionist Doc Gibbs and drummer Ted Thomas Jr. taste as the core players of one of the hottest TV house groups, The Emeril Live Band.

Gibbs' and Thomas' job as the rhythmic force behind the highly popular Food Network cooking show *Emeril Live* puts them in a very elite circle of musicians that includes the bands on *The Late Show with David Letterman,* Jay Leno's *Tonight Show, Late Night With Conan O'Brien, Saturday Night Live,* and possibly a few other programs. The number of players who draw a regular paycheck from a national TV network is decidedly tiny.

"You can count the TV bands on your hand," says Doc Gibbs, the bandleader of the four-piece, and yin to the master chef's yang on the set. "To take it a step further, most of your TV bands are on entertainment shows, and this is a cooking show. It's very difficult to get a gig like this."

Unusual as it is for a show about the joys of melted butter and merlot to lay out for a live band and the expensive support structure that goes along with it, Thomas points out that the group is a natural extension of Emeril Lagasse, who may be the most popular chef in the world today. "Everybody loves food, and everybody loves music; that's why I think it works with this live band," he says. "When a lot of people cook, they play music, it goes hand in hand. Emeril himself does that."

For anyone who has seen *Emeril Live,* the world beat-flavored funk of the band, who perform just a few feet stage right from Emeril's fully-equipped kitchen, is an essential ingredient to the show's unique character. Gibbs and Thomas, whose long history together has helped them to form an exceptionally deep pocket, are joined on the set by keyboardist Cliff Starkey, bassist Charles Baldwin, and saxophonist Louis R. Taylor, Jr. They provide an added dimension of energy that few TV shows can come close to matching.

Although the high-energy funk that the Emeril Live Band pumps out during the show's intro, outro, and as it segues in and out of commercial breaks, is fun and packed with spontaneous jams, making music that works for TV is an exact science. Besides being incredibly fickle and armed with remote controls, viewers may be watching on anything from a tiny TV with one mono speaker to a home theater with 5.1 surround. As a result, the band's arrangements have to be exciting enough to get immediate attention from as many people as possible, and played on instruments that can be mixed properly to sound snappy and well-balanced on almost anything.

"TV is always about trying to pull you in and keep you there," says Gibbs. "We have to be conscious of playing up-tempo music that's accessible to everybody. We couldn't do free playing or ballads for too long, because people just won't go for it. Plus, sometimes we only have five seconds of total playing time—that's one chord!"

Before every show, the band makes a set list of sorts by going over collections of their own grooves that Gibbs and Thomas have laid down on CD. Once the grooves have been decided on, they'll simply count in when the cameras are on, giving this tight, fast-thinking unit hundreds of different possible variations to play off of. The fact that the band is asked to play its own original material, instead of covers, is another reason why the "Emeril Live" gig is a live TV music job unlike any other. "I think because you can sit there and watch cats play and create with real instruments, that adds another unique element that people enjoy," Gibbs says. "We're not playing anybody else's music, we're playing something we create. We have to stay within some parameters, but what we have to pick from is huge in terms of music and what we can visit. We're like, 'Let's do something with a Latin feel, or an island feel—or something corny!'"

"There's certain shows where we're asked to pick a specific feel for that show, like Italy or Hong Kong," Thomas adds. "But usually we play want we want to play, and that's time to create some other textures. That's great because Emeril will be talking to the kitchen staff, then turn around and just smile because he hears something he likes, and because he's a drummer, during the breaks he'll just have a drum clinic and we'll get into a nice little jam."

It's not quite accurate to say that doing *Emeril Live* is a dream come true for Doc Gibbs and Ted Thomas, Jr.—getting a gig like this is such a long shot, it never even occurred to them. "When we were in my basement shedding every day, working on that clave, we had no idea where it was going to go," Gibbs admits. "We knew it would have some validity, but we didn't know nine years ago we would eventually end up on a TV show. Not just any TV show, but a popular one with a viewing audience that crosses all genders and boundaries."

By David Weiss. Originally printed in Drum! *magazine (www.drummagazine.com).*

CHAPTER eleven

The Future of Music Supervision

Time flies, and technology flies even faster. By the time you finish reading this book, your new (even more scaled-down in size) computer may have become obsolete, and there will be a new standard software program to replace the previous one in some sector of the audio/video world.

Convergence Returns

As we saw in Chapter 1, The Evolution of Music Supervision, media convergence is constant—phones, films, TVs, computers, and music are constantly folding into each other in new ways and morphing into something new. There are key areas in the world of entertainment and business that music supervisors must constantly observe to see how technology is affecting them, and they include the following: The studio, gaming, restaurants/bars, cell phones/hand-held electronic devices, concert venues, broadcast television, the World Wide Web, and even the streets.

The challenge is to bring all these areas together in one medium, and for now that process is called "convergence." Tomorrow it may be called something else. The future of music supervision relies primarily on where technology is headed at any particular point in time, so it's important to stay intimately aware of the *technol*—all things technological—trends that affect all of the businesses music supervisors work in today.

The most important areas to watch are the ones that most directly affect your business, and you are not expected to be a psychic, fortune-teller, or tarot card-reader to find out what's next! Knowing what developments are most important to your work is simple, and we're going to talk about that in this chapter.

Continuing Education

As a working music supervisor, you owe it to yourself to commit to continuous self-education on new and more advanced digital editing and composing software being used in studios throughout the world. Knowing what's happening technologically speaking will help you communicate effectively when dealing with producers, composers, and engineers.

How about gaming? Gaming technol moves extremely fast, and it's becoming more advanced every day. Music supervisors will always be a critical part of the gaming business, and it's your job to keep an eye on the daily advances in this business with hopes that you'll have something important to bring to the table at some point.

How about that great dinner you went out to last night at that cool new hotel in New York City? Did you happen to notice who the DJ was? Maybe there wasn't a DJ at all, but rather a program pre-produced by a music-supervision services company. Services like MuMa (see Chapter 3, Tools of the Trade, profile on David Schwartz) are constantly being refined to improve retail/restaurant ambience and create an environment tailored for the customer. Scheduling, playlists, and other features that haven't been thought of yet will soon be in the pipeline, because better ambience means better sales and repeat customers.

How about that cell phone in your pocket? Who is choosing, licensing, and programming those dance, jazz, hip-hop, pop rock, and R&B ringtones? As new delivery systems for ringtones are developed, rights holders of marquee titles will gradually drop their resistance to having their music licensed for cell phones, and even more music will be available. It may very well be up to the aggressive, forward-thinking music supervisor to help develop these formats, and then put them in front of choosy pop stars for a breakthrough in ringtone licensing.

Licensing Transformed

Ultimately, music supervisors of the future must stay aware of technology and how it affects the distribution, and subsequently the licensing, of music and sound effects in their projects. When your phone is also your digital audio player, Internet access portal, and home movie player all in one, then that will mean you can watch or listen to any movie, concert, or TV show you want to at any time.

Music supervisors have to be aware that this kind of convergence brings up complications in license negotiations like never before. All media will be negotiated simultaneously in music licenses because they're all being released at the same time. That means deals will involve even more money than before, and music supervisors will have a commensurate responsibility as well. The good news is that more responsibility usually means a higher value on—and better pay for—your services. Make sure you're on top of where digital music licensing is going.

Format Evolution

Right now there are any number of ways to put music into a project. Due in no small part to the perpetual rise in microprocessor capability (and their falling prices), the audio component in video-editing suites like Avid and Final Cut Pro is constantly being improved, allowing music supervisors to insert audio in various formats and to then edit, effect, and otherwise manipulate in new ways.

As HDTV (high-definition television) becomes the standard, even the lowest-level systems will be capable of working in that format. For music supervisors, that will mean an increased migration to Surround 5.1 and 7.1 formats. Music acquisition and licensing will get more complex when both surround and stereo formats must be researched and acquired, and music supervisors will all need at least a basic surround setup to audition surround music and sound effects.

In conjunction, user interfaces and manageability are being simplified further to give more creative people access to the editing process. Mac's iMovie is just one example, allowing even a novice computer-user to upload footage from a personal digital camera easily, and then edit in music and sound effects. As software suites become even easier and more efficient, music supervisors will be expected to deliver results even faster—but then, so will all of our colleagues!

Even the audio-editing suites are facing competition from simpler, easier-to-use programs. New Macs come with GarageBand, a loop-based composition program that is easy to use and creates great-sounding mixed tracks. The capabilities in GarageBand don't come close to those of high-end DAWs like Pro Tools, but music supervisors can expect to see audio programs getting easier and easier to use. At the same time, video editors can expect to have the music-editing portions of their programs become fully capable and easy to use, a convergence leading to one powerful software suite that provides video and music-editing capabilities that are easy to use and can handle everything in one environment.

Music storage/playback is another critical area where there is tremendous potential for change and growth. MP3s, .aiff, and .wav files are the currency of music supervision searches, and they can eventually claim all of the real estate on our computer hard drives—no matter how many gigabytes our machines can hold. But iPods have shown us how small and affordable external music storage devices can be, and talented music professionals are constantly finding new and high-powered applications for them. The next step is for devices this small to hold thousands of *uncompressed* audio files, as opposed to MP3s. When CD-quality audio becomes that portable, music supervisors are bound to benefit.

Online searches are going to continue to get more refined, easier, and faster as well. With bigger and faster connections available, online music and video services geared to the music supervisor will be able to offer us more. Hopefully, more components of licensing will also be executable on line.

Likewise, the constant improvements to wireless technology are redefining the concept of a workspace. Enhancements and wider coverage for AirPort and other WiFi networks will probably allow music supervisors to search for, audition, and implement uncompressed audio from just about anywhere in the world—once again increasing our efficiency, but probably shrinking our deadlines.

The World of Music

One of the music supervisor's chief responsibilities is to be a music expert, with the better ones sporting an encyclopedic knowledge of as many styles, genres, and artists as possible. The world of recorded music is growing at an extremely fast—some would say exponential—rate. There will always be more music that you are expected to know.

Despite the record industry's many financial problems, there are more people making high-quality, usable music than ever before. There is an ever-growing number of licensable commercial tracks, and to the musicians making them, your attention and approval are even more crucial—the vast majority of them can no longer depend on record sales alone to survive.

In addition, an increasing number of musicians are dedicating themselves to composition for media, either by making music on demand or creating incredible music libraries. The affordability of professional recording equipment means that they can open up a music-production facility that is fully capable of making music to your standards, no matter what level you work at. More composers mean more high-quality (as well as low-quality!) music for you to navigate.

With more music to sift through, and more commercial artists and composers competing for your attention, expect the time demands on music supervisors to be stretched to the outer limits. Meanwhile, expectations of your capabilities will be higher than ever before. Get ready for the pressure, and do your best to handle it.

Where Does This Leave the Music Supervisor?

The world of entertainment is only going to keep expanding, and with it, the music supervisor's role will continue to become even more important. We will have to keep finding the perfect music, envisioning how it will be used in the project, negotiate the licenses, coordinate with the production team, and handle the legal issues.

In all probability, licensing and copyright issues will get more complex before they get simpler. As the sea changes that come with digital distribution are resolved, the short-term future of music copyright will be fraught with court battles and legal wrangling for how, when, and why copyright licenses are issued. The performing-rights organizations will change and evolve, while companies that provide file-sharing technology will grow, morph, appear, and disappear. This battle is as much cultural as it is technological and legal, and it is impossible to predict the final outcome.

Tracking music usage is another huge part of the music supervisor's job where serious streamlining is in order. If the performance-rights societies can come to agreeable terms with digital watermarking initiatives like Verance (See Chapter 3, Tools of the Trade), music supervisors will be relieved of submitting cue sheets for watermarked music, and composers will enjoy completely accurate reporting of their performances in the process.

For the foreseeable future, music supervisors can expect to have to personally negotiate every piece of music separately with all of the various rights holders. Hopefully, the future holds a more standard, efficient licensing model. Keep in mind, however, that we might not want the process to get *too* efficient—part of the necessity of the music supervisor is that we know how to navigate all of the pitfalls! Along the way, expect there to be a more standardized method of payment.

Another important change that must happen in music supervision is that we must forge better alliances with each other. Right now, music supervisors are loosely organized, at best, compared to other professional entertainment trade associations like cinematographers with ASC (American Society of Cinematography). By forming a united front, music supervisors can advance our profession by sharing best practices and networking with each other.

One of the aims of this book is to create a central hub for music supervisors to meet, interact, and organize. Visit this book's companion Website, *www.musicsupervisioncentral.com,* to see how local, national, and international connections for our trade are being established.

Music Supervision is Innovation

There are a lot of predictions in this chapter, but the rate of change in today's world means today's predictions can quickly become yesterday's news. Ultimately, music supervisors must not lose sight of the benefits of innovation. The music supervisors who will succeed are the ones who are willing to adapt—and quickly—to new sounds, techniques, attitudes, and technologies.

Those positioned best to succeed are music supervisors with an open mind and a broad understanding of the multiple platforms and possibilities of creative multimedia. They pay attention to developments, not only in their immediate profession, but to the professions that are related. For a music supervisor, those professions include audio editing, video editing, 3-D design, film, HD, compositing, composing, gaming, wireless technology, PDAs, video on demand, cell phones, computer hardware and software, audio hardware, and the music industry as a whole. Pay attention to the smaller and broader trends everywhere in order to understand how you can best manage your niche.

There has been plenty of talk about the opportunities for innovation in music supervision here. While you're in the field, don't sit around waiting for a solution to your music-supervision problem. If there's something you need that hasn't been invented yet to make your job easier, maybe you can be the one to create it and bring it to market. Chances are that if you need or want this innovation, your fellow music supervisors do, too. The rewards for creating a killer media application can be tremendous—just ask Evan Brooks and Peter Gotcher, who in 1984 wanted to expand the sounds on one of their drum machines. That need, and their determination to meet it themselves, spawned Digidesign and subsequently Pro Tools, the single most significant piece of audio software yet.

Important as technology is, however, many things aren't really so different in today's electronic media-driven world from the Greek amphitheaters and Renaissance opera houses: In order to look great, it has to sound great. It takes a music supervisor to bring the vision of today's great storytellers to life, and inspire their audiences with the richest experience imaginable. Are you ready? Then get organized, be innovative, and have fun!

What's your choice for a career in music supervision? For Damon Williams it was Music Choice (*www.musicchoice.com*), where, as Senior Director of Programming, he oversees the music that gets played on more than fifty TV channels going out to thirty-five million households via cable and satellite. It's a music-supervision gig that's all about matching music to people's tastes, in their homes or offices.

"It's incredible for consumers—we can target almost everybody," Williams says of his music-driven media outlet. "Music Choice has a wide array of channels that appeal to people of all demographics. Our base is huge, because TV is the medium in the home. People turn on TV to be entertained, and people can turn on this great music service and get everything. Radio is so segmented and formatted—not only in your hometown, but on vacation you hear the same fifteen songs you hear at home. We're offering something for everyone in the home, and other networks can't compete against that."

A flip through the Music Choice channels—which are accompanied on the TV screen by graphics that list the current artist and song, plus interesting trivia about them—gives evidence to the variety that Williams mentions. Rock, rap, gospel, classical, Radio Disney, country, Americana, metal, 1970s, 80s, 90s, party favorites, reggae, Latin hip hop, and much more are all available—and all commercial-free.

Filling more than fifty channels 24/7 with quality music that's truly compelling, doesn't repeat often, and goes beyond what radio can offer, requires expert music supervision and nonstop research. "We try to offer a package that is going to appeal to segmented targets that all fit together in one system," Williams states. "Let's look at our urban cluster, for example. How do we pick what urban channels to program? We look at the marketplace from teens to adults and study lifestyle trends—when people grew up, what they grew up on, what kind of music they need in their homes—and then make a package.

"So, in that cluster you have classic R&B like late sixties Motown that will appeal to someone forty-five and up, and then smooth R&B for the working female with a hard day who wants to come home and hear Luther Vandross and Anita Baker. Likewise, you have a child who's fourteen years old that wants MTV, so we're programming hip hop. We're trying to design a package for tastes, and not just a channel. You have to constantly examine lifestyles to know when and how to shift the programming. That's what programmers do! We do a lot of research."

The music supervisors with the critical task of turning research into playlists are called programming managers at Music Choice, and they oversee more than just one channel. "We take on everything by 'cluster,'" says Williams. "We develop a programming philosophy for the cluster that relates to how we look at it. So for the genre of rock, we want to break it out eight different ways. How do we have something for the twelve to twenty-four year olds, twenty-five to thirty-five year olds, etc. We look at those lifestyles and find the music that makes sense."

In this equivalent of music-supervision nirvana, a thirst for great sound is equally important to number-crunching ability. "We look for people who are very passionate about music," Williams confirms. "We have a guy programming metal, and we expect him to be in the mosh pit! We look for people that live or have lived the lifestyles."

The programming director builds playlists with music and information that come from a variety of sources. "We're sent music by the major labels and independent artists, and we pay attention to the same industry trades as radio. In the fourth quarter, for example, the new Eminem comes out and we want that on the appropriate channels, including the current hit channels, which are driven by what's happening now. But the other channels that are more targeted, like classic rock, that programmer will delve into the music and lifestyles. So when it comes to the Rolling Stones, we'll play 'Satisfaction,' but there may be a great album cut that, if you were a casual fan, you might not know.

"Typically, on a current format we try to give a song a four- to six-week run. We put it in a test rotation, where it's limited in how much you play it a week. Then we watch and say, 'Is it showing up on radio lists? Is the video getting played? Is there a buzz on the street?'"

According to Williams, Music Choice is a service with the potential to make a real difference in media consumption. "I think we have the opportunity to be on the forefront of how people consume music," he says. "Technology will allow us to move onto different platforms. Our slogan is 'Your music, your choice,' and I think we'll be able to deliver music-related content in so many different ways that people will be comfortable with Music Choice as their source. And we have star power, delivering interviews with the Beastie Boys, Courtney Love, etc., so artists will come here and say 'Music Choice is where I want to come to promote my album.' And the next generation of users will look to us as their source for new music. The direction things are going is that I think people are going to be able to get their music in products and services that adapt to their lifestyles."

For Damon Williams, it all adds up the ultimate music-supervision rush. "I love it," he concludes, "because it's exciting and very challenging. I'm doing something that's never been done. I can say I'm leading the way in programming with the next-generation music service. There are no rules here. What we're doing here has not been done. It's safe to say that we are in a position to be at the forefront of music delivery in all media."

PROFILE
Chris Harvey, Creative Director
SonicVision

• Music supervision for inventive media
• Twenty-three-channel surround
• Creating new experiences with music and graphics

One place to find the future of music supervision is in entirely new media. Sophisticated experiences, many of which have yet to be invented, will require cutting-edge music supervision to capture public interest. What groundbreaking new media can you be a part of in the near future? Check out one of the most advanced entertainment options on the planet: SonicVision.

Is your current universe lacking zip? Could your energy level be boosted with safe transport to an alternate dimension—to the sound of an enveloping rock/electronica soundtrack? If the answer to these questions is yes, then it's time to book a trip, not with NASA, but to New York City to experience *SonicVision* at the American Museum of Natural History (*www.amnh.org*).

An awe-inspiring thirty-eight-minute, digitally animated music show with a playlist picked by Moby, *SonicVision* is playing out for the foreseeable future in the museum's Hayden Planetarium Space Theater. Aptly described by the AMNH as one of the world's largest and most powerful virtual reality simulators, the 6,550-square-foot dome is now the home of a mind-and-body experience that has definitely never been done before, bolstered by an ambitious surround mix featuring twenty-three channels of discrete sound and the music of artists such as Radiohead , U2, Coldplay, Queens of the Stone Age, Goldfrapp and many more.

"Our goal is to bring people to new visual and auditory spaces that they can visit," says Anthony Braun, executive producer. "For the visitor who's experiencing it, this is a new kind of audio/visual experience, in which you're truly immersed in the content and feel like you're there."

"I wanted to really elevate the music—that was my ambition for the show," adds Chris Harvey, *SonicVision* creative director. "I didn't want to talk to anybody about religion, but give people a glorious, transcendental experience. It's a new form of entertainment in that it's not a high-impact edit, not a movie, not a narrative. Its power lies in how intimately connected it is to the music, and how integrating the experience in the circular theater is."

Created in association with MTV2, *SonicVision* was the result of the dedicated work of a diverse team of sound mixers, animators, video jockeys (VJs), editors, and media artists up against a short deadline— approximately six months—that would have been unthinkable only a year or two ago. But with a staff of museum artists who had already designed two previous planetarium shows, along with the huge gains in available computer firepower, Braun and Harvey's group were able to hit the ground running in April of 2003.

"Up until then, the museum animators had only produced science shows, and of course there you're held to scientific-accuracy restrictions," Harvey says. "But they're all artists, and had been playing with ideas that wouldn't fit into a science show. Then, taking those ideas for possible scenes or moments, I designed a kind of flowchart for this show, an overall structure that I felt would be open and modular enough that I could plug a lot of things into it, but would give the show a beginning, middle and an end. To make this flowchart I also used a very long list of songs they were already considering, some of which had been recommended by MTV, some of which the staff had chosen, and some of which Moby had recommended."

Harvey and Braun worked closely with re-recording mixer Peter Hylenski, sound designer Paul Soucek, audio editor Russell C. Baird, Jr., director of Engineering Benjamin Bernhardt, and chief video engineer Jeff Gralitzer to make sure that the audio and video components of the show would translate in the unique environment of the planetarium's dome. Hylenski, who already knew the dome intimately after mixing the planetarium show *Search for Life,* had the equivalent of twenty-three channels of surround, plus ample low-end reinforcement, to motivate him.

To add to the solid sense of synchronization between the music and the dazzling imagery, Harvey's VJ friends, who often operate in the real-time performance realm, had some additional tricks up their sleeves when creating the animation for two specific scenes. "They use a lot of audio-responsive software to drive the animation," he says. "I know from experience, one of the most expensive and labor intensive things you can do is synchronize to audio, so I thought this would be a clever way to do it.

"One program we used is software called Filmbox [by Kaydara], which had already been customized for their planetarium to work in real time through their seven [Barco 812s] projectors, for the White Zombie song 'Blood, Milk and Sky'. On top of the dome there's a huge, beautiful sunwheel of sparks that was in fact driven by the audio—it's subtle but definitely connected. The other audio-responsive tool is actually a plug-in for After Effects called Trapcode Soundkeys, in the 'Heroes' scene. The birth of all these home movies is triggered by David Bowie's voice."

The resulting show is loud and extremely crisp without being anywhere near deafening. It's all the better to appreciate the subtle acoustical placement and visual amazement that constantly takes place throughout *SonicVision,* which deserves recognition as an important advancement in the field of digital art.

"Early on, I said that I wanted to use science without mentioning science, evoke spirituality without mentioning religion, and give people a psychedelic experience without drugs," Chris Harvey concludes. "I feel very strongly that audiences are ready for a new kind of entertainment. The kind of short-attention-span that we've all been trained to expect has its place, but that's not all there is, and I think that it's in music that most people find an alternative. *SonicVision* appeals to that appetite—we give audiences all the shock that they want, but with a real respect for their ability to appreciate beauty."

By David Weiss. Reprinted by permission of Mix *magazine.*

Resources

Suggested Reading

Audio Postproduction for Digital Video by Jay Rose (CMP Books)

The Indie Guidebook to Music Supervision for Films by Sharal Churchill (Filmic Press)

Music, Money, and Success: The Insider's Guide to Making Money in the Music Business by Jeffrey Brabec and Todd Brabec (Schirmer Trade Books)

Music Publishing by Tim Whitsett (Artistpro)

Advertising

AdTunes.com
Insightful ad music Weblog

SongTitle.info
List of music used in television commercials (North America)

SoundFamiliar.info
British database of music in television ads and movies

WhatsThatCalled.com
Library and forum devoted to music used in television commercials

Artists

AllMusic.com
Valuable artist bio/music database

ArtistDirect.com
A-to-Z artist bio/music database

BroadJam.com
Indie artist hub

GarageBand.com
Indie artist hub

Music-Map.com
Artist/genre identification tool

MusicPlasma.com
Artist/genre identification tool

MySpace.com
Indie music/artists post here

SonicBids.com
Locate artists, call for music, submit music

The Kin
www.thekin.tv
Example of a visual media-friendly band site

Digital Watermarking
Digimarc.com
WatermarkingWorld.org
Verance.com

Employment
CrewNet.com
Film employment

The Employment & Career Channel
www.employ.com
General job site

EntertainmentCareers.net
Entertainment-industry employment

FilmStaff.com
Film employment

Mandy.com
Film and TV employment

Music Jobs
www.music-jobs.com
Music employment site

TVJobs.com
Broadcast employment site

General Music Supervision Sites

Music supervision and music supervisors
www.bobthompsonmusic.com/music_supervisors.html
Music supervision info/news

Film Music Network
www.filmmusic.net
Film music hub

The Entertainment Industry Directory
www.filmmusicdirectory.com/pages
General entertainment-industry directory

Studio Systems, Inc.
www.inhollywood.com
Film and TV research management tool

SensesofCinema.com
Cinema hub

www.crimsonuk.com
TV, film, video news for Great Britain

Licensing

DigitalmiX.com
One-stop music licensing

HFA (Harry Fox Agency)
www.harryfox.com
Mechanical licensing agency

SongFile.com
Online mechanical licensing

Music Clearance

EMG (Evan M. Greenspan, Inc. Music Clearance
www.clearance.com
Music clearance outsourcing firm

Music Libraries

MeetYourBeat.com
Downloadable loops, one shots, sound effects, and music

Mi7Libraries.com
Online/CD music library (formerly Prime Sounds)

Performing Rights Organizations

ASCAP.com
BMI.com
SESAC.com

Equipment and Technology

Guitar Center
www.guitarcenter.com
Chain seller of guitars, audio gear, and more

Sam Ash
www.samashmusic.com
Brick-and-mortar stores, as well as online sales

Scotch Plains Music Center
www.spmusic.com
Famed music store

Sweetwater Sound
www.sweetwater.com
Online store featuring pro audio gear and instruments

Trusonic.com
Business sound solutions

YCD.net
Business sound solutions

Trade Publications
AdAge.com
AdCritic.com
AdWeek.com
Billboard.com
BrandWeek.com
CMJ.com
FilmMusicMag.com
FilmScoreMonthly.com
HollywoodReporter.com
MediaWeek.com
MusicNewswire.com
PCRNewsletter.com
PromoOnly.com
Variety.com

Video Games
G.A.N.G. (Game Audio Network Guild)
www.audiogang.org
Video game music hub

Music4Games.net
Video game music hub

Bibliography

Books

Brabec, Jeffrey and Brabec, Todd. *Music, Money, and Success: The Insider's Guide to the Music Industry.* New York; Schirmer Trade Books, 2004.

Churchill, Sharal. *The Indie Guidebook to Music Supervision for Films.* Los Angeles; Filmic Press 2002.

Erickson, Gunnar; Tulchin, Harris; Halloran, Mark. *The Independent Film Producer's Survival Guide.* New York; Schirmer Trade Books, 2002.

Farinella, David John. "Music Supervisors: Selling the Movie, Selling the Song." *Mix* magazine. April 2001.
Gordon, Rick. *Digital Journalism: Emerging Media and the Changing Horizons of Journalism.* Lanham, Maryland; Rowman & Littlefield, 2003.
Huber, David and Runstein, Robert. *Modern Recording Techniques.* Boston; Focal Press, 1997.

Mancuso, Anthony. *How to Form Your Own New York Corporation.* Berkeley, CA; Nolo Press, 1998.

Porter, Hayden. "Phone It In!" *Electronic Musician.* February 2004.
Kirn, Peter. "Step Away from the Sampler", *Keyboard,* January 2005.
Rose, Jay. *Audio Postproduction for Digital Video.* San Francisco; CMP Books, 2002, 133-135, 298, 300.

Websites

Copyright and the Public Domain
www.pdinfo.com

Chinese Opera: A Brief History
www.hamilton.edu/academics/Asian/OpProg2.html

Adventures in Cybersound,
www.acmi.net.au/AIC/

Early Recorded Sounds & Wax Cylinders
www.tinfoil.com

Television History—The First 75 Years
www.tvhistory.tv/1946-1949.htm

The Development of Radio Networks
earlyradiohistory.us/sec019.htm

Broadcast History
www.oldradio.com/current/bc_am.htm

The Broadcast Archive
www.oldradio.com/current/bc_fm.htm

American Bandstand—Broadcast History
www.fiftiesweb.com/bandstnd.htm

The Ed Sullivan Show
www.tvtome.com/tvtome/servlet/ShowMainServlet/showid-1156

The History and Nature of Stereophonic Technology
bryant2.bryant.edu/~ehu/h364proj/fall_98/pepin/stereohistory.html

The History of Production Music
www.classicthemes.com/50sTVThemes/prodMusHistory.html

PARC History
www.parc.com/about/history

A Brief History of Home Video Games
www.geekcomix.com/vgh/first/atpongarc.shtml

Player 2 Stage 1: The Coin Eaters
www.emuunlim.com/doteaters/play2sta1.htm

History of CD Technology
www.oneoffcd.com/info/historycd.cfm

Eric Clapton Frequently Asked Questions
*www.ericclaptonfaq.com/questions/Has_Clapton_ever_appeared_in_a_tele
vision_commercial.htm*

Hobbes' Internet Timeline v8.0
www.zakon.org/robert/internet/timeline

DVD Introduction & History
www.disctronics.co.uk/technology/dvdintro/dvd_intro.htm

Howard Shore Biography
www.allmusic.com/cg/amg.dll?p=amg&sql=11:kpfwxqegldfe~T1

Frequently Asked Questions About ASCAP Television Licensing
www.ascap.com/licensing/tvfaq.html

SESAC FAQS
www.sesac.com/licensing/broadcast_licensing_faq1.asp#sesacl

Do I Need a Mechanical License?
www.harryfox.com/public/mechanicalLicense.jsp

Index